D0700412

A PASSION FOR
CHRISTIAN UNITY

A PASSION FOR CHRISTIAN UNITY

Essays *in* Honor *of* William Tabbernee

JOHN M. IMBLER, EDITOR

CHALICE PRESS

ST. LOUIS, MISSOURI

Copyright ©2009 by Chalice Press.

All rights reserved. For permission to reuse content, please contact Copyright Clearance Center, 222 Rosewood Drive, Danvers, MA 01923, (978) 750-8400, www.copyright.com.

Bible quotations marked NRSV are from the *New Revised Standard Version Bible,* copyright 1989, Division of Christian Education of the National Council of the Churches of Christ in the United States of America. Used by permission. All rights reserved.

Those quotations marked RSV are from the *Revised Standard Version of the Bible,* copyright 1952, [2nd edition, 1971] by the Division of Christian Education of the National Council of the Churches of Christ in the United States of America. Used by permission. All rights reserved.

Those quotations marked KJV are from the *King James Version.*

Those quotations marked INT are from *The Inclusive New Testament,* copyright ©1994, Priests for Equality. Used by permission. All rights reserved.

Cover and interior design: Elizabeth Wright

Visit Chalice Press on the World Wide Web at
www.chalicepress.com

10 9 8 7 6 5 4 3 2 1   09 10 11 12 13 14

Library of Congress Cataloging–in–Publication Data

A passion for Christian unity : essays in honor of William Tabbernee / John M. Imbler, editor.
    p. cm.
ISBN 978-0-8272-3010-1
1. Church--Unity. I. Tabbernee, William, 1944- II. Imbler, John M. III. Title.
    BV601.5.P37 2009
    262'.72--dc22   2009024090

Printed in the United States of America

Contents

Preface

The date was May 11, 2007. The place was a ballroom at the Radisson Hotel in Tulsa, Oklahoma. The event was the Friday dinner party typically held during the Annual Meeting of the Board of Trustees the evening before graduation at Phillips Theological Seminary. But that year the event was different—it was the kickoff for the year-long celebration of the seminary's centennial. In addition to trustees, faculty, staff, and spouses who normally attend, numerous special guests were invited to join in the festive occasion, bring greetings, and reminisce.

As appropriate, the organizing committee scheduled President Tabbernee to speak after the introductions were made and before the main program began. He briefly but engagingly reflected on the seminary's history and its future. Referring to its beginnings, the president characterized the school's founder, Ely Vaughn Zollars, as an innovative and daring educator, Disciples of Christ minister, and biblical scholar who carried "a passionate zeal for the goals of Christian unity." That ecumenical approbation of one hundred years past rings more true for Phillips Theological Seminary today than it did even then—true in ways that Dr. Zollars probably never could have imagined.

This book, however, is not about the centennial or Ely Zollars as important as they both were to the institution. Rather, this *festschrift* is a gift to Bill Tabbernee as he celebrates his sixty-fifth birth year and his retirement from PTS. Under the theme of *A Passion for Christian Unity,* the authors have introduced aspects of ecumenical and interfaith life from their respective disciplines, experiences, and scholarly interests. Each chapter was written by a current or former member of the regular faculty at PTS who worked with Dr. Tabbernee in Enid, Tulsa, or both, between 1991 into 2009. Some of the professors preceded him in time at the seminary, some came during his presidency; yet all have served with him as teachers of ministers.

Dr. William Tabbernee, this book is dedicated to you with appreciation for your leadership, ecumenism, scholarship, and colleagueship.

Contributors

Joseph A. Bessler is Robert Travis Peake Associate Professor of Theology and Associate Dean for Assessment and Faculty Development. Dr. Bessler's research interests in the history of Christian thought and contemporary methods of theological analysis are currently expressed in the study of religion and politics, especially on rhetoric. Raised Roman Catholic, he is active in a United Church of Christ congregation.

Duane R. Bidwell is Assistant Professor of Pastoral Theology, Care, and Counseling and Director of Presbyterian Ministerial Formation. Dr. Bidwell, holding a licentiate in spiritual theology and direction, informs his academic discipline of pastoral care and pastoral theology through spirituality and gives attention to intercultural and interfaith contexts. He is managing editor of the *Journal of Pastoral Theology* and an ordained minister in the Presbyterian Church (USA).

Ellen Blue is Mouzon Biggs Jr. Associate Professor of the History of Christianity and United Methodist Studies and Director of Methodist Ministerial Formation. Among her interests are studies in ministry, particularly women's issues, and Christianity in Latin America. Due to her pastoral experiences and education in Louisiana, she has devoted recent research to the effects of Hurricane Katrina on communities and churches. Dr. Blue is an ordained elder in full connection with the Louisiana Conference of the United Methodist Church.

Mady Fraser is Assistant Professor of Spirituality and Chaplain. She addresses her work to Celtic Christian cultures, hospitality, and the disciplines of simple living. With the renovation of the seminary's campus, Dr. Fraser was instrumental in the creation of the labyrinth located in the seminary's meditation gardens. She is an ordained minister in the Christian Church (Disciples of Christ).

Harold Hatt is Professor of Theology and Philosophy, *emeritus.* Dr. Hatt was called to the seminary in 1962. He later became academic dean of the Enid campus and served as interim president 1990–91 after which he was appointed Vice President for Academic Affairs. His academic pursuits are theology and popular culture, especially film. He is an ordained minister in the Christian Church (Disciples of Christ).

John M. Imbler is Associate Professor of the History of Christianity and Disciples Studies, Executive Vice President, and Director of Disciples Ministerial Formation. His interests include Christianity in the United States, especially in the nineteenth, twentieth, and twenty-first centuries and the development of ministry as seen through various denominations and faith communities. He is an ordained minister in the Christian Church (Disciples of Christ).

Sandra Costen Kunz is Assistant Professor of Educational Ministries. Employing such techniques as meditation and drama, she focuses her work on teaching church leaders to teach the Bible to all ages. Dr. Kunz centers attention on intersecting interfaith relations and spiritual formation in an international context. She is a lay leader in the Episcopal Church and serves as secretary for the Society of Buddhist-Christian Studies.

Richard H. Lowery is Johnnie Eargle Cadieux Professor of Hebrew Bible. For the past two years he has been "on loan" to Lexington Theological Seminary in the capacity of Interim Dean and Vice President for Academic Affairs. Dr. Lowery works in the texts and contexts of the cultures of Ancient Israel, which he connects to the contemporary world focusing on justice and the mission of the church. He is an ordained minister in the Christian Church (Disciples of Christ).

Gary E. Peluso-Verdend is Associate Professor of Practical Theology and Vice President of Stewardship. Joining PTS in 1993 as director of the D.Min. program, then academic dean, he left in 2000 for service at another seminary. Returning in 2005 as a vice president, he concentrates his academic work in areas compatible with his administrative functions, engaging in social analysis, congregational cultures, and transformative leadership. Dr. Peluso-Verdend is an elder in full connection with the United Methodist Church.

Don A. Pittman is William Tabbernee Professor of the History of Religions and Vice President for Academic Affairs and Dean. His research is directed toward cross-cultural and interfaith studies with interests in Chinese Buddhism. Under the Common Global Ministries Board of the Disciples of Christ and the United Church of Christ, he taught at Tainan Theological College and Seminary in Tainan, Taiwan, a Presbyterian school. He is an ordained minister in the Christian Church (Disciples of Christ).

Nancy Claire Pittman is Associate Professor of the Practice of Ministry and Director of the Doctor of Ministry program. With an emphasis in New Testament studies Dr. Pittman also gives attention to the art and practices of ministry, women in ministry, and congregational leadership. Under Common Global Ministries, she taught New Testament at Tainan Theological College and Seminary. As an ordained minister in the Christian Church (Disciples of Christ), she is also a certified spiritual director.

Elizabeth Box Price is Professor of Christian Education, *emerita.* Dr. Price was called to the seminary in 1989 to serve as dean of the Tulsa Campus, and later was appointed Vice President for Faculty and Student Development. She stresses the interconnectedness of religion and science as a means of understanding creation with an appreciation for the whole created order. She is a United Methodist diaconal minister in the Oklahoma Annual Conference

Dennis E. Smith is LaDonna Kramer Meinders Professor of New Testament. Editor of the *Chalice Introduction to the New Testament* (2004), Dr. Smith has focused his studies on the ancient social world, especially Greco-Roman meal customs. He brings his understanding of the New Testament in its context into the church in the twenty-first century. Additionally he is involved in storytelling as proclamation and interpretation. He is an ordained minister in the Christian Church (Disciples of Christ).

Foreword

Budapest, Hungary, 1989. Dr. William Tabbernee, principal and lecturer in church history at the Churches of Christ Theological College in Melbourne, Australia, proudly showed me pictures of his new campus. Highway construction forced the theological college to abandon its facilities and build a new life in a new setting. The transition had been complex, utilizing multiple teaching sites during the interim period. It was apparent to me that Bill's visionary leadership had been critical to the development of a new, unified campus that would serve the churches of southern Australia well.

We had come to Budapest that summer to attend a meeting of the Faith and Order Commission of the World Council of Churches. I had met Bill some years earlier at other Faith and Order meetings. He was a member of the commission, and I served as staff and later as plenary secretary. In those international, ecumenical settings, we were drawn together by our common ties to churches in the Campbell-Stone tradition. I had come to know Bill as a highly regarded scholar, church historian, and ecumenist. The pictures and the story of his new campus also marked him as an adept and innovative theological administrator.

Tulsa, Oklahoma, 1990. John Imbler, then vice president of the Division of Higher Education of the Christian Church (Disciples of Christ), and I sat in Tulsa International Airport waiting for a flight back to St. Louis. We had just finished the first meeting of a search committee to nominate a new president of Phillips Graduate Seminary. John was serving as consultant to the process, and I had been selected by the board to chair the committee. As we waited, we reflected together on the bewildering array of issues confronting the seminary. It was a school with a proud history and, at the same time, a fledgling institution with an uncertain future. We knew that it would be a challenge to find someone with the skills, the commitment, and the creativity to move the seminary forward and secure its future.

For eighty years, the seminary had existed as an integral part of Phillips University in Enid, Oklahoma. The university, facing a financial crisis that would ultimately result in its demise as a teaching institution, had sold its campus to the city of Enid to raise operating capital. The district court in Garfield County, while approving the arrangement, subsequently ruled that the city could not own a theological seminary.

As a result, Phillips Graduate Seminary, suddenly separated from Phillips University, was in the throes of rebirth as Phillips Theological Seminary—a freestanding institution with a new board of trustees, a new president, and eventually a new campus in Tulsa. At that moment in the spring of 1990, however, its existence was tenuous. Its very survival would require truly extraordinary leadership.

The incoming president would need to devise a strategic plan and oversee a variety of administrative programs attendant to stabilizing finances, increasing student recruitment and services, improving faculty development and retention, and building an infrastructure suitable for a freestanding, yet church-related, school. Fund raising would be a priority, as would establishing the confidence of numerous constituencies. Operating with a geographically fragmented faculty and student body in rented spaces on two campuses separated by 120 miles, the seminary was not meeting its budget. It owned no facilities, precious little endowment, and virtually no physical assets beyond the books in the library (also housed in rented space). An inexperienced board of trustees required guidance and training. We needed operational policies. We were facing issues of accreditation. And, of course, we had no campus of our own.

In addition, the small but exceptionally talented and dedicated faculty would demand that the new president be a reputable scholar. Highly desirable, too, was a president who understood the unique traditions and structures of the Christian Church (Disciples of Christ) with which PTS is historically affiliated and, at the same time, be committed to the ecumenical vision that is at the heart of its mission.

Who in the world could do this job?

As John and I sat in the cafeteria at the airport, I remembered Budapest and said, "I know one person who could do it, but I can't imagine that he would be interested. He just successfully completed building a new campus in Australia, and I am sure that he will want to stay and enjoy it."

The response was, "Why don't you try?" So with John's encouragement, I returned to my office and put in a call to Australia to speak with William Tabbernee. I tried to be more or less honest about the seminary's situation without sounding desperate or discouraging. To my surprise, Bill was immediately interested. Having played a pivotal role at a critical juncture in the life of one historic institution, he was energized by the thought of claiming such an opportunity again. Following interviews with him and other excellent candidates, the search committee unanimously and enthusiastically offered to Bill the presidency of Phillips Theological Seminary. To my eternal gratitude, he accepted the challenge. Following lengthy negotiation with immigration officials, President Tabbernee assumed office in April 1991. The rest, as they say, is history.

Tulsa, Oklahoma, 2009. The task has, perhaps, proven to be even more of a challenge than Bill imagined. However, he has succeeded in measures beyond anything we anticipated. With incomparable leadership, charm, wisdom, and dedication, Bill has brought the seminary to its current state: a beautiful new campus in Tulsa, thirteen consecutive years of balanced budgets, an enlarged and diverse faculty and staff, assets exceeding $40 million, an enthusiastic student body, and a very grateful board of trustees.

With the students, friends, faculty, trustees, staff, and alums of Phillips Theological Seminary, we join in a prayer of thanksgiving for the ministry of William Tabbernee.

Bill, you are our friend and our leader. This volume is for you.

Stephen Cranford
Trustee Emeritus
Phillips Theological Seminary
Summer 2009

Introduction

JOHN M. IMBLER

In 1832 those who appropriated the name Christian, as advocated by Barton Warren Stone, and the Disciples or Reformers, as promoted by Alexander Campbell, came together to form what ultimately became the Christian Church (Disciples of Christ). Anthony Dunnavant listed four ideals of this union: restoration, unity, liberty, and mission.[1] These ideals framed a plea known as the restoration movement. That plea was essentially a call for the return to biblical principles wherein all Christians could find a common ground of faith, which would, presumably, foster unity. Unity, Campbell and Stone contended, could not be achieved through the creeds and confessions developed by denominations, nor from ecclesiastical pronouncements or human inventions. Such unity would come only through the witness of the scriptures. Among the popular slogans that marked this restoration emphasis was "No creed but Christ, no book but the Bible," and "Where the scriptures speak, we speak, and where the scriptures are silent, we are silent." Eugene Boring captures the importance, and distinctiveness, of biblical interpretation for Disciples, "*Examine the role the Bible has played in Disciples thought, and you have your hand on the pulse of denominational theology*"[2] (emphasis by Boring).

Aspects of the Plea

Alexander Campbell, his father Thomas, and Barton Warren Stone all were competent biblical scholars. Although not recognized as such in the halls of the academy, as that was not their environment, each was familiar with biblical languages and did significant exegesis for his own depth of understanding as well as for sermon preparation and public writing. Each of these men argued that Christianity had been corrupted by sectarian influences and ecclesial restrictions, and so they demanded a return to the Bible.

Liberty was foundational both in the United States from its inception as well as in the church. Independence and self-determination were held inviolate, as control was to be exercised by each congregation rather than directed under denominational hierarchies or forced through relationships with civil governments. The "plain meaning" of scripture without the imposition of human authority would free the church to be the church Jesus intended. The Campbells, especially, were heavily influenced by the Scottish reforming spirit, which urged the separation of church and state, the autonomy of local congregations, the restoration of the New Testament as the essential pattern for church organization, and an evangelical zeal to proclaim salvation through Jesus Christ and him alone. Informed by such theologians as Greville Ewing, Robert Sandeman, John Glas, and James A. and Robert Haldane, the Campbells brought those ideas to the States, believing that a democratic nation would be sympathetic to a democratic church. Stone proposed that the Bible was clear but that later uncritical interpreters interjected their own opinions between the text and the reader.[3] Having been born in the U.S. and coming from a different religious experience than the Campbells, Stone, nonetheless, found agreement with them, claiming the authority of the Bible and only the Bible as the proper rule of faith and practice.

Another aspect of the movement was the blending of faith and reason. Thomas and Alexander Campbell were drawn to scientific thought espoused by such philosophers as John Locke, Francis Bacon, Isaac Newton, and as advocated by Thomas Reid through the Scottish School of Common Sense. Harmonizing European intellectual thought with their North American religious reformation, both Campbells appropriated empirical evidence to affirm the facts of the Bible. From Locke's writings they expressed disdain toward speculative theology in favor of the truth of scripture. The blending of faith and reason was never considered in conflict with authentic faith; it was a reformation of both heart and head. Disciples scholar Ronald Osborn described this perspective in its historic and current contexts:

> What do we mean by the Disciples mind? It is a way of approaching the Scriptures with reverent intelligence. This

style of professing Christian faith has accepted the reproach of advocating a "head religion" hurled by those who profess a "heart religion." Emphasizing faith with understanding, the Disciples mind puts the highest premium on rationality and faith in action.[4]

Locke's notions of sensory and experiential learning and Reid's concept of natural philosophy created a foundation on which Alexander Campbell built his educational principles–principles that incorporated both classical and modern thought. Those building blocks consisted of instinct, sensation, reason, and faith.[5] Exhibiting the "Disciples mind" in their own times, ministers, teachers, and administrators in educational institutions, following Campbell's prescription, made the Bible a primary text in certain curriculums. Within both the Hebrew and Christian stories were the richness and expanse of literature, history, geography, social dynamics, and anthropology. In addition and more importantly, the New Testament, specifically, presented guides for moral living as well as the essentials for faith and salvation.

If the first mission of the nineteenth-century Stone-Campbell movement was planting churches on the North American frontier, the second mission surely was the building of educational institutions to prepare both clergy and laity to assume leadership for those churches. In 1853 Alexander Campbell observed, "Next to Christianity itself, stands Education, in its proper import."[6] After the first school was established in 1836, four years after the merger of the Disciples and the Christians, 209 colleges and 205 academies and institutes were founded.[7] As they spread throughout the Northwest Territory and the western frontier, Disciples schools offered the breadth of liberal arts, biblical studies, and vocational courses that produced well-rounded individuals, capable civic leaders, and responsible church people.

In his "Address on Colleges" delivered at the dedication of a new church building in Wheeling, (West) Virginia, in 1854, Alexander Campbell proclaimed, "Colleges and churches go hand in hand in the progress of Christian civilization."[8] Campbell wrote and spoke widely on the values of education, and his philosophy of education extended into the twentieth century, informing planners for both religious and secular schools. Briefly stated, his seven points were:

1. *Wholeness of person* was not simply for the well-bred or for males but for all citizens. Proper education develops body, mind, and spirit.

2. The *moral formation of character* was not an idea unique unto him, but undergirded his proposition that educated citizens are dutiful citizens to one another and in society.

3. *Biblical studies* clearly informed social values, but also moved people beyond right human interaction into right relationship with the redemptive God.

4. *Non-sectarianism* was a mark of true education, referencing the Bible as the core text neither from a denominational nor purely historical perspective but from its revealed truths for all people for all time.

5. The *perfectibility of the individual* exhibited Campbell's millennial disposition convicted of the ability of humanity to reconstruct itself sufficiently to usher in the reign of Christ.

6. The importance of *lifelong learning* engaged and sustained individuals physically, intellectually, morally, and religiously from infancy through adulthood.

7. A seventh point, not always listed and discussed, was that education should be *international,* conceding that, for him, international referred to the British Isles and, to a lesser extent, the European continent.

The curricular format of Disciples schools throughout the westward expansion found basis, in some form, around these educational principles.[9]

New Ecumenical Impulses

Energized by the impulses of Barton Warren Stone in *The Last Will and Testament of the Springfield Presbytery* in 1804 "that this body die, be dissolved, and sink into union with the body of Christ at large";[10] and of Thomas Campbell in his 1809 *Declaration and Address of the Christian Association of Washington* that "the Church of Christ on earth is essentially, intentionally, and constitutionally one";[11] these churchmen challenged the existing parochialism—arrogance?—of denominations. These two foundational documents of the Stone-Campbell people are still considered unity documents because of their appeal to the cause of oneness in Christ. Adherence to the simple—primitive—gospel rather than creeds, confessions, or human theology was the only way to be truly Christian.

Disciples forebears showed no patience with sectarianism. While not specifically seeking merger or organic union of Christian organizations as attested by Thomas, "That although the Church of Christ upon earth must necessarily exist in particular and distinct societies, locally separate one from another, yet there ought to be no schisms, no uncharitable divisions among them. They ought to receive each other as Christ Jesus hath also received them, to the glory of God...,"[12] the Campbells promoted an understanding of spiritual unity.

To press a point, Alexander Campbell wrote a parable about churches on the hypothetical Island of Guernsey as a response to disunity and factionalism. An evangelist planted six churches on the island and, with the approval of the congregants, appointed elders and deacons for each. Having left the six churches to their own administrations, the evangelist returned some five years later only to find no cooperation among any of the six. "The communities A, B, C, D, E, and F, constituted the whole church on the island of Guernsey, but as yet they did not act as one church."[13] The evangelist then convened a council of the various church leaders. They discussed the problems and resolved their disunity through a set of propositions and recommendations. Contending that one church should not interfere in the business of another, all were, nonetheless, drawn together as one body under the Messiah, "That all Christian communities on earth, however numerous, constituted but one church of Christ."[14] The story went on to state that each organized community had two great classes of duties–"one performed to itself (private) and one to the world (public)"–neither of which was in conflict with each other but complemented the church of Christ on earth.[15]

As time passed, the unity of the church proclaimed by the Campbells and Stone evolved to a new plane. In 1908 the Disciples of Christ, along with thirty other denominations, formed the Federal Council of Churches of Christ in America[16] to address social, political, and economic concerns occasioned by the unprecedented growth of cities in an industrializing nation. Rapid urbanization challenged traditional forms of ministries and stretched the abilities of individual churches to provide services. Many denominations and church groups were struggling to assist the influx of immigrants from foreign lands and migrating peoples from within the United States with housing, food, education, child services, medical care, and other human necessities, not the least of which was spiritual nurture. With the realization that together the churches could do more, and do it more effectively, such cooperative ventures signaled not only the emergence of the modern ecumenical movement in the United States but also an active recognition in the twentieth century that recast words of Barton Warren Stone for modern times–unity is our polar star.

The period around the establishment of the Federal Council of Churches was also a time of deep internal conflicts and separations.

Dating back to the national division in the 1850s and 1860s, many denominations experienced schisms that carried into the turn of the century and were exacerbated by theological, scientific, and sociological developments. Disciples were not immune to these strains, and the new ecumenical work was not received well in all quarters. As churches grew and new generations of leaders emerged, understandings of restoring the primitive gospel, expressions of unity, approaches to mission, and protection of congregational liberty became as divisive as they had been formative. Differing views on biblical interpretation, church organization, and social witness pulled churches and individuals apart. In 1906, what became the body known as the Churches of Christ claimed an independent standing from the Disciples of Christ in a special religious census conducted by the U.S. Census Bureau. This action unofficially but effectively separated two major sections of the church along theological, ecclesiological, and significantly geographical lines. At odds were the quest for unity and the restoration of the primitive gospel, two ideals which contributed to the union of the Campbells' churches and Stone's churches in the first place.

College of the Bible–Oklahoma

Between the competing forces of restoration and unity, Ely Vaughn Zollars, also a noted biblical scholar, opened a school in the Oklahoma Territory two months before Oklahoma statehood. Among the schools, academies, and institutes established under Disciples auspices and influenced by Campbell's educational philosophy was Oklahoma Christian University in Enid.[17] Growing out of Zollars' ecumenical vision, with the support of the Oklahoma and Indian Missionary Societies of the Disciples of Christ, this school, through its College of the Bible, was about educating ministers for the developing churches in the Plains. Admissions began in the spring of 1907, and the first classes of the College of the Bible opened the following September. Even before classes met, the 1907–08 catalog defined its purpose this way:

> For several years prominent men in the Christian church in Oklahoma and Indian Territory, recognizing the great need of high grade institutions of learning in this new and rapidly developing country, and feeling that the disciples of Christ, like other religious peoples, had a great duty to perform in this direction, contemplated the establishment of a College or University, and while the general public need made the importance of such a school apparent, yet the necessity was

further emphasized by the great dearth of preachers among all religious bodies, throughout the United States, and especially among the disciples of Christ, this shortage being particularly felt in the Southwest.[18]

A promotional statement reinforced the founder's and supporters' commitment to unity:

Oklahoma Christian University belongs to, and is controlled by, the religious body known as the Christian Church or Disciples of Christ. This does not mean that the school is sectarian in character. On the contrary, if true to the principles of the people it represents, it must be non-sectarian.... The promoters of the school believe that Christian education is the only true education because it is the only education that recognizes the whole man, physical, intellectual and spiritual, and provides for the development of his threefold nature. No denominational tests will be imposed, and no sectarian tenets will be inculcated, but the aim will be to offer liberal courses of instruction in a healthy Christian atmosphere.[19]

In the 1950s yet another rift occurred within Disciples, although the antecedents of dissolution dated back to the 1920s, occasioned by encroaching denominational structures and differing views on the theology of missions and practices in the mission fields. The Christian Churches/Churches of Christ, more commonly known as the Independent Christian Church, claimed a separate identity from the Disciples.

In the throes of expanding missions and advancing structuralism, Dean Stephen J. England, a biblical scholar as well, issued a challenge to the faculty of the College of the Bible in the form of a question. The minutes of the February 5, 1951, faculty meeting, of what was shortly to become the Graduate Seminary of Phillips University, record, "Dean England pointed out that we were training a number of ministers of other communions—Two or three Methodists and several from other churches. *How far should we encourage this?*"[20] (emphasis in original). His question continued moving the seminary on a decidedly intentional path of openness to the extent that in subsequent meetings, the faculty positioned itself to seek non-Disciples candidates when teaching positions came open.

Continued Ecumenical Activities

Despite the pain of divisions within its own tradition, Disciples have understood that the concept of unity was in keeping with its biblical theology. Work with many denominations through common missions both in the United States and throughout the world has produced shared resources such as Sunday school curriculums, youth ministry programs, and adult study materials including lectionaries.

In 1953, the publication of *Christian Worship: A Hymnal* by The Bethany Press, a joint venture of the Disciples and the American Baptist Convention, was considered by some a prelude to union, although that did not eventuate. Then, authorized by the General Assembly meeting in Indianapolis in 1989, the church embarked on a formal Ecumenical Partnership with the United Church of Christ. Salient among the points of Resolution 8915 were the mutual recognition of membership "under the one universal church of Jesus Christ," and the mutual recognition of ministers as "truly ministers of word and sacrament."[21] Furthermore, point 5 advocated that "both churches search for mutual ways of manifesting the common mission of witness and service."[22]

Beginning with the 1832 Stone-Campbell merger, to the formation with the Federal Council of Churches, and into a chartering role with the World Council of Churches (1948), Disciples have pursued their convictions toward unity. From involvements with local, regional, national, and world ecumenical bodies to its early participation in the Consultation on Church Union (COCU, 1962) and with its successor Churches Uniting in Christ (CUIC, 2002), Disciples find themselves not only participating but giving significant leadership. In addition to untold numbers of board members and commissioners over the years, notable examples are that Suzanne J. Webb has served a term as president of CUIC. Thomas F. Best has recently retired as executive staff for the Secretariat of the Commission on Faith and Order of the World Council of Churches; Michael Kinnamon is presently general secretary of the National Council of Churches; and Richard L. Hamm, former General Minister and President of the Christian Church (Disciples of Christ), is executive administrator for the recently-organized Christian Churches Together.[23]

Specific to Stone-Campbell heritage, Disciples also are actively engaged in the World Convention of the Churches of Christ now comprised of Christian Churches (Independent), Disciples of Christ, and the Churches of Christ. Currently Erick D. Reisinger, an officer of Disciples Church Extension, is secretary/treasurer of that organization. A major collaboration resulted in the publication of *The Encyclopedia of the Stone-Campbell Movement* (Wm B. Eerdmans) in 2004. This notable volume was edited by Douglas A. Foster, Churches of

Christ; Paul M. Blowers, Christian Churches; Anthony L. Dunnavant (deceased prior to publication), Disciples of Christ; then followed by D. Newell Williams, Disciples of Christ. Contributors of articles, like the editors, represent all three streams of the movement.

Phillips Theological Seminary

From its beginning, Phillips Theological Seminary through its many configurations—College of the Bible, Graduate Seminary of Phillips University, Phillips Graduate Seminary—has maintained a constant, vigorous commitment to ecumenism. Even though generations of people far removed from its founding have taught, studied, worked, and governed there, the ethos remains the same. The first of three core values of the seminary in the catalog reads: "rooted in the ecumenical life of the Christian Church (Disciples of Christ)." In addition, the institution's current nondiscriminatory statement affirms: "In the administration of its policies and procedures related to admissions, financial aid, and academic programs, the seminary does not discriminate on the basis of race, color, national or ethnic origin, age, gender, gender identity, sexual orientation, disability, or theological perspective." Such a commitment is also evidenced in hiring practices and in services to community and church.

Although located in a state proud to claim its link in the Bible Belt and in a city that regards itself as the belt's buckle, PTS is able to foster a cooperative spirit within its student population and among churches throughout a multi-state region while maintaining its commitment to Disciples values and traditions. Extracurricular programs and lectureships for the community as well as courses within four degree programs and a certificate in graduate theological studies display an inclusive understanding of the Christian faith, from honoring specific denominational traditions to ecumenical explorations to interfaith engagements. At the heart of the seminary's mission is education—education in its broadest context. To this educational institution William Tabbernee was called to be president in 1991.

The Tabbernee Legacy

Born in Rotterdam, Holland, during World War II, Tabbernee was the only child of a Salvation Army officer mother.[24] His father worked in city government until captured by the Germans and sent to a labor camp where he was interned during the time of his son's birth. Along with other Dutch and central Europeans in a wave of post-war immigration, the family relocated to Warrandyte, Australia, a community in the state of Victoria outside the city of Melbourne. This was in the mid–1950s when young Tabbernee was about eleven years of age. Interested in architecture and design as a career, he was nonetheless intrigued by religion. Attending the local Gospel Chapel, he found the allure of the gospel appealing. At age sixteen he enrolled in Emmaus Bible College in Sydney, a school affiliated with the Brethren Assembly, a fundamentalist sect of the Plymouth Brethren. He was invested in evangelism, and the streets became his church. Preaching and playing music toward the conversion of many, he was known as the "boy wonder preacher."

Needing other employment to sustain his ministry, he attended teachers college where he became certified in primary and secondary education. Upon completion of his studies, he taught grades three, four, five, and six in one room while concurrently serving as headmaster of the school in Swan Reach, Victoria, Australia. In 1967, he joined the faculty at Newlands High School in Melbourne. During this time he became attracted to school chaplaincy, coupling his educational interests with that tug to ministry. To fulfill that dream, he needed recognized theological training plus the endorsement of a mainstream denomination. Accordingly he found himself drawn to the Churches of Christ (the Australian equivalent of the North American Disciples of Christ).

The educational system in Australia follows a British model; therefore, the nomenclature, sequencing, and credentialing of degrees are not entirely compatible with those in the United States. After obtaining a Diploma in Religious Education and Licentiate in Theology from the Melbourne College of Divinity in 1968, he enrolled in the College of the Bible[25] in Glen Iris, Victoria, Australia, where he began his studies in a theological environment that set him on yet another vocational track.

Tabbernee discovered his academic niche in the history of the early Christian church and was particularly attracted to the Montanists, a little-known, and to some critics heretical, sect concentrated in Asia Minor. In 1970 he was called to the College of the Bible as a lecturer in Christian thought and history while concurrently serving as senior minister at Patch Church of Christ in Melbourne. In the same year he received his Diploma in Ministry and was ordained in the Churches of Christ. He deferred his quest for chaplaincy and continued his education. In 1972 he was awarded the Bachelor of Arts (with honours) from the University of Melbourne. Traveling to the U.S., he completed the Master of Sacred Theology from Yale Divinity

School in 1973. Later, he earned two postgraduate degrees from the University of Melbourne: the Doctor of Philosophy in 1979 and the Doctor of Letters in 2002. Phillips University conferred upon him an honorary Doctor of Divinity in 1993.

Maintaining his faculty appointment in the College of the Bible, he became principal (president) in 1981 and eventually oversaw the building of a new campus and the renaming of the school to the Churches of Christ Theological College. In February of 2007, he was invited to return as a lecturer as part of that school's centennial celebration. Ironically, the theological college in Glen Iris, like PTS, traces its beginning to 1907.

Tabbernee's experiences as a child at the end of the war in Europe, then growing up in Australia, secured within him a large world view. Isolationism, sectarianism, and nationalism were not seen as positive attributes. His religious journey from the Salvation Army heritage of his mother to the Dutch Reformed Church of his birth land to the Plymouth Brethren of his adopted homeland then finally to the Churches of Christ broadened his theological perspectives. His education reinforced his love of learning and validated his journey. The more he learned about the Australian Churches of Christ, the more impressed he was with its progressive stances on biblical interpretation, women in ministry, theological dialogue, issues of justice, values in education, and ecumenical work.

Tabbernee's term as president of the Australian and New Zealand Association of Theological Schools enhanced his appreciation of cooperative work and a desire to communicate with those whose theological dispositions, liturgical practices, and biblical orientation were different from his. Grounded in the historic faith and committed to the expansion of Christianity, he advocated the promotion of quality ministerial education regardless of denominational affiliation.

With such openness, he naturally participated in and eventually gave leadership to Commissions on Faith and Order in the Victorian Council of Churches (deputy chair), the Australian Council of Churches (moderator), and the World Council of Churches. He has co-moderated the International Bilateral Commission for Dialogue between the Disciples Ecumenical Consultative Council and the Pontifical Council for the Promotion of Christian Unity (Roman Catholic). Boards and commissions on which he serves include the International Bilateral Commission for Dialogue between the Disciples Ecumenical Consultative Council and the World Alliance of Reformed Churches, the Oklahoma Center for Community and

Justice of which he is a member of the Jewish-Christian Dialogue, and Tulsa Metropolitan Ministry where he chaired the Christian Unity Issues Committee.

Among his past and present academic memberships are the American Academy of Religion, Society of Biblical Literature, American Society of Church History, American Catholic Historical Association, Association Internationale d'Études Patristiques (International Association of Patristic Studies), Association of Disciples for Theological Discussion, and the North American Patristic Society. While in Australia, he was part of the History Institute in Victoria and the Fellowship for Biblical Studies.

Tabbernee is widely published through books, chapters in books, journal articles, encyclopedia entries, and scholarly reviews. Many of his writings resulted from his numerous speaking engagements both in the United States and overseas. Interested in a variety of subjects, his topics range from critical interpretations of Montanism to historical perspectives on women in ministry to theological analyses of the Disciples of Christ to engagements with unity and interfaith dialogues. One of his early books was an edited work on *Ministry in Australian Churches* (Joint Board of Christian Education, 1987). Perhaps his magnum opus to date is *Montanist Inscriptions and Testimonia: Epigraphic Sources Illustrating the History of Montanism* (Mercer University Press, 1997), number 16 in the Patristic Monograph Series. Having recently completed a six months' sabbatical, he finished work on *Fake Prophecy and Polluted Sacraments: Ecclesiastical and Imperial Reaction to Montanism* (Brill, 2008). He collaborated with Peter Lampe from the University of Heidelberg in writing *Pepouza and Tymion: The Discovery and Archeological Exploration of a Lost Ancient City and an Imperial Estate in Phrygia* (Walter de Gruyter, 2008). Published in 2009 is *Prophets and Gravestones: An Imaginative History of Montanists and Other Early Christians* (Hendrickson).

As Steve Cranford noted in the Foreword to this volume, inviting Dr. Tabbernee to consider moving to the United States to assume the presidency of Phillips Theological Seminary was a logical choice, if a seemingly remote chance. His experiences in theological leadership, his gifts for administration, and his academic integrity were precisely what the school needed in a stage of transition. With a campus in Enid and a center in Tulsa, the seminary to which he was introduced had two faculties, two administrative units, and essentially two student populations. Among the first of many decisions was how to bring coherence to these separate entities.

Along with settling into an unusual institutional context and adapting to a foreign culture, Tabbernee discovered within the student populations significant strains of evangelical fervor that were not consistent with the overall philosophy of the faculty and administration, nor with the ecumenical tradition of the school. One risk of an open theological environment is that it invites discussions that can become confrontational. While those differences did not appear problematic on the surface, they carried undercurrents that created dissention in the classrooms and had the potential to disrupt the seminary altogether. Tabbernee had to direct his attention to these challenges, as well as the demands of governance, finances, and operations. An educator with proven administrative capabilities and an ecumenical bent, he proved able to reach out to students of differing viewpoints, church people beyond the Disciples of Christ, and various constituent groups who were anxious about the viability of the seminary. He generated confidence at a critical time when the school needed to reconstitute itself.

This disposition enabled him to meet with the contentious student leaders to resolve the disagreements. The results were not theological consensus—for that was not the goal—but respect for differing viewpoints.

During an executive session of the Board in the winter of 1996, toward the end of his first five years, the Trustees celebrated his contributions as president with a commendation that recognized his accomplishments as an academician and ecumenist. The declaration concluded with "the Board of Trustees is grateful to Dr. Tabbernee for the model of excellence in ministry and scholarship."

In a personal interview with me, Tabbernee observed, "Christian unity is ultimately rooted in the basic underlying unity of all human-kind. As we are all creatures of the one creator, there is something which we all have in common, and we should understand each other and be in relationship with each other even though each of us has a different understanding of how God is revealed to us."[26] In the interview, he went on to say, "We need to educate in a post-denominational age as we live in proximity with each other."[27]

This disposition is manifest in the public arena as well. In 2006, having lived in Tulsa less than ten years, he was one of three recipients of the Interfaith Understanding Award sponsored jointly by the Islamic Society of Tulsa, Jewish Federation of Tulsa, Oklahoma Center for Community and Justice, and Tulsa Metropolitan Ministry. Indeed, living out the question of how far we should encourage ecumenism, posed by Dean England to the faculty in 1951, forms a guiding principle of what the seminary was then and is still called to be. It is no accident that in addition to being president, Tabbernee is also the Stephen J. England Distinguished Professor of the History of Christianity.

Maintaining its historic and current non-sectarian commitments, Phillips Theological Seminary has expanded into interfaith conversations with the living religions of the world. Currently the faculty and staff represent ten different faith groups, and students claim affiliation with twenty-plus denominations, including a handful who designate themselves as nondenominational. Under Tabbernee's tenure, the curriculum has expanded to include specific courses in spirituality, non-Christian traditions, ecumenism, and the study of world missions as well as opportunities for national and international study tours to promote cross-cultural exposure.

Bill Tabbernee epitomizes the Campbellian dictum that "Colleges and churches go hand in hand in the progress of Christian civilization."

1

The Ecumenical Paradox in Three Linguistic Strategies

HAROLD HATT

One of the often-overlooked sources of zeal for the goals of Christian unity is what we might call the "ecumenical paradox." We are zealous about Christian unity because it is a gift from God in which we can rest secure, and we are zealous about Christian unity because it is a goal that lures us into new and uncharted waters.

This study proposes to explore that ecumenical paradox as it gains expression in three linguistic strategies—the symbolic language of popular discourse, the conceptual language of theology (represented by Wolfhart Pannenberg), and the confessional language of affirmation in the Progressive Christianity movement. This distinctive treatment of three strategies is not intended to suggest that we have to commit to one strategy, nor is it intended to suggest that there is no crossover, as if, for example, those developing a confessional language could do so without reclaiming symbols of the faith and without having engaged in conceptual language about the faith.

Symbolic Language and Ecumenical Paradox

The linguistic strategy of symbolism is to communicate through what Paul Ricoeur calls "a surplus of signification."[1] Symbols generate a richness and fullness of meaning, which we never exhaust, but from which we can draw that which is meaningful for our particular context.[2]

Today the cross is by far the most commonly used symbol of the Christian church. But it was one of many symbols of the faith in the early days. Two of those symbols have been very popular in the contemporary ecumenical movement: the house and the boat.

The House

The image of the church as a household is found in 1 Peter 2:5: "Like living stones, let yourselves be built into a spiritual house, to be a holy priesthood, to offer spiritual sacrifices acceptable to God through Jesus Christ."

Stones are hard, cold, and seemingly inanimate, yet they can be brought together to build a house. That process becomes a figure of speech for the way in which individual Christians and congregations can be brought together as living stones to build the church.

The word *oikoumene,* from which we get our word *ecumenical,* is derived from the Greek word *oikos,* which means "house" or "household." From this same root we get our word *economics,* which originally referred to the management of the finances of the household. For the church, the whole household of faith embraces people from all races, genders, sexual orientations, classes, and creeds. We are all over the map, and yet we are one in Christ.

The Boat

Paradoxically, the church is also thought of as a boat. We do not know for sure how the symbol of the boat originated, but most think that it stems from two incidents in the life of Jesus—calling his disciples beside the Sea of Galilee and stilling the storm on the Sea of Galilee. Whatever its origin, its suggestion of a destination makes the point that the church is en route. The World Council of Churches put the cross and the boat together to form its logo.

Why Both Symbols Are Needed

Holding together all the diversity that God has placed in our world can be a challenge, and sometimes a very tough challenge. But here we are with two images of the church—as a stone house built on a solid foundation on which to stand secure, and as a boat in which to sail forth, perhaps into uncharted waters. The affirmation of both images is necessary, and so we have the paradoxical symbols of the church as a house built of living stones that floats like a boat.

Granted, some people have a clear preference for one image over the other. For example, think of the hymns, "The Church's

One Foundation" and "Standing on the Promises," and of course there is Martin Luther's famous declaration: "Here I stand, I can do no other."[3]

On the other hand, we have the spirited statement of Archbishop Helder Camara, of Brazil: "Pilgrim: when your ship, long moored in harbour, gives you the illusion of being a house; when your ship begins to put down roots in the stagnant water by the quay: put out to sea! Save your boat's journeying soul, and your own pilgrim soul, cost what it may."[4] Certainly churches and congregations vary, some resembling more closely a house and others, a boat.

The image of the house expresses the faith that God is our shield and defender, who calls the church to live in a covenant of mutual respect and support, bearing one another's burdens and celebrating one another's joys. The image of the boat expresses the faith that God is the wind in our sails, inspiring the church to launch out into the deep and calling the church to speak truth to power, to liberate the oppressed, to care for the poor, and to comfort the afflicted.

Both figures of speech are necessary for a full expression of the faith. We live in a house built of living stones because God has spoken, and our foundation is sure. We sail in a stone house that floats like a boat because God is still speaking and because we have not completed our journey, nor have we learned all that God has to teach us nor done all that God calls us to do.

Sometimes tension rises between those who want the church to stand firm against the forces that assail it and those who want the church to be willing to change so that it can launch out into new territory. But not only are both images necessary, they both face a common enemy. The common enemy is sand. On the one hand, we build on the rock, because sand shifts so that a house built on sand will sooner or later collapse. On the other hand, we sail in the deeper waters, because if we sail on the sand we will sooner or later become stuck.

Conceptual Language and the Ecumenical Paradox

The linguistic strategy of theology, notwithstanding the wide variety of methodologies employed and differences over the sources to be drawn upon, is to use conceptual language to communicate the faith. This kind of formulation facilitates greater precision and critical reflection.

However mind-boggling paradoxical symbols may be, they are often what we get stuck on when we try to move from the euphoric language of symbol to the rigorous language of theology. Can the symbols of a house built of living stones that floats like a boat survive a translation into the language of theology?

In this study, Wolfhart Pannenberg is taken as the representative of theological discourse. One of the particular characteristics of Pannenberg is his emphasis that theology is a kind of science and that it is incumbent upon the theologian to adhere to the scientific method.[5] Pannenberg's discussion of the ecumenical paradox is undertaken, not in-house where faith may rule, but in the open public arena, where logic rules.

Chapter 2 of Pannenberg's book, *The Church*,[6] is entitled: "The Unity of the Church: A Reality of Our Faith and an Ecumenical Goal." A reality and a goal—the paradox is alive and well in theology, at least in Pannenberg's version of it.

Pannenberg offers a logical argument for the paradox of the unity of the church as both a gift and a goal. "Therefore, prior to all human efforts, unity already exists because Christians are Christian, because, that is, of their 'union' with Jesus Christ."[7] This conclusion entails that

> the efforts of the ecumenical movements are directed toward the reunion of Christians, not in the sense of a return to the historical state of Christianity before the divisions arose, but something much more urgent, a reunion in the sense of turning to that unity which already exists in our Christian faith and is one of its constituent elements.[8]

Pannenberg discerns, in this givenness of unity, not only a word of assurance but also a word of judgment. He attributes a large measure of responsibility for the decline of the church to its complacent acceptance of divisions in spite of this constituent element. He will not let us off the hook with the specious claim that "my" branch of the church is the only true embodiment of the church, nor even with the claim that the church manifests a transcendent and invisible unity. An unseen unity will not do; it must be visible.

On the other hand, Pannenberg sees the unity of the church as a goal. As a settled reality, unity assures us; but as a goal, unity allures us. As a settled reality, unity judges us; as a goal, it nudges us, operating as a hope and promise rather than as a constituent element and standard of judgment.

Just as Pannenberg finds a word of judgment in unity as a reality, so also he finds a word of judgment in unity as a goal. We corrupt the sense of this theological affirmation if we take it as a justification for going slowly on achieving mutual recognition and for meeting "ecumenical enthusiasm" with "calm reserve."[9] Even as a goal, unity is an essential, not an optional, feature of the church. It is not merely desirable, but essential.

The eucharist poses a particular problem since it has tended to polarize the reality and the goal of Christian unity. We have some traditions arguing that celebration of the eucharist is only appropriate for those who have already achieved unity, whereas other traditions encourage us to break bread together because that helps us in our efforts to break down the walls that divide us. Pannenberg's discussion of the eucharist seeks to retain, not resolve, the tension. Christian unity is, on the one hand, a settled reality that is a source of confidence and strength attested through participation in baptism and the eucharist. For Pannenberg, the eucharist has the greater clarity as a manifestation of the unity of the church and its signification of the kingdom of God.[10] The eucharist is a dramatic expression of the paradox of the unity of the church since it both witnesses to the unity of the church and strengthens our resolve to work toward its realization.

Pannenberg closes his chapter on "The Unity of the Church: A Reality of Our Faith and an Ecumenical Goal," by identifying four areas in which fruitful progress may be attained.[11]

First, recognition of the positive contributions of other churches can be developed if each group will commit itself to an enlarged self-consciousness that finds room for the contributions of others.

Second, the Roman Catholic Church and the churches separated from Rome can progress by affirming what is held in common and by exploring ways of replacing older anathemas by contemporary blessings of one another.

Third, progress can be achieved by mutual recognition of and participation in baptism, eucharist, and ministry,[12] with a view to larger cooperation at every level, and even agreement on the form and conditions for an office that is responsible for the whole of Christianity.

Fourth, progress can be made by the organization and convocation of a new ecumenical council in which Catholics, Orthodox, and Protestants share equally.

Pannenberg seemingly recognizes that he has proffered a highly ambitious proposal. So he closes by proposing an intermediate goal. Even in the state of separation, the churches

> have the opportunity of making their own organization, their worship, and their faith so rich, and so to strengthen their unity with Christ, the one Lord of all Christians, that in their

own life they would become capable of participating in a council, become capable, that is, of coming together in such a council in the fellowship of the Holy Spirit.[13]

In the final chapter of *The Church,* Pannenberg addresses the important issue of the relationship between furthering the unity of the church and furthering the unity of humankind. He cautions that fostering this relationship risks secularizing the ecumenical movement. To give this a positive spin, he says: "The most important contribution that Christians can make to human unity would certainly be to regain their own unity."[14] He softens his stance even more by adding: "To be sure, the church is not an end in itself. It already manifests the future fellowship of the Kingdom of God, which is to include all mankind, a renewed mankind that has passed through the judgment of God."[15] Pannenberg's guiding principle is that the church is a sign—he even speaks of it as a sacrament—and instrument of the future unity of humankind in the kingdom of God.

Things really begin to open up when Pannenberg talks about what is necessary for the church to be effective. A church that achieved uniformity would not be an effective sign and instrument but would instead be "a source of trauma for all non-Christian religions and world views."[16] To be diverse is not the same as to be fragmented. The latter is contrary to the unity of the church and the unity of humankind. Diversity is here to stay, and diversity in polity, liturgy, and theology should be welcomed, not resisted, by the church even in—especially in—its quest for the unity of the church. Pannenberg's vision involves "a unity of Christians through reciprocal recognition in faith and love, accompanied by continuing differences in doctrine and polity because of the shared knowledge that one's own faith and polity are provisional—this kind of Christian unity would have no need to shut itself off from other religions in an exclusivistic attitude."[17]

A basic issue this vision raises involves the contending claims that religion is a private matter and that religion has a social function. The debate over these competing claims is complicated by a variety of historical, political, and economic influences.[18] Pannenberg observes that when religion is considered a private matter, substitute religions arise so that the state can provide religious authorization for its authority. But these substitute religions are not independent of the ruling authority, and they lack the dimension of transcendence that gives genuine religion its potential for critical reflection. If all of our beliefs and claims are provisional, we must have some way to test them. That task can only be performed by a religion that operates in the public sphere. Pannenberg celebrates the ecumenical movement, with its dual commitment to unity and multiplicity, as a force that can reverse the trend toward private religion and that can promote the development of the church as a sign and instrument of the future unity of humankind.

Because our beliefs and claims are provisional, we cannot fix them in the present. This does not mean that we are set adrift, tossed about by whatever wind happens to be blowing at the moment. We can, in each present, look to the promised future kingdom of God for guidance in our quest for the unity of the church.

Confessional Language and the Ecumenical Paradox

The linguistic strategy of confessional affirmation rests on neither the richness of symbols nor the precision of concepts but seeks rather to affirm a shared common ground. In the confessional language of the movement of Progressive Christianity, this affirmation of common ground is not narrow and protective but expansive and welcoming. Progressive Christianity is a contemporary movement indirectly living out of Pannenberg's vision of a church that recognizes the reasonable, but provisional, nature of all beliefs and that welcomes the goal of seeking justice and peace in cooperation with all humankind.

The original plan for this essay was to take Crosswalk America with its "Phoenix Affirmations"[19] and The Center for Progressive Christianity with its "Eight Points"[20] as representatives of this contemporary development within the church. However, during the period of research, Crosswalk America became incorporated within The Center for Progressive Christianity. So these will now be considered as two compatible thrusts within one organization that is typical of the Progressive movement in contemporary Christianity.

Crosswalk America was co-founded in Phoenix, Arizona, by the Rev. Eric Elnes and Rebecca Glenn. It brought together both clergy and laity from a variety of mainline denominations, all of whom shared a concern that people with a genuine Christian faith increasingly find themselves marginalized, and even spiritually homeless, in the narrow and often intolerant form of religion that commonly passes for Christianity in the late twentieth and early twenty-first centuries.

The first public action of this group was to formulate "The Phoenix Affirmations," a set of twelve spiritual principles that express Jesus' core values and that form a pledge to express Christian love by loving God, neighbor, and self. Elnes authored the initial draft and also wrote the book, *The Phoenix Affirmations: A New Vision for the Future of Christianity*[21] –his personal elaboration of what this shared set of core beliefs means for him and a first step to stimulate others to reflect on the twelve affirmations. The name has a double source. It refers to the mythological bird adopted by Christians because of its rising out of the ashes–and which symbolizes the contemporary resurrection of the historic Christian faith in the Progressive movement. The other source is the city of Phoenix, the geographical center of the movement.

The second public action began in Phoenix on Easter 2006 (April 16) as six people, joined at times by others, set out walking on a 2,500 mile journey through the heart of America, ending in the nation's capital on Labor Day weekend. En route, they communicated with church groups who shared their message of compassion and inclusion and with others who resisted their degree of openness. This journey of faith and witness is analogous to the journey symbolized by the boat in the logo of the World Council of Churches, but it was conducted by foot and on land. The walk across America has given rise to another book by Eric Elnes, *Asphalt Jesus: Finding a New Christian Faith Along the Highways of America*,[22] and a ninety-minute documentary produced by Scott Griessel, *The Asphalt Gospel.*[23]

The Rev. Jim Adams founded The Center for Progressive Christianity in 1994 in Washington, D.C., in response to statistics showing that mainline churches are in steep decline. Adams sought to provide an alternative to those for whom organized religion was irrelevant or even repressive. The Center for Progressive Christianity established a network for sharing resources and publicizing opportunities for Progressive churches, organizations, and individuals. This network has expanded dramatically and soon became an international network. The Center also formulated the Eight Points as a succinct, but defining, statement of the essence of the Progressive Christianity Movement.

The Twelve Affirmations and the Eight Points do not mention some of Pannenberg's ideas; they carry some of his ideas even further; and they modify yet others. For example, Pannenberg conceives of theology as a kind of science, but Point 6 describes progressive Christians as people who "find more grace in the search for understanding than we do in dogmatic certainty–more value in questioning than in absolutes." Affirmation 10 talks about "recognizing that faith and science, doubt and belief serve the pursuit of truth." So Pannenberg employs logical argument, even for the paradox. The Affirmations and Points, however, are more on the order of invitations to taste and see.

We can see parallels in the first two areas that Pannenberg identifies as areas for fruitful progress–finding room for the contribution of others and replacing anathemas with blessings. For example, Affirmation 8 values "seeking to understand and call forth the best in others, including those who consider us their enemies." Pannenberg has no desire to return to the primal unity of the church. Nor do the Affirmations lead us there. For example, Affirmation 2 speaks of "listening for God's Word, which comes through daily prayer and meditation, studying the ancient testimonies which we call Scripture," and then it continues: "and attending to God's present activity in the world." On top of that, Affirmation 4 speaks of "expressing our love in worship that is as sincere, vibrant, and artful as it is scriptural." In general, the Bible is often mentioned in the Affirmations, but it is something to work from, not something to be restored in the contemporary world.

Pannenberg contends that unity is essential and must take visible form. Point 5 emphasizes that "the way we behave toward one another and toward other people is the fullest expression of what we believe." A little more sense of living a kind of life that stems from the sense of unity with others, rather than of working toward ways of living that give visible form to our sense of unity, appears here.

Pannenberg's emphasis on the eucharist as the prime symbol of Christian unity is echoed in Point 3, which describes Progressive Christians as people who "understand the sharing of bread and wine in Jesus' name to be a representation of an ancient vision of God's feast for all peoples." However, Pannenberg's specific suggestions of promoting mutual recognition of baptism, eucharist, and ministry, and of convoking a new ecumenical council are not the major means employed by Progressive Christianity for advancing Christian unity. I certainly do not see any echoes of Pannenberg's call for a person or office to represent the whole Church.

On the other hand, there are many echoes of Pannenberg's insistence that religion is not private, but social. Point 7 says:

> By calling ourselves progressive, we mean that we are Christians who form ourselves into communities dedicated to equipping one another for the work we feel called to do: striving for peace and justice among all people, protecting and restoring the integrity of all God's creation, and bringing hope to those Jesus called the least of his sisters and brothers.

Affirmation 6 speaks of standing with the oppressed and seeking peace and justice; Affirmation 7 of "preserving religious freedom and the church's ability to speak prophetically to government by resisting the commingling of church and state."

Does Progressive Christianity retain the paradox that we talked about in our discussion of symbolic language? Note Affirmation 1: "Walking fully in the path of Jesus without denying the legitimacy of other paths that God may provide for humanity." This continues the paradox of reality and task. The reality of the quest is expressed as "walking fully in the path of Jesus" and its goal is expressed as "without denying the legitimacy of other paths that God may provide for humanity." Walking fully opens us up to a fulfillment that lies in the future as we embrace God's children whose walking fully has taken a different form from our own.

Point 2 does something similar: "Recognize the faithfulness of other people who have other names for the way to God's realm, and acknowledge that their ways are true for them, as our ways are true for us." Note again Point 6, which affirms that those who call themselves progressive Christians "find more grace in the search for understanding than we do in dogmatic certainty—more value in questioning than in absolutes."

Conclusion

The Progressive Christianity movement of the twenty-first century is characterized by an increased emphasis on diversity and on interfaith dialogue. Ironically, the twenty-first century is also marked by a resurgence of strife generated, or at least justified, in the name of religion. Religious leaders want a voice in the public discourse, but some go further in each's efforts to be *the* spokesperson for all "legitimate" religious faith. Arguably the mutual respect and appreciation of the Abrahamic religions—Judaism, Christianity, and Islam—have been most deeply damaged as a fallout from the 9/11 attack and the invasion of Afghanistan and Iraq.

So the paradox lives on. An all-embracing love is the root, but much work remains to be done before we realize the fruit of mutual recognition and appreciation of different denominations, different religious faiths, and of different human beings. It is better to speak of "schismatics" than of "heretics"; better yet to speak of "separated brothers and sisters" than of "schismatics"; but we can still do better than that. As Peter Steinfels wrote: "What was once the scandal of division now looks more like the virtue of diversity."[24]

The house built of living stones that floats like a boat continues its voyage. En route, it has picked up new sails and new sailing companions. Thanks be to God, who has increased the zeal of the quest for the unity of the church and the unity of humankind.

2

"Give Me Thy Hand"

Practicing Ecumenical and Interreligious Theology at a United Methodist Campus Ministry

ELLEN BLUE

Even in Louisiana, where Huey Long and his colorful brother Earl are among the characters who have occupied the Governor's Mansion, the 1991 gubernatorial election stands out as bizarre. It was a near miss for Louisiana that year, when bumper stickers urging "*Vote for the Crook—It's Important*" helped return the ethically challenged Edwin Edwards to the state's highest office.

My husband and I voted absentee in the fateful open primary because we would be away on Election Day. That night we sat beside a bonfire on an Arkansas lakeshore listening to returns on a distant radio station and gleaning enough information amidst the static and station bleed to realize that what I had predicted and dreaded was coming true. I vividly recall saying, "David Duke's going to make it into the runoff. We're going to remember this night forever."

Duke's supporters complained that the press accompanied every mention of his name with the appositive, "former Grand Wizard of the Ku Klux Klan"; however, that was, and remains, a compelling description of the man. Circulation of a photograph of Duke wearing a Nazi uniform at Louisiana State University and his insistence that the

Holocaust never really happened motivated the Jewish community to activism. A broad coalition of Jews, liberal Christians, and secular humanists united to support Edwards against his far less acceptable opponent in the run-off.

It seems ironic that the evening by the bonfire occurred during the annual Intercultural Retreat organized by the campus ministry at the University of Louisiana, Monroe (ULM), where my husband was pastor.[1] Although most people associate the KKK with violence toward African Americans, the Klan's resurgence in the early twentieth century was also a product of widespread anti-immigration and anti-Catholic sentiment that led to riots against various immigrant groups, along with physical attacks on nuns and the burning of convents in several locations.

The students with us in Arkansas were from all around the world and came from a wide variety of faiths. The importance of every issue we'd taken them to Arkansas to discuss—religion, culture, custom, race, nationality, ethnicity, values, fear, acceptance, sameness, and difference—was being highlighted back home in Louisiana that night. David Duke's popularity was a tragically appropriate part of the evening's discussion.

* * * * *

When I was in seminary—way back in the early 1990s—my friends and I never answered our e-mail while our professors lectured. This was not because we were so well mannered or because we were tired out from walking to class uphill both ways through the snow. None of us *had* e-mail. We had never dreamed of a time when serious presidential contenders would announce candidacies on their Web sites and when campaigns might fall over a video posted on YouTube, or of a time when Christians might choose a "virtual" church instead of a "real" one, or at least catch a missed Sunday sermon the next Tuesday via podcast.

Although technology has dramatically altered the shape and speed of the public discourse, when seminary students become ministers, they are automatically going to become participants in and contributors to that discourse. Further, they will not be participants in the "fifteen-minutes" sense. Week after week and year after year, they will be opinion shapers who influence not only their parishioners but also others who attach import to the words and actions of a woman or man of the cloth.

Laity and clergy both are obligated to address many of the ideas and opinions being disseminated in the public arena today. Put another way, material circulates "out there" that the church of Jesus the Christ ought either to support and nourish or to critique and undermine. The concept of ecumenical and interreligious tolerance, understanding, and cooperation is clearly among them. The problem is that some devout Christians think this concept should be nurtured, while others are sure it should be challenged.

Unfortunately, usually those against the concept usually speak more frequently and louder. Phrases like "ecumenical and inter-religious tolerance, understanding, and cooperation" do not make for good sound-bites. It requires a long investment of time and effort to change attitudes about fundamental matters such as "us and them" religion. A level of career risk remains involved in promoting something that many vocal church people do not approve of or even understand.

Thus the National Campus Ministry Association's occasionally bestowed Richard Ross Hicks Award was instituted to honor a lifetime contribution to the field of campus ministry and, more especially, to recognize outstanding ministry that cuts across ethnic and other lines. In 2008, my husband, Jim Wilson, received the award for decades of cutting edge work with people from various kinds of marginalized communities.[2] This chapter in a book on unity seems a fitting location to chronicle and discuss a few things that Jim's creative ministry revealed about the practice of ecumenical and interreligious theology. The contribution that such ministry makes toward changing the temper and character of public discourse flows into that discussion.

In 1969 Jim was appointed to the Wesley Foundation on the campus in Monroe, Louisiana. Relatively soon his efforts led to establishing a formal ecumenical partnership at what had been a United Methodist ministry. When he left twenty-six years later, the ministry was supported by Presbyterian Church USA, Christian Church (Disciples of Christ), and Evangelical Lutheran Church of America (ELCA) congregations and, more surprisingly, a congregation of the Lutheran Church–Missouri Synod. (This unusual affiliation resulted from a relationship built over several years between Jim and a Missouri Synod pastor. It did not imply "full communion" or deep doctrinal shift on either's part–it evidenced a recognition that aims which both agreed were part of the larger church's mission were being fulfilled through ministry activities.)

Ministry partners benefited the work in numerous ways, potential for increased funding being only one of them. Camps belonging to participating non-Methodist judicatories permitted events such as the Intercultural Retreat, which would otherwise not have been financially feasible. When Jim arrived in Monroe, Presbyterians operated a separate campus ministry in a former private residence located across the campus. After an ecumenical partnership was established, that Presbyterian site was put to use as a co-op day care and child development facility operated by the campus ministry. When it opened in the mid–1970s, the availability of safe, affordable day care was very much a justice issue for women students. Large numbers of divorced women had put their husbands through college, only to have those husbands then leave them. Single mothers who lacked education were hard-pressed to support children and even harder pressed to attend college while those children were young. Day care ministry allowed women to volunteer several hours a week as care-givers and thereby significantly decrease the price of their children's care. By the 1990s, fathers often used it as well. The facility also served as a training site for students in child development programs at the university. It required a large investment of time and effort to ensure a high quality of care. Neither United Methodists nor the Presbyterians could have sustained the ministry alone.

Furthermore, the existence of the ecumenical framework for campus ministry allowed for quick creation of ecumenical flood relief agencies after disasters in the mid–1970s and the early 1990s. Pastors affiliated with the ministry and the local rabbi formed a board of directors, and the campus ministry building provided a site for operations. The pooling of resources that enabled hosting scores of volunteer work teams and disbursal of funds from many denominational sources to hundreds of area families certainly could not have been accomplished as effectively, and possibly could not have been accomplished at all, if the groundwork for ecumenical cooperation had not been laid on campus.

Ecumenical work was not without problems of course. Accountability to multiple judicatories, with attendant report-writing and paperwork, increased work loads for Jim and his administrative assistant. Jim attended many more meetings, and many more congregations needed to have campus ministry interpreted to them on a regular basis. The entity of "Northeast Campus Ministry" was created and the name added to the letterhead and the front of the building when Presbyterian-Methodist cooperation began. Still, the term "Wesley Foundation" continued to be used alongside it. In time, as other denominations joined the work, it became clear that using "Wesley Foundation" was no longer appropriate, and the name was simply dropped. Some former students and some area laity found the change unsettling, so a time-consuming program of interpretation was necessary to minimize loss of Methodist support.

Jim judged all the extra effort required for ecumenicity to be worthwhile—and not just for the additional resources it provided. He deeply valued the broad spectrum of students drawn to the ecumenical ministry and the opportunities this provided for teaching and learning. He came to believe that increased ecumenical awareness is tied to a more profound understanding and appreciation of one's own tradition.

Over the two-and-a-half decades that Jim spent in Monroe, he moved the ministry beyond inter-denominational cooperation and into a significant level of interreligious work. The Intercultural Retreat project mentioned in the opening paragraphs began in the early 1990s with a suggestion from a non-Christian Asian student. She had noticed others experiencing the same adjustment difficulties that she recalled from her first year in the United States. It is a tribute to Jim that she chose a Christian pastor to approach, but, by then, Jim had developed a vital ministry among international students.

His credibility in that arena was further enhanced when he extended welcome and free office space to Dr. Kok-Liang Gan from Singapore. A practicing Buddhist, Dr. Gan was an elderly but extremely energetic physician who came to the United States to study gerontology, choosing ULM because his two children were already students there. Gan worked with international students, counseling and assisting them in any way he could, and he used Jim's campus ministry as his base of operations. He was respected and beloved by the community there.

Jim's assistant, Lanette Carroll, would later earn a master's degree in Latin American Studies from the University of New Mexico. During her career at the campus ministry, she displayed a special interest in and gift for working with the international students who spent time there. She built strong relationships with many of them.

Jim, Lanette, and Dr. Gan headed the committee to organize the first Intercultural Retreat and drew upon all their knowledge of the campus population to make it a success. We took twenty newly arrived international students, twenty international students who had been at ULM for at least a year, and twenty students from the States for a weekend in a camp setting. They heard of each other's customs and faiths and learned from experts and from one another about what it is like to live in a different country and then go back home. (Many did not realize that going home generates more severe culture shock than leaving.)

Members of the ministry's Board of Directors (including the Dean of Student Affairs), and sociology, anthropology, and communications faculty served as small group facilitators. Students were assigned so as to ensure as much diversity as possible within each unit. Every year Christians, Hindus, Muslims, and Buddhists attended. Most years other groups were represented, including followers of Judaism and Confucianism. The small groups met throughout the weekend to compare religious backgrounds and value systems.

No formal worship was included since the spectrum of beliefs was so broad. The most religious aspect of the gathering was the remarkably honest and thoughtful sharing in the group settings, enabling the students to discover similarities in the core values of all their faiths. Most participants considered the event to have been profoundly meaningful from a religious standpoint.

Some years after the retreats began, Jim and I moved to new ministry settings in New Orleans. Several years after that, we were surprised to hear that the campus ministry had recently ended its sponsorship of the retreats. A newly appointed pastor—call him Rev. John Doe—reasoned that the ministry should not put resources into any event that did not attempt to convert non-Christians. Jim had recruited secular organizations such as the Student Government Association to help finance the retreat. This guaranteed that many stateside students involved were campus leaders, a not insignificant benefit. Rev. Doe told the other sponsors that he intended to conduct uniquely Christian worship during the retreat, and if they objected, he would refuse to let the ministry, which performed most of the organizational work involved, participate. They did object, and he refused.

While I completely disagree with Doe's decision, I understand it to have been an act of integrity, given his theological understandings. If one genuinely believes that students will burn eternally in hell because they have not accepted Jesus as Savior, then spending the weekend without providing opportunity for them to "be saved" would indeed be failing in one's Christian responsibility.[3]

Jim saw that international students were often among the brightest and most affluent citizens of their countries and could therefore be expected to fill leadership roles after returning home. He thought interacting with them in such a way as to live out his own Christianity— as over against trying to convert them to it—was making the best of the opportunity to work with them. He was, in other words, in ministry with them not in order to make *them* Christian, but rather because *he* was Christian. However, more conservative Christians such as Rev. Doe tend to see the students' potentials for leadership as reason to expend greater effort in "converting them now, while we have a chance."

Those who share Doe's theological viewpoint are usually willing to back their doctrine with their practices. I argue that those of us whose viewpoint looks toward openness are equally bound to do what we can to move others in that direction, even though that task is significantly more complicated than fanning prejudice or denouncing heterodoxy. I make this assertion because following an apparently enlightened "think and let think" policy fails to address a concomitant responsibility for tragic consequences that can spring from religious exclusivism.

Many Christians labor under the misconception that only two points of view present themselves about the unique efficacy of Christianity for salvation. They think they must either: (a) believe that Christianity is the only true religion; or (b) believe that anything anyone calls "religion" is acceptable—an "anything goes" approach. Schubert Ogden challenges the assertion that the only two options are "one is true" and "all are true."[4] He maintains certain criteria about what constitutes a "true religion" can help us decide that certain religions are "true" while others are not. Certainly no consensus exists about what such criteria might be. Still, grasping the basic idea that if one had sufficient information at hand, one might be able to make some judgments about the "acceptability" of some other religions and the "unacceptability" of others may offer some individuals enough freedom to think more clearly about whether Christians must believe in the unique efficacy of Christianity.

As a Methodist historian, I find it ironic that the campus minister who withdrew sponsorship of the retreats was, like my husband, ordained in a tradition founded by English cleric John Wesley and shaped by his theology. What most United Methodists know about Wesley's stance on ecumenism is the oft-quoted conclusion to his work, "The Character of a Methodist." He believed that disagreements about doctrine should not stop Christians from working together. He wrote:

> But from real Christians, of whatsoever denomination they be, we earnestly desire not to be distinguished at all.... And I beseech you, brethren, by the mercies of God, that we be in no wise divided among ourselves. Is thy heart right, as my heart is with thine? I ask no farther question. If it be, give me thy hand. For opinions, or terms, let us not destroy the work of God. Dost thou love and serve God? It is enough. I give thee the right hand of fellowship.[5]

This should not be taken to mean that John Wesley did not have strong opinions about the correctness of his own theology. An unwavering Armenian, he was especially convinced of the wrong-headedness of Calvinism and proclaimed at every opportunity, both orally and in print, how and why it was utterly wrong. However, he believed that even Calvinists could be true Christians because he knew Calvinists who displayed what seemed to be genuine fruits of the Spirit.[6]

While Wesley's admission that non-Methodists could be Christians is not shocking, it does surprise many to learn that he was unwilling to insist that only Christians could be in right relationship with God. After the rebellion of the thirteen colonies occasioned removal of Church of England priests, John Wesley accepted the necessity of forming an official Methodist organization in America. This occurred in 1784. Because he personally created the basic theological documents for that body by means of editing those of the Church of England, we can use a form of redaction criticism to know which aspects of the Church of England's stance he thought needed modification. When he edited the Thirty-Nine Articles for Methodist use, he completely omitted Article XVIII, "Of obtaining eternal salvation only by the name of Christ," which states that according to Holy Scripture, it is "only the name of Jesus Christ, whereby men must be saved." While the articles he edited for Methodism continue to insist that the Christian canon contains everything needed to be saved, there is no remaining claim about the uniqueness of Christianity as a vehicle for salvation.[7]

Scholars talk about Wesley's sometimes contradictory stands, and some discern Early, Middle, and Late stages of his theology. John Wesley was born in 1703. By the time he edited the Articles of Religion, a lifetime of study and reflection had produced a mature theologian. The omission of Article XVIII is clear evidence of his belief that the hope of salvation exists both inside and outside the Christian faith.

It is also worth examining one aspect of Wesley's theological method, which Albert Outler deemed the "Wesleyan Quadrilateral" and which Charles Wood suggests might more aptly be called the "Wesleyan Quartet"–the mix of scripture, tradition, reason, and experience as sources and norms for theology.[8] Though "experience" has become controversial in recent years, it is evident that John Wesley did use his own personal experience in his theological reflection, from his "heartwarming" experience in Aldersgate Street to his acceptance that Calvinists might be Christian because he was personally acquainted with Calvinists whom he judged to be genuinely Christian.

While Wesley lived centuries before the rise of liberation theology, I think he would have been receptive to the idea that theological reflection is a second-order activity. I believe he would agree that our theologies are affected by our (first-order) practices and by our experiences. Precisely because experience can be such a powerful force in the development of theological understandings, some would like to exclude it from "orthodox" theology. I maintain that working on events such as the Intercultural Retreats is an effective way to create wider acceptance of theological diversity because it fosters the creating of personal relationships with people from different backgrounds, and experiencing them as equally beloved children of God.

My own first pastorate was a cross-racial appointment to an African American congregation in Monroe, which was known as one of the most intransigent southern cities in terms of resistance to the Civil Rights Movement and one of the most dangerous locations for activists to work. I was not surprised that my appointment made local television news.[9] One reporter held a microphone in my face while she asked what made me think this kind of appointment would work. I responded that many of the parishioners and I knew each other through civic and political activities and already had good working relationships. "It's a shame," I added, "that it works that way. It would be so much better if I were telling you that we can work together in a civic organization because we know each other from church."

The study of peacemaking is becoming a more established discipline, and the concept that it is as necessary to "wage peace" as it is to "wage war" is gaining acceptance. Many are coming to believe that the primary hope that exists for peace among the nations is citizen diplomacy—the changing of public opinion one person at a time by exposing individuals to international travel and introducing them into relationships with people from other lands.

Jim's efforts in relationship-building certainly nurtured the intercultural and interreligious aspects of his ministry. He worked to create helpful relationships with international students, offering them not only a welcoming space in which to study and visit, but also use of the kitchen so that they could prepare some of the foods they missed. He allowed use of the building for Hindu festivals, earning the appreciation of Hindus in a city where there were too few of them to support a temple but too many to hold celebrations in the confines of a home. These members of the local community in turn influenced Hindu students as they arrived at school. In the early 1990s, the regular participants at the ministry's Sunday morning Christian worship included a young Hindu student (along with a fifty-something Jew who taught at the university.)[10] Both Sunni and Shi'ite Muslims held observances there, as well.

Jim began the journey toward this kind of openness at the ministry quite simply, without issuing a challenge so dramatic as to be counterproductive. It started with lunch—more specifically the lunch on Thanksgiving, a holiday linked to U.S. history and family gatherings. When colleges close dorms for Thanksgiving, domestic students tend to head home for turkey. International students rarely fly home for just a few days when the long Christmas break is near. As Thanksgiving approaches, they may wonder where they will eat when dining halls and even most restaurants are closed. So, Jim began serving Thanksgiving dinner to international students.

As the guest list expanded over the years from a few students whom he knew, to all the university's international students, and finally to all students left on campus, the venue moved from the campus ministry building to a university dining hall. The scant formal programming included a non-sectarian grace offered by Jim and addressed to the Creator "whom we call by many names." Students were asked to identify their countries of origin, and all present applauded each country's representatives. As Jim noted, it may have been the only occasion when students from countries at odds, such as Taiwan and the People's Republic of China, could greet each other's presence so positively. A more substantive and beneficial activity was the rich sharing, not just among the students at the tables, but also among the many volunteers from local congregations and from the university's faculty and staff who labored in the kitchen all morning to ready the food.

Thanksgiving is almost always a very slow news day. Stories about lines at the airport and volunteers serving dinner to the poor are inevitable segments on the evening news. In a world where suspicion of the Other is the norm, active pursuit of intercultural interchange offers reporters something different. On a day when the media have minutes to fill, international students provide an interesting visual scene. This almost guarantees that the city at large will be exposed to an image of international fellowship.

All pastors are contributors to the public discourse, whether they wish to be or not. The discourse occurs at many levels. Not everyone has a call to step past the pulpit to mass media and the public arena. Those who do venture beyond the pulpit make a powerful contribution, whether for good or for ill. A Thanksgiving dinner for students from other countries is but one of many relatively uncontroversial places to start a public ministry of tolerance, and perhaps acceptance. Maybe, one day, the ministry will even deepen to one of love for one anOther.

* * * * *

Over seventeen years have gone by since we sat by the bonfire and listened to the news about David Duke. Both Duke and former Governor Edwin Edwards have been imprisoned since then—Duke on charges of tax evasion, and Edwards on...well, one of the many charges finally stuck, though I forget which one.[11] Despite Edwards' later conviction or criminal activity, it was indeed important that more Louisiana citizens voted for him than for Duke in 1991.

My hope is that the students who participated in Jim's ecumenical Christian ministry and who attended the Intercultural Retreats have reason to appreciate the richness that relationships with persons outside their own denominations and religions can bring to their spiritual lives. I hope this despite the unlikelihood that more than a few, if that many, will ever practice the same level of theological reflection as John Wesley. My hope is built instead on the knowledge that they have had face-to-face and perhaps even heart-to-heart encounters with Christians of different theological persuasions and with devout practitioners of other faiths.

I also hope that those experiences will affect their decisions about more temporal matters. I hope they will be among those who resist the sort of "wall-building" political rhetoric in which Duke and others like him engage. Fear and resentment of immigrants are harder to maintain once you have shared a small part of the lives of people who have come here from different homelands.

I hope that Jim's students might even undertake some work of their own to teach others how to open their lives to Others. Though some can bring off even more ambitious projects, organizing an event such as the Intercultural Retreats is not something everyone in favor of openness can accomplish. Just feeding the group is complicated, since practitioners of some religions have dietary restrictions, and some, like those of Hindus and Muslims, may actually conflict.

Perhaps this description of work at one campus ministry will spark ideas for other projects that will help to counter the fear that is afoot and encourage hospitality instead. Asking one couple, or two or three students, from a different background to dinner is a start and, truth be told, much more than that. Civil rights proponents sometimes assured segregationists that while integration would level the playing field in schools and workplaces, it would *not* mean that people of different races had to socialize together. Being Christian, however, does mean exactly that, for Jesus repeatedly annoyed the powers-that-be by eating with Outsiders. If we follow him, then we must do the same, and do it not to make *them* Christians, but rather because *we* are.

3

Seeking Wholeness

Biblical Visions of Separation and Unity

RICHARD H. LOWERY

"We are Disciples of Christ, a movement for wholeness in a fragmented world."

Thus begins the identity statement[1] formulated by a group convened by Sharon Watkins, General Minister and President of the Christian Church (Disciples of Christ) in the United States and Canada, four decades after Disciples first established a formal denominational structure. The new identity statement is an early step in a process of institutional transformation of the church.

The primary point of this chapter is to offer biblically grounded theological reflection on the idea that Disciples of Christ are called in this time to be "a movement for wholeness in a fragmented world." The bulk of the chapter will be devoted to a theologically focused analysis of the mythic traditions of the human world's beginning and end, found in the early chapters of Genesis and in the final chapters of Revelation.

These sections of scripture are, by virtue of their mere placement, the bookends of the Christian canon. The links between them run deeper than that. John's vision, like the early chapters of Genesis, is rooted in the imagery of ancient Near Eastern creation mythology. The closing scene of Revelation alludes to the opening chapters of Genesis: earth's final destiny is a return to Eden. The long-deferred realization of the human desire for intimacy with God is expressed with tragic consequence in Babel's project to escape the confines of mortal earth by building a tower to heaven where immortal beings dwell. In the new earth of John's vision, God bridges the gap between human and divine by pitching camp with humans. These stories of origin and of final destiny offer, not a glimpse into the historical past or future, but a hint of what human life might and should be in the here-and-now. The utopian visions they offer are both prophetic critique and statement of hope for a world that is broken and, by the will and power of God, is in the process of being healed.

Origins

The first twelve chapters of Genesis, often called the Primeval History, thread together a series of mythic tales about the origins of human civilization by genealogies full of fantastic life spans that ultimately link Israel's ancestral father and mother with the original human couple and situate Israel among the peoples of the earth. As the Genesis narrative later makes clear, the point of all this is that the story of God's interaction with the family of Abraham and Sarah has universal human significance. By this story, all the families of the earth are meant to find blessing. The narrative paints a picture that is at once very lofty in its view of human potential and very sober about our propensity toward alienation and self-destructive violence. We are simultaneously created in the image of God and driven away from God and from one another by our own jealousy, violence, and greed.

The creation story that opens Genesis 1 describes the world as God intends it to be: fundamentally benevolent and able to produce more than enough to sustain prosperous life. As I have argued elsewhere,[2] the word translated "create" in Genesis 1 connotes "fatness," prosperity, and well-being.[3] Abundant wholeness lies at the very heart of the world, an assertion underlined by the story's climax in sabbath rest. Six days of work yields seven days of wealth. In the world of God's desire, abundance overflows. We have more than enough for life to thrive, for humans and all the living creatures of the earth to "be fruitful and multiply" as God commands (Gen. 1:28).

A number of parallels join the biblical narrative and the imperial creation stories of ancient Mesopotamia. Even more striking than the similarities, however, are the contrasts. In the imperial myths, creation is conquest, the victory of a divine king over the raging god/dess of chaos.[4] Humans are created to serve and feed the gods. The mythic drama thus reinforces the imperial claim that human life finds its meaning and purpose in subservience to divinely ordained royal authority, grounded in military might and structured to ensure the unimpeded flow of wealth toward the imperial center.

The Bible's first creation narrative, by contrast, envisions creation without violence. No cosmic battle is fought; no gods die. Earth springs to life through the unchallenged word of God. By divine command, human beings are created male and female, not as subservient slaves, but as governors of the earth, stamped with the very image of God and thus empowered to rule. The syntax of the Hebrew sentence is clear on this point: "let us create a human being in our own image, according to our likeness, so they can rule."[5] The "image of God" is the power to govern, the power to rule in the earth—power shared by men and women by virtue of their common humanity.

Human gender difference is significant in this context. Other creatures reproduce sexually, but the narrative explicitly mentions "male and female" only when it describes the creation of human beings in the image of God. This suggests that the narrative is doing more here than merely stating the obvious biological fact that humans have two sexes. By emphasizing that humans are created male and female, the narrative stresses the complementary diversity of human beings who are at once the same and necessarily different. Humans cannot exist as isolated, wholly self-contained individuals. They are inherently social, different from one another yet joined together in common life.

The essential pluralism of human beings is further underlined by the unique mode of speech God employs in this part of the story. The rest of creation unfolds with a singular command—"let there be..." Till now, God stands alone on the narrative stage. When God creates the human being, however, other divine actors appear; and God's speech shifts: "Let us create a human being in our own image, according to our likeness" (Gen.1:26). The narrative picture is that of the ancient Near Eastern royal court. God sits enthroned before divine courtiers set to do the bidding of the monarch. God rules, but God does not rule alone. God exercises power in community. In the creation of human beings, male and female, "in our own image," a feature of God's character previously hidden in the narrative is revealed: God is by nature social. God's power, though concentrated in the person of the divine monarch, is nevertheless shared. Humans, in their social nature, in their complementary and interconnected difference, in maleness and femaleness, in their mutual sharing of power, reflect the communal character of God.

Finally, God gives the vegetative produce of the earth to the humans and to all living creatures as food (Gen.1:29–30). Meat is not on the menu. In this creation drama, God makes a bloodless, vegetarian world. No living creature must die for another to survive. This striking vision echoes the "peaceable kingdom" passages in the Isaiah tradition: "the wolf will live with the lamb; the leopard will lie down with the kid; the calf, the young lion, and the fatling together; and a small child will lead them" (Isa.11:6); "the wolf and the lamb will graze together, the lion will eat straw like the ox, and the snake's food will be dust. In all of my holy mountain, they will not injure or bring to ruin, says YHWH" (Isa. 65:25). With this final touch of creation business before the inauguration of the seventh day rest, the narrative underscores the fact that the world envisioned in this story is utopian. This is a picture of the world as it should be, not the world as it is. Creation in this story is a vision of hope, a dream of wholeness, of abundant life commonly and peacefully shared.

A Fragmented World

Many scholars think that the creation story at the beginning of Genesis was written sometime after the Eden story (Gen. 2:4b–3:24) and attached to it as an introduction.[6] Whatever the literary prehistory of the current biblical text, the shift in theme, perspective, language, and literary style that begins in the middle of Genesis 2:4 is clear. The story that follows marks a transition in the narrative. While the first story describes the abundant and peaceful world of God's intention, the stories that begin in Eden and end in Babel seek to explain the radical disjuncture between the world as God created it to be and the world of actual experience—a world of scarcity, cruelty, and violence.

In Genesis 1, human beings are said to be created in the likeness of God. The stories that follow this striking proclamation give the fine print commentary on what that means and does not mean. By the end of the Eden story, humans are declared by God to be "like god/s" (3:22) because they have acquired the power of moral discernment. Ironically, however, their possession of this godlike power prompts God to set a clear line between the divine realm and the human. Each of the subsequent stories in the Primeval History deals with this separation and explores the self-destructive consequences of attempts to blur the line.

The Eden narrative is structured as a universal human story. The original human is simply Adam (ha-'adam), "the Human." His wife is

Eve (chavah), "Living One" or "One Who Brings Life." The precise but impossible geographical coordinates that chart the courses of the four branches of Eden's river (2:10–14) define the outer boundaries of the known world. Eden stands at the source of the whole inhabited earth. Adam and Eve are Everyman and Everywoman. This story is not about a specific event in the past. It describes the human condition in every place and time.

Two basic problems move the plot: the earth is barren (2:5), and the human is alone (2:18). The departure from the first creation story is striking in this regard. In chapter 1, humans are created from the very beginning in community, male and female. They inhabit a world teeming with plants and animals. The Eden story, by contrast, begins "in the day that YHWH God created the earth and the heavens" (2:4a) with the antithesis of the verdant world of Genesis 1. The earth is universal desert, desolate because "YHWH God had not yet made it rain on the earth, and there was no human to till the ground" (2:5).

God creates a human and places the person in a garden paradise, with only one rule: do not eat the fruit of moral discernment from the tree of knowing right and wrong. Up to this point, God has only declared the works of creation "good" or "very good." For the first time in the Bible, however, God offers a negative assessment: "It is not good for the human to be alone" (2:18). After a trial-and-error search for a suitable companion, which results in the creation and naming of all the animals, God solves the problem of human loneliness by creating "a helper, as a corresponding partner" from the side of the human. Now for the first time the narrative uses gender-specific language. The new creature is "woman" ('ishshah), "because this one was taken out of man ('ish)" (2:23). Though distinct, the two are one flesh and bone and therefore are drawn to each other. This splitting of the human into woman and man and their need to reconnect forms the cornerstone of human social order, the household couple. "For this reason a man leaves his father and his mother and clings to his wife and they become one flesh" (2:24). Separation becomes the occasion for union; but it also sets up an ongoing dynamic between the two, as husband and wife become father and mother to children who will leave them for other unions. Human unity, in this telling, is not a state finally to be achieved, but an ongoing activity, a never-ending process of coming together even as the natural cycles of life pull us apart.

By story's end, the human couple are alienated from one another, from God, from the serpent who urged them to seek wisdom, and finally from the garden paradise and its tree of immortal life. At the root of this series of disasters is the human desire to be wise, to know the difference between right and wrong.

The man is not entirely off the mark when he points out that God shares part of the responsibility for the way things turn out in the story–"the woman that you put with me, she gave to me from the tree, and I ate" (3:12). Note the progression of the pronouns: you, she, I. The man's comical attempt to deflect blame highlights an important truth implicit in the narrative sequence itself. The desire to know right and wrong becomes an issue only after the human is no longer alone. It is precisely the social nature of human being that makes moral discernment necessary. God's solution to the problem of human loneliness leads inevitably to the human desire, the need to know the difference between right and wrong. Human community is impossible without some sense of justice. The plurality of human being requires moral discernment.

In one sense it is appropriate to speak of the Eden story as a "fall" story. Humans pay a steep price for the power of moral judgment. But this is a fall upward. Humans exchange endless life in paradise for the wisdom to live in human community, for the joy and the pain that come with human companionship, and for the knowledge of right and wrong.

In the end, the story comes full circle. Banished from Eden, the man and the woman go out into the barren world to till the ground. By choosing wisdom and leaving utopia, the human couple becomes the solution to the problem that introduced the story. They enter the desert world where there is "not yet any plant of the field or herb of the field," because "there was no human to till the ground" (2:5), and they farm. With utopia forever out of reach, humans venture into the world. Wise to what is right and wrong, they bring a bit of paradise to the wasteland. They make the desert bloom.

The Eden story is closely connected linguistically and thematically to the Cain and Abel story that follows in chapter 4. The triad of characters Adam earlier blames for humans acquiring wisdom—"you" (God), "she" (woman), and "I" (man)–appears in reverse order at the beginning of this story. Newly equipped with the ability to know right and wrong, the man "knew" his wife. She conceives and gives birth to Cain; and she says, "I have acquired[7] a man with YHWH" (4:1). The human couple lost immortal life when they gained the power to know right and wrong. Now, by "knowing" one another, they acquire a new life, with the help of God.

A second child, Abel, is born. The brothers grow to adulthood and settle into the two basic forms of social-economic organization in the ancient Near East: farming and herding. A difference of religious practice rooted in their different forms of labor becomes a source of tension (4:3–5). Despite God's warning (4:6–7), Cain allows his own resentment to grow to the point that he murders his brother (4:8). As Adam and Eve had usurped the power of wisdom formerly reserved for divine beings, Cain now usurps the power of God to give or take human life.

God's response to this transgression is telling. Rather than take Cain's life in return, God breaks the potential cycle of violence and protects the murderer from violent retribution: "Anyone who kills Cain will suffer sevenfold vengeance" (4:15). Echoing themes of the Eden story, God curses Cain's ability to farm and sends him out to wander the earth (4:10–14). As in the Eden story, punishment becomes the occasion for blessing. With separation comes the opportunity for unity. The wanderer founds cities, communities of common purpose. His offspring multiply and learn to produce the various artifacts of culture (4:17–22).

The genealogy of Cain closes on an ominous note, however. Lamech, Cain's descendent five generations later, boasts to his two wives: "I have killed a man for bruising me, a young man for hitting me. If Cain is avenged seven times, Lamech will be avenged seventy-seven" (4:23–24). What God intended for good–divine protection of a human life–Lamech arrogantly twisted to evil, taking for himself the prerogative of God and offering it as an excuse to escalate violence.

The cycle of violence and retribution that God sought to prevent in the case of Cain spins out of control. By chapter 6, the violence and corruption have become so pervasive and severe (6:11) that God decides to wipe the human slate clean. Borrowing extensively from the common ancient Near Eastern legend of a prehistoric universal flood,[8] the biblical narrative portrays a reversal of Genesis 1. God opens the windows of heaven, uncorks the fountains of the deep, and allows the waters of primordial chaos to "uncreate" the world (7:11). At the end of the flood, when creation once again emerges from the deeps, God restocks the human race with the offspring of Noah, an upright and just man (7:1). God reissues the charge given to the original humans to be fruitful, multiply, and fill the earth (9:1), and strictly forbids the killing of human beings, created "in the image of God" (9:5–6).

In the final episode of the Primeval History, the technological power of human civilization threatens to cross the boundary between the human and the divine. This story is in part etiological, told to explain an observable fact of the world: human beings speak different languages, which leads to miscommunication, often with tragic consequences. This story also reiterates the deeply ambiguous portrayal of the human condition that emerges from the stories so far: human beings are in some ways godlike and therefore powerful, but that very quality reveals their deepest flaw. They are simultaneously aware of their own awesome potential and dangerously insecure about it.

As in the Eden story, the humans in this story begin in a state of utopian harmony: "Now, all the earth had a single language and the same words" (11:1). People migrate to the plain of "Shinar," another name for Babylon (cf. Dan. 1:2), and begin to build a great city. They start to construct a tower "with its top in the sky" (Gen. 11:4), where God and the other divine beings live. The purpose of this attempt to cross the divine-human border is to "make a name for ourselves, so we are not scattered over the face of the earth" (11:4). God goes down to see the city and the tower humans are building. Echoing the end of the Eden story, God exclaims to the heavenly court, "Look! They are one people, and all of them have a single language. This is only the beginning of what they will do. Now, nothing they plan to do will be impossible for them" (11:6; cf. 3:22). So God "confuses their language." Unable to communicate, the human community is fractured. They abandon the project and scatter to the ends of the earth. Even in the midst of human tragedy, hope remains. Once again forced out of utopia, the human community spreads throughout the world to fill it, till it, and make it bloom.

A Movement toward Wholeness

The final vision of the book of Revelation (chapters 21–22) draws images and themes from the stories of the Primeval History. We know from the opening letters to the churches of Asia (chapters 2–3) that the visionary's Christian community is experiencing varying degrees of pressure to participate in the imperial cults of Rome. Some Christians apparently have even died as a result (Rev. 2:13; cf. 6:9–11). John's revelation is a vision given by God to the resurrected Christ to show the faithful "what must soon take place" (1:1). It is a revelation "of Jesus Christ." It both belongs to him and is about him. By uncovering the spiritual reality that undergirds history, Jesus shows John and those who hear his report that the Risen Christ, though unseen with the naked eye, in fact stands with the churches as they struggle to keep faith in a time of distress (1:12–20).

A repetitive cycle of visions follows the letters to the churches, in various ways dramatizing the current predicament of the faithful as the tip of the iceberg in a cosmic battle between the forces of good and evil. The visions come to a climax with the disappearance of the current world of injustice and suffering. In its place, a new heaven and earth appear (21:1). In contrast to the tower of Babel (and to popular apocalyptic scenarios today), humans do not "go up" to be with God. God "comes down" to be with humans. A new Jerusalem descends to earth from heaven, the gift of God who leaves heaven to live with mortals on earth, literally to "pitch tent" with them (21:3). The renewed earth, the renewed Jerusalem, has no temple, because God's presence is immediate, unmediated, through all and in all (21:22). Nations walk by the city's light, and the rulers of the earth bring their glory through its gates that never close (21:24–25). Like Eden, the city of God has a river. It flows out from God. Unlike the river of Eden, it does not leave paradise. It flows through the middle of Main Street to water the tree of life, which is for the healing of the nations.

Thus the biblical story comes full circle. The end returns to the beginning. The desire for intimacy with God and with one another, derailed in the first times, is finally achieved in the last, not by reaching to the heavens, but by living now in the unmediated presence of God who descends to earth and pitches tent with mortals. In the final analysis, unity– nations healed, people reconciled, God and humans at one–is not a goal to be achieved by human effort, but a gift to be received from the hand of God. As the heavenly vision makes clear, that gift is not a heavenly reward in a far-off future. It is immediately near (22:6–12). Wholeness is not a distant result we may someday achieve. It is a way of living on earth now in the presence of the Risen Christ.

A Movement for Wholeness in a Fragmented World

This brief survey of narratives from the Bible's beginning and end offers several theological insights relevant to the opening words of the new Disciples identity statement. The Primeval History describes the human condition as a constant tension between wholeness and fragmentation, unity and division. Humans are simultaneously at one with God and separated from God, bearing God's own image and driven by our own arrogance and insecurity from God's presence. We are at the very same time united in common humanity and split apart from each other. Our coming together often becomes the occasion for our moving apart. Our attempts to maintain uniformity and thus preserve our oneness typically fracture our community. Our separations often offer new opportunities for reunion. To be human is to live in the constant dynamic between fragmentation and wholeness.

In this sense the wording of the vision statement gets it exactly right. At our best, Disciples of Christ must be a *movement*. We are in process, on a journey, ever moving toward the vision of wholeness we receive as the revelation of Jesus Christ. Wholeness is for us less an elusive result in a distant future than a daily discipline in the here and now. It is a faith commitment, a way of life. The measure of success is not whether any particular effort at wholeness works or fails but whether we have kept faith each day with the vision of a world of open gates, where the warring nations of earth are received for healing care.

Finally, humans bear the image of God. As the stories of Genesis attest, however, human attempts to "be like god/s" often yield impressive results, but they finally lead to disaster. In the end, wholeness is the gift of God, the daily presence of the Holy One who chooses to cross the boundary between the divine world and the human, and who, as we see in the revelation of Jesus Christ, pitches tent with mortals and lives among us on earth even now being made new. For this reason, the opening words of the vision statement hold the key to its power. We are a movement for wholeness in a fragmented world precisely because we are Disciples of the Risen Christ by whose faithful witness the world is transformed.

4

The Idealization of Christian Origins in Acts of the Apostles

DENNIS E. SMITH

At least as far back as Eusebius, Acts of the Apostles has been considered the primary source for the official story of Christian origins.[1] As a result, the story Acts tells has firmly embedded itself within the church's self-understanding.[2] To be sure, scholarship on Acts has long questioned Acts' reliability as a historical resource on a variety of points. Yet the overall storyline in Acts has still prevailed, not only because it was the only story we had, but also because it was a story with which we had become comfortable.

New research on Acts has challenged this paradigm to such a degree that it is now debatable whether any reliable details about Christian origins can be derived from Acts. Although the debate is still in process and far from being resolved, the issues raised are substantive and the implications far-reaching. Such a process can only be helpful, I would argue, for it will cause us to reexamine critically how we tell our story, and in the process, take account of the ways in which the Acts story has shaped our self-understanding as Christians.

The Redating of Acts and Its Implications

The cornerstone of the proposed new paradigm on Acts is a reassessment of the date of Acts. The consensus in scholarship for some time has been that Acts was written ca. 85 C.E. This tended to be a compromise date and was rarely, if ever, supported by detailed scholarly argument.[3] Recently this date has been challenged in a massive, groundbreaking study by Richard Pervo.[4] After over 300 pages of detailed analysis of the issue from every possible angle, Pervo concludes: "Acts should be dated ca. 115." Based on "the various social and ideological orientations of the book...one can better understand Acts as a product of the decade 110–120 than of the decade 80–90."[5] Building on Pervo's work, Joseph Tyson has argued that the social context for Acts was most likely the developing controversy surrounding Marcion and his teachings about Paul and the central thrust of Christian theology.[6]

Dating Acts in the early second century, rather than the late first century, dramatically changes the playing field. For example, it undercuts arguments that the author could have been a companion of Paul, a position still maintained by a number of scholars.[7] Furthermore, by the early second century, the letters of Paul were being widely circulated, thus making it more likely that the author of Acts did, in fact, use the letters of Paul as a source for his story. After all, given that the author defines himself as one who has done his research (Lk. 1:3), it is unlikely that a story that gives so much attention to Paul would have overlooked the letters of Paul as a source. Indeed, several recent studies of Acts make compelling cases for the use of Paul's letters.[8] As we will see, the same author who radically edits Mark for his story of Jesus could be expected to edit radically Paul's letters for his story of Paul; one has only to look as the Acts version of Paul's conversion, for example, to see how free the author can be in editing his sources (compare Gal. 1:15–17 with Acts 9:1–31; 22:1–21; 26:2–23).[9]

These two hypotheses, that Acts was written ca. 115 and used the letters of Paul as a source, require a radical reassessment of Acts as a resource for Christian origins. In particular, all prevailing theories about the sources of Acts will have to be rethought. An important cornerstone of all previous theories about sources of Acts was its presumed reliability as a source for Paul, since it is found to agree closely with the biographical details found in the letters of Paul.[10] According to this argument, if Luke can be assumed to have sources that are exceptionally reliable where we can check him against Paul, then he must have had reliable sources in those instances where we have no sources other than Acts. This hypothesis only works, however, if one assumes that the author did not have access to Paul's letters. On the other hand, if the author used Paul as a source, then scholars must rethink how we go about reconstructing the sources of Acts. In addition, an early-second-century date instead of a late-first-century date increases significantly the burden of proof for hypotheses that assume that historically reliable data for Christian origins was easily available to the author of Acts. For one thing, by the early second century it is highly unlikely that any figures from the first generation were still alive. Finally, the dating of Acts in ca. 115 is strongly supported by the close fit of the argument and theology of Acts with issues under debate in the early second century.[11]

How the Author of Acts Edits His Sources

The author of Acts is often assumed to be a careful historian whose reliability can be trusted.[12] However, a close look at how he actually used his sources undermines this view. From the very beginning of Acts, we can see the author editing, even manipulating, his sources and shaping his story to fit an apologetic purpose. For example, at the beginning of Acts the author presents a resurrection appearance narrative, one that recapitulates the ending of the gospel of Luke. In this way, the narrative is made to flow seamlessly from the story of Jesus in the gospel of Luke to the story of the church in Acts and, in the process, support Luke's theological purposes.

In this case, we can clearly identify Luke's source, namely, the gospel of Mark. Mark's story of Jesus ends with an empty tomb narrative, in which a heavenly messenger commands: "Go, tell his disciples and Peter that he is going ahead of you to Galilee; there you will see him, just as he told you" (Mk.16:7). All three of the other canonical gospels use this story, but, since Mark does not have a resurrection appearance narrative, all three of the others add appearance stories. Their stories, however, are distinctive to each gospel. Matthew and John, following Mark's emphasis on Galilee, both provide stories of appearances of the risen Jesus in Galilee. In Matthew, the appearance in Galilee is the only one he presents (Mt. 28:16–20). In John, the Galilee appearance narrative is one among many (see Jn. 20:1–29), but it is the last one he presents (Jn. 21:1–14).

The gospel of Luke, however, takes the pieces of Mark's empty tomb story and makes it say something entirely different. Galilee is once again referenced by the heavenly messenger at the empty tomb, but this time for a different purpose: "Remember how he told you, *while he was still in Galilee* (italics mine), that the Son of Man must be handed over" (Lk. 24:6–7). Luke's story only references Galilee as the place where Jesus was when he predicted his death, not the place where the apostles are to go. The risen Lord finally appears to the apostles, but in Jerusalem. In what is, in effect, Luke's version of a "great commission," the risen Lord instructs the apostles that "repentance and forgiveness of sins is to be proclaimed in his name to all nations, *beginning from Jerusalem*" (italics mine), and commands them to "stay here in the city until you have been clothed with power from on high" (Lk. 24:47, 49). After giving this commission, he ascends into heaven (Lk. 24:50–53). The narrative of Acts begins by repeating this resurrection story with the commissioning of the apostles and the ascension (Acts 1:1–11). The ascension story is found only in Luke-Acts and serves to reduce all resurrection narratives to this final one. That is to say, not only does Luke not include a Galilee appearance, he rules out any possibility of one. The Luke-Acts resurrection/ appearance story also sets the stage for the rest of the story in Acts, following the outline enumerated by the risen Lord, namely: "you will be my witnesses in Jerusalem, in all Judea and Samaria, and to the ends of the earth" (Acts 1:8).

The contrast between Mark and Luke is stark and should not be glossed over. Mark's story emphasizes departing from Jerusalem immediately and starting over again in Galilee. Luke's story says the opposite: stay in Jerusalem because everything will begin from there. Luke makes this revision to support his case for a single origin of Christianity and a singular connection with Jerusalem as the point of origin.

This beginning lays the groundwork for important themes in Acts. First, the singular origin establishes the theme of a unified Christian movement from the very beginning, a movement begun by a miracle of God and led by a specially chosen apostolic leadership. Second, it connects that origin with Jerusalem, which allows the author to build his case that Gentile Christianity will be the legitimate heir to Judaism. None of the other gospels is familiar with this story; they imagine early Christianity getting its start somewhere other than Jerusalem. In its language and themes, the story of singular origins in Jerusalem emerges as a creation of the author of Luke-Acts and an important component of his apologetic purpose.[13]

Acts as a Myth of Origins

The genre of Acts has long been debated. Theories range from Acts as history to Acts as a novel to somewhere in between.[14] Genre identity can be a red herring, however. Perhaps more important is a sober and detailed assessment of the purpose of Acts. As a contribution to this effort, Joseph Tyson has recently argued that Acts may be considered a myth of Christian origins.[15] He defines such myths as "charters for social organization and behavior." He decries the fact that "the myth of Acts continues to exercise great power even among modern critical scholars who are allegedly searching for history. Scholars have not so much confused the non-historical with the historical," he argues, but "the power of Acts as a charter myth has been hard to escape." For example, he points out, "some older studies of Christian origins are, for the most part, uncritical replications of Acts."[16] Studies of Paul routinely use Acts as a source, even while acknowledging the problems with Acts.[17] Tyson acknowledges that the myth of Acts was necessary to compete with other myths of its day—most notably, in Tyson's view, that of Marcion. To appreciate Acts as myth does not mean we should accept it as valid history. Tyson's point is a good one, and his argument is quite useful in helping us sort through the story of Acts and how it functions, both for the ancients and for historians today.

The Myth of Divine Guidance

From Pentecost to Rome, the Acts story is imbued with the miraculous, a theme that must be assessed in terms of the apologetic aims of the book. Luke consistently views Christian origins within the framework of what is, in effect, a myth of divine guidance.[18] That this was the author's construct can be seen by the heavy-handed way in which he applied it throughout his story. Virtually every major move takes place through the direct guidance of divine agency. The result is an apologetic one: what "the church" became (that is, "the church" as defined by Luke) happened because God willed it. More often than not, it took place contrary to the desires or expectations of the human characters themselves.

A quick catalogue of these references will illustrate how important this theme is to Luke's story. At the very beginning of Acts, the apostles are portrayed as effectively clueless—they ask the risen Lord: "Lord, is this the time when you will restore the kingdom to Israel?" (Acts 1:6). But he has already told them "not to leave Jerusalem, but to wait there for the promise of the Father" (1:4; see also Lk. 24:49). The point is that God has a plan, namely that "you will be my witnesses in Jerusalem, in all Judea and Samaria, and to the ends of the earth" (1:8; see also Lk. 24:47–48), a plan about which the disciples themselves are still unclear. Consequently, God must start the ball rolling by sending the Holy Spirit on the day of Pentecost, causing the apostles to speak miraculously in other languages (Acts 2:1–4) and, as a result, to set in motion the origin of a new community of believers (Acts 2:37–47). As the story proceeds, God will guide each phase of the process "to the ends of the earth."

The phrase "to the ends of the earth" promises a Gentile mission. This mission is foreshadowed by an angel-directed encounter of Philip with an Ethiopian eunuch (8:26–40), who represents a well-known "end of the earth" location in geographic lore of Luke's day; and by the divine intervention to bring Paul on board (9:1–19), since Paul will soon take over the Gentile mission in Luke's story. According to Acts, however, Peter, not Paul, introduces the Gentile mission, illustrating another rewriting of Luke's received tradition. Peter must be cajoled by means of a dream into accepting a Gentile as worthy of inclusion (Acts 10:9–29). Then he must convince a skeptical Jerusalem community that this is okay (Acts 11:1–18). The amount of space given to this story in Acts, extending from 10:1 to 11:18, indicates its importance to his overall purpose.

Luke maintains the single-origin story by stating that the church in Antioch was founded by exiles from Jerusalem (11:19). This church then commissioned Paul and Barnabas to be missionaries to the larger Gentile world. They chose them only after the Holy Spirit told them to do. The Spirit spoke to their leaders en mass with the words, "Set apart for me Barnabas and Saul for the work to which I have called them" (13:2). Later, God specifically directed Paul through a dream to leave Asia Minor and bring the gospel for the first time to mainland Macedonia and Greece (16:6–10). The story ends with Paul effectively at "the ends of the earth"—namely Rome, where he has arrived after a miraculous escape from a shipwreck (27:13–44), and where, though a prisoner of the Roman government, he is able to preach unhindered (28:31).

Few scholars would argue that these stories of divine guidance should be taken at face value. The question that must be raised is whether any of the data in these narratives has historical credibility once this theme is excised.

The Myth of a Harmonious Christian Community

According to the writer of Acts, the founding community was a model of orderliness and obedience. Immediately after Peter's inaugural sermon, a large community is formed (3000![19]) which Luke describes in glowing terms: "They devoted themselves to the apostles' teaching and fellowship, to the breaking of bread and the prayers" (2:42). Furthermore, they "had all things in common" and used the common purse to care for all the needy in the community (2:44–45). This is clearly an idealization, as most scholars freely acknowledge.[20] It was intended to provide a model for Christian unity in Luke's own day. In the context of an emerging sense of heresy in his world,

Luke defined the ideal community as one that submitted itself to the teachings of the certified leaders, namely "the apostles," and did so without any hint of disagreement.

As the movement spread into new areas, tensions developed. The existence of a growing Gentile community, represented by the church in Antioch, caused nervousness among the leaders of the "mother church" in Jerusalem. An "apostolic council" was gathered to address this issue, as recounted in Acts 15:1–35. This is the same event as the one Paul described in Galatians 2:1–14. If Acts used Paul as a source, we really only have one source for this event, that of Paul. The version in Acts is a rewriting of Paul's story, changing it to fit new concerns.

Whereas Paul's account speaks of what must have been a raucous debate and an uneasy compromise, Luke's story speaks of an orderly discussion with a harmonious outcome. Especially remarkable is the way in which Luke has Peter and James become the spokespersons for the Gentile mission, completely reversing Paul's account. Indeed, the positions taken by both Peter and James are actually molded out of snippets from Paul's own distinctive theology, as William O. Walker has argued.[21] Walker notes how Acts presents a "transfer of roles" in contrast with the account in Paul. In Galatians Paul presents himself as the "apostle to the Gentiles" and Peter as the "apostle to the circumcised" (Gal. 2:7). In Acts, on the other hand, Peter is presented as the primary apostle to the Gentiles (Acts 10:1–11:18; 15:7–11).[22] Furthermore a close analysis of Peter's speech in Acts 15 reveals how arguments and even phrases that can be shown to derive from Paul have been placed in Peter's mouth. Whereas in Galatians Peter, James, and finally Barnabas oppose Paul, in Acts 15 both Peter and James warmly join Paul in his mission. Barnabas only splits with Paul over a minor issue. Walker concludes that the author of Acts used Galatians as a source for this story and revised it so as to present Peter as the initial "apostle to the Gentiles" instead of Paul.[23] Even though Paul's story is an eyewitness account and Luke's clearly is not, scholars have been wont to correct or harmonize Paul's story with that of Acts.

Elsewhere in Acts, Christian assemblies are consistently characterized as congenial gatherings. Pervo points out that, whereas Acts characterizes the gatherings of Christians as orderly and harmonious (1:15–26; 6:1–7; 11:1–18; 15:6–29; 21:18–25), the meetings of others are characterized as dangerous and disorderly, sometimes even riotous, whether they be Jews (4:5–21; 5:21b–40; 6:12–7:60; 22:30–23:10) or a Gentile mob (19:21–40). This rhetorical device serves to support key themes of Luke's narrative.[24] Pervo concludes:

Examination of these meetings in their social context underscores the extent to which Acts presents the early Church
in Jerusalem and elsewhere as a *political* organization that
elects officers, holds formal meetings, promulgates decrees,
and engages in ambassadorial exchanges. Description of
its constitution, structure, and proceedings is one means of
showing that the "Christian church" is the "true Israel."[25]

Consequently, the burden of proof has now shifted to those who
would claim that reports of meetings in Acts, either of Christian groups
or non-Christian groups, have any historical basis to them.

An Uneasy Relation to Judaism

A major theme of Luke-Acts is to defend the legitimacy of Gentile
Christianity. Luke apparently considered it important to establish
Gentile Christianity, not as an aberration, but as central to the ministry
of Jesus and to God's plan for the church. In his gospel, Luke takes
on this issue directly by rewriting a story he derives from Mark, the
story of Jesus' rejection at Nazareth (Mk. 6:1–6). First, contrary to
his usual practice, he changes Mark's order of events and places this
story at the very beginning of Jesus' ministry (Lk. 4:16–30). Then he
rewrites the story to give it a different emphasis than it had in Mark.
In Luke's version, Jesus first proclaims in the synagogue that his
mission is to fulfill Isaiah's prophecy: "The Spirit of the Lord…has
anointed me / to bring good news to the poor" (Lk. 4:18). Then, in the
sermon that follows, Jesus interprets what Isaiah meant by providing
two examples of prophets who were sent to heal Gentiles instead
of Israelites (Lk. 4:24–27). In this way, Jesus effectively equates the
"poor" with Gentiles (Lk. 4:24–27) and makes the Gentile mission
central to his ministry. This message causes the synagogue worshipers
to reject him. They are all Jews, of course, and are insulted by Jesus'
sermon (4:28–29). To be sure, Jesus' ministry in the gospel of Luke
does not actually follow this path; rather, his ministry is to the Jews.
In Acts, the sequel to the gospel, the prophecy is fulfilled. In Acts
10–11, in an elaborately constructed story, the centurion Cornelius
becomes the first official Gentile convert and thereby sets in motion a
Gentile mission that will dominate the rest of Acts. Clearly, Luke-Acts
wants to draw a direct line from the beginning of Jesus' ministry to
the Cornelius story and eventually "to the ends of the earth," which
to Luke meant the Gentile mission as a whole. The saga of Luke-Acts
is therefore largely constructed to defend the Gentile mission. For
the most part, Luke-Acts is made up of stories created by Luke out

of bits and pieces from his sources and, in some cases, perhaps, out of whole cloth.

In recounting this story, Luke struggles not only to connect with Jesus' ministry but also with Jewish tradition. On the one hand, he wants to make a connection between the Gentile mission and Jewish scripture and tradition. Thus Jesus, Peter, and Paul are all presented as observant, pious Jews.[26] Joseph Tyson has recently argued that Luke's insistence on fulfillment of scripture marks a direct and intentional contrast with the theology Marcion championed. In contrast with Marcion's view that the Christianity of Paul was a separate religion and not related to Judaism at all, Luke-Acts wants to argue that a consistent story runs from Adam to Christ to the Church. Luke wants to hold onto the Jewish scripture and tradition while at the same time affirming the Gentile mission.[27]

On the other hand, part of the thread that holds together Luke-Acts is the theme of conflict with Judaism. Just as Jesus was rejected at Nazareth, so also Jewish rabble-rousers opposed the apostles at virtually every turn.[28] In Paul's last speech in Acts, he addresses a Jewish delegation, "testifying to the kingdom of God and trying to convince them about Jesus both from the law of Moses and from the prophets" (28:23). When they refuse to accept his message, he turns away from them, as if for the last time. His last words are: "Let it be known to you then that this salvation of God has been sent to the Gentiles; they will listen" (28:28). Thus Acts ends with a strong affirmation of what is basically a doctrine of supersessionism. Judaism has been replaced by Christianity, but, according to Luke and unlike Marcion, Christianity is to be understood as the proper heir of the Jewish heritage.[29]

Why Rewriting the Story Is Important

The idealization of Christian origins in Acts was developed as an apologetic motif to defend Luke's community in the context of controversy and debate in the larger Christian movement. In this brief sketch I have argued that it is a story created by the author for apologetic and theological rather than historical reasons. Consequently, the Acts story offers very little data that can be considered historically reliable. This point needs to be dealt with directly. If we are to uphold historical accuracy in recounting the earliest history of Christianity, we must separate ourselves from the hegemony of Acts.

One perspective that Acts glosses over is the great diversity in Christianity virtually from the beginning. Without the story Acts provides, we would probably find ourselves telling a much different story, one that reflects the great diversity that scholars have begun to discover at the very origins of Christianity. Many scholars today, for example, point to the document Q and its stratified history as a record of what must have been one of the earliest documented Christian groups. As Burton Mack has said, "Q will put us in touch with the first followers of Jesus."[30] What is remarkable about Q, Mack argues, is that it testifies to a Jesus movement that revered the sayings of Jesus but did not include any death and resurrection stories in their collection, thus indicating that the death of Jesus played no major role in their theology and piety. Mack goes on to identify other groups of Jesus followers who represented diverse streams in the movement and who left traces in the pre-Markan literary data.[31] Separate from the Jesus followers was another strand Mack identifies as the "Christ cult" movement, identified by its emphasis on the significance of Jesus' death.[32] Paul interacted with this group and developed out of it.[33]

As a result of this new research into Christian origins, a wealth of new data is being amassed. It tells a different story than that of Acts. Instead of a "big bang" story in which the Christian church began with one big miracle and progressed in an orderly and singular manner through history, we now have evidence of a virtual explosion of diversity from the very beginning, a diversity that continued into later periods as evidenced in the noncanonical literature and the heresy disputes of the second and third centuries.

We can gain much from this rewriting of our history. It will help us escape some of the excesses of our traditional founding story, the story that Acts tells. That story proclaims Christian triumphalism, punctuated by a heavy-handed theme that God ordained it all. It affirms supersessionism, the doctrine that "Christianity" superseded Judaism. It affirms a specific form of orthodoxy that justifies the authority of a centralized leadership and legitimizes the suppression of alternative movements and theologies.

On the other hand, if we can begin to rewrite our history of origins free of the Acts story, we can do justice and honor to the human achievement that was the church. Real history is "messy." It does not follow a divine, preordained script. So also today we deal with the "messiness" of ministry in a real world. Correcting the story of our history can empower us with a more convincing and ultimately more powerful sense of who we are and where we came from. It can free us to acknowledge the *vitality* of early Christian diversity and thus enable us better to face our increasingly global and diverse twenty-first-century world.

5

Clippings from *World Call*

Disciples Perspectives on Religious Pluralism 1919–1940

DON A. PITTMAN

Paul F. Knitter asserts that while the "replacement model" of theological exclusivism represents the position most Christians within contemporary evangelical and fundamentalist churches affirm, the "fulfillment model" of theological inclusivism represents the dominant stance of those affiliated with Roman Catholicism, Greek Orthodoxy, and mainline Protestantism.[1] If, in fact, inclusivism accurately characterizes the theology of religions of the majority of current members of the Christian Church (Disciples of Christ), and if, as Mark Toulouse has argued, the Disciples theology of mission developed slowly through four distinct phases from an evangelical toward a more progressive form of Christian piety—culminating in the *Principles and Policies of the Division of Overseas Ministries* (1981) and the "Report of the Commission on Theology in Response to Resolution No. 8728 'Concerning Salvation in Jesus Christ'" (1989)—we might ask what Disciples were reading in their denominational publications in the twentieth century that contributed to the shaping of more "liberal" theological perspectives on global mission and interreligious dialogue.[2]

If Disciples leaders were increasingly prepared to row their boat "toward the left fork" of the diverging "progressive" and "conservative" tributaries of American Protestantism, we ought to be able to find signs of where their oars were stirring the waters.[3] The thesis of this particular essay, the scope of which is limited to clippings from the monthly magazine *World Call* published in the years between World War I and II, is that we can identify such ripples of theological change, even if we cannot judge on the basis of their appearance alone the extent to which any one of them was effective in redirecting the boat.

In the Wake of the "Great Century of Mission"

The resilient optimism regarding the evangelization of the whole world that marked the so-called "Great Century of Mission" (the nineteenth) and prepared the way for what was to be the "Christian Century" (the twentieth), was clearly evident at the first international conference on Christian mission held at Edinburgh in 1910.[4] As William Richey Hogg has noted, "When the Great Century began (1815 [with Napoleon's defeat at Waterloo]), several hundred persons would amply have accounted for the total Protestant missionary force. When it ended (1914 [with the start of World War I]), there were some 22,000 missionaries–half of them women."[5] However, according to Stephen Neill, theological reflection on these developments was virtually missing from the Edinburgh conference:

> There had seemed to be little need for it, when all were at one on all the fundamentals. All were agreed that Jesus Christ the Son of God was the final and decisive Word of God to men; that in Him alone is the certainty of salvation given to men; that this Gospel must be preached to every living soul, to whom God has given the freedom to accept or reject and who must stand by that acceptance or rejection in the last day.[6]

North American Disciples in the period shared the prevalent optimism about the evangelization of the world "in this generation," as John R. Mott would express it, while, at the same time, they lacked a well-developed theological perspective concerning global mission.[7] On the other hand, the sense of Western and especially American "manifest destiny" was grounded for virtually all Americans in a complementary nationalism and Christian triumphalism. As David J. Bosch has commented:

The Western missionary enterprise...proceeded not only from the assumption of the superiority of Western culture over all other cultures, but also from the conviction that God, in his providence, had chosen the Western nations, because of their unique qualities, to be the standard-bearers of his cause to the uttermost ends of the world.... Was their motivation nationalist, or was it religious? Little debate was conducted on this question, since most contemporaries saw no need for a choice. "Christian obligation and American obligation were fundamentally harmonious."[8]

The magazine *World Call,* the first issue of which appeared in January 1919, was the successor to five distinct Disciples periodicals: the *American Home Missionary* (of the American Christian Missionary Society, ACMS), *Missionary Tidings* (of the Christian Woman's Board of Missions, CWBM), the *Missionary Intelligencer* (of the Foreign Christian Missionary Society, FCMS), *Business in Christianity* (of the Board of Church Extension, BCE), and the *Christian Philanthropist* (of the National Benevolent Association, NBA). The new monthly magazine became a publication of the United Christian Missionary Society (UCMS) when that new organization was formally established in June 1920. The magazine ceased publication at the end of 1973, succeeded by *The Disciple* in January 1974.

From the outset, readers of *World Call* learned that leaders of the denomination shared a sense of a newly reinforced obligation and divinely granted opportunity for worldwide missions in the post-war era. In accord with theological exclusivism, the editors stated in the opening essay:

This magazine is meant to be a channel through which the call of the world's supreme needs and the challenge of the Christ's supreme leadership may reach the people of God.... After seven years of preparation it comes "in the fullness of time," both for the great day that has now dawned in the world and for the uniting of our efforts to meet this day. The world war was waged and won for the intangible verities for which the Church of Christ stands, and which only the Church of Christ can propagate. The free nations by their combined might could stop the sweep of murder and rapine, but it is left to the gospel of God's grace to transform the mind of murder into a heart of love.... The hour came when we had to fight Germany or become her victim. Now the hour has come when we must evangelize Asia, Africa and Latin America or eventually fight them. Just as we saved both men and women by throwing our whole strength into the conflict, so shall we find it both easier and surer to make quick work of winning the world to Christ.[9]

Stephen J. Corey, leader of the FCMS, argued similarly that for America, "the foremost nation of the world," all foreign doors were now open, and that missionary service overseas should be understood as a "worthy and heroic" equivalent to military service.[10] It was "the high noon of missionary opportunity," others asserted, and in many lands, including the United States, "never were prospects so bright or burdens so heavy."[11] In the call to global ministries, "Americanization" and "Christianization" were often closely related. As Christian educator Cynthia Pearl Maus argued with regard to home missions, "we must Christianize our democracy and Americanize our foreign peoples, build the church into the life of every neglected and isolated group, see that social and economic justice is the portion of the masses, and thus make it possible for America to be used of God in lighting the world to Christ's kingdom of universal Fatherhood and universal brotherhood."[12]

Three concerns expressed in the findings of the Edinburgh conference of 1910 especially resonated with Disciples responses to the new sense of urgency and opportunity.[13] First, in the decade prior to the 1928 Jerusalem conference of the International Missionary Council, Disciples were clearly motivated by the "great commission" in Matthew 28 but were also firmly committed to a broadly envisioned social gospel. That is, on the one hand, the essence of the church's mission was widely interpreted to mean worldwide evangelization, "to make Christ known to all the non-Christian world," as the concern was expressed at Edinburgh.[14] Disciples evangelist Jesse M. Bader argued passionately that personal evangelism was the method of Jesus and the key to the early frontier success of the Disciples of Christ. In fact criticizing those in the church who were comfortable with an emphasis on congregational fellowship at the cost of evangelism, Bader wrote the following in a 1920 essay titled "Won to Win:"

> Even though we have a rich evangelistic heritage back of us yet we are not as faithful in soul winning as we should be.... It does not take any Christianity to turn an ice cream freezer but it does take Christianity to win precious souls to Jesus Christ. Those who are won must win; those told must tell; those saved must save another.... The church evangelical many times means the church on ice, but the church evangelistic means the church on fire.[15]

Especially compelling contributions to issues of *World Call* included stories of actual conversions such as that of the Jewish immigrant from Poland, Elimelech Korn, who was converted through the work of the Chicago Hebrew Mission and later baptized in the Central Christian Church in Kansas City,[16] photographs of baptisms on the mission fields[17] or of overseas Christian leaders and churches,[18] sharply contrasting descriptions or photographs of "heathens" and Christians,[19] or stories from mission fields written not by Western missionaries but by foreign "recipients of Christianity."[20]

Yet on the other hand, in addition to acknowledging the need for evangelistic preaching, Disciples unquestionably understood that a Christian mission to the world rightly involved a multifaceted, compassionate outreach in education, medicine, and agriculture. Accordingly, they established schools, hospitals, dental clinics, orphanages, printing and binding facilities, and food distribution centers.[21] Believing that people were "more likely to criticize the church than to criticize Christianity,"[22] and, with Stephen Corey, that "no oriental religion has a social gospel" and are "bankrupt before human needs,"[23] denominational leaders typically interpreted engagement with social tasks as "evangelizing without sermonizing," an idea that had broad appeal to potential missionaries, especially women who could not, or were not encouraged to, imagine themselves as evangelists or pastors.[24] The only qualification for legitimizing its various social ministries, according to E. S. Muckley, is that the church must put "the distinctive Christian note into the service." Muckley concluded:

> The church should enter no field of service where it cannot differentiate its service from that rendered by nominally non-Christian institutions in the same field by putting the Christian mark on what it does. Everything the church does should advertise Christ and His ideals.... The church should educate and has educated the state to apply the ethics of Jesus in its realm of service, and it is right here where the new social consciousness is largely finding expression, for it was here in the state's realm of service where the greatest defects were found—where injustice and greed and crime sought entrenchment and protection in exploiting the masses.[25]

Second, the Disciples were in fundamental harmony with the call articulated at Edinburgh for a greater measure of ecumenical cooperation in mission. The findings of the 1910 conference stated, "As the missionary forces are divided into numerous independent organizations which are conducting foreign missions in different lands and with diverse methods, it is of utmost importance that they should be in close touch with each other, that they should be familiar with each other's work and methods, and that they should profit by each other's failures and successes."[26] Shortly after the Edinburgh conference, Peter Ainslie called for Disciples to reconfirm their historic commitment to Christian unity. Ainslie led the way in establishing a "Council on Christian Union," later renamed the "Association for the Promotion of Christian Unity," and ultimately the "Council on Christian Unity." In 1919, the editors of *World Call* described the work of the organization by quoting John R. Mott, "An unbelieving world is the price we pay for a church divided," and A. J. Brown, "A divided church cannot evangelize the world."[27] For Disciples leaders, sectarianism was consistently seen as a scandal that would one day be overcome, even if for many in the church faith in such an outcome was flagging. H. C. Armstrong wrote:

> Division and redivision, having run their unhallowed course for four centuries, have reduced denominationalism at last to the uttermost extremity of absurdity, until reproach has been brought upon the very church itself, and the supreme claims of Christianity have become so obscured that the majority of men feel that they can get along without the Church. Not only so, but for a century or more those sovereign bonds of the Holy Spirit and Holy Scripture have become so relaxed among Christians that it has been possible for groups and coteries of men for one doctrinal reason or another, instance after instance, to withdraw and start "new churches" and commit the supreme heresy without fear or compunction of conscience.
>
> Yet in full face of these scandalous facts there seems to be a faltering of faith in the grand ideal of Christian unity. It is being said that we have now the only kind of unity possible or desirable. "Cooperating denominationalism is the best possible order for the Church in the present age." Possibly so, but it is a "second best" order, and God gives his "second best" only to those or to that age which will not have His best.[28]

Third, despite the growing recognition of the importance of indigenous leaders, Disciples leaders resonated with the critical need expressed at Edinburgh for more educated candidates for commissioning as overseas missionaries.[29] Indeed, in 1910, as a direct response to the Edinburgh conference, the denomination's Christian Woman's Board of Missions founded the first graduate school specifically designed for the training of mission staff, both women and men, to serve at home or abroad—the College of Missions near the Butler University campus in Indianapolis. Under the direction of Charles T. Paul, a former missionary to China, the college accepted students sponsored by a number of different denominations and mission boards.

Students attended classes at Butler University in biblical languages, literature, history, and theology. The College of Missions offered general courses including comparative religion, social reform, philosophy, ethics, linguistics, international relations, and folkways, as well as special area studies such as modern missions in India, China, and Africa, religions of Japan, literature of Hispanic America, and modern languages (Chinese, Hindi, Urdu, Spanish, etc.). Having graduated more than one hundred students by 1920, the instructional program was transferred to the Kennedy School of Missions of Hartford Seminary Foundation in Connecticut in 1927–1928. Director Paul assured readers of *World Call* that the decision had not been made hastily but had been under consideration for some years as the number of "student-candidates" for overseas service decreased significantly and the financial requirements of independently operating the extensive educational program of the College of Missions mounted. He also confirmed that the institutional identity and goals of the College would be preserved through the new ecumenical arrangement with the Congregationalists and that beyond the seminary foundation's more than ninety courses, with the addition of "special instruction relating to the history, ideals and mission fields of the Disciples, the important work of preparing our missionary candidates will proceed in the Halls of Hartford."[30]

Considering a New Challenge

As a result of the Edinburgh conference in 1910, the International Missionary Council (IMC) was established in 1921. In the spring of 1928, the IMC convened in Jerusalem for the first of its five international conferences on mission (1928, 1938, 1947, 1952, and 1958). The meeting stimulated a decade of considerable debate among churches around the world. Stephen J. Corey, Samuel Guy Inman, and E. K. Higdon represented the Disciples. Two issues were especially central to the conference agenda. The first concerned the asymmetrical relationships between the "older" and "younger" churches; the second concerned Christian perspectives on other faiths.

UCMS Vice President Stephen Corey reported that while approximately three thousand persons had attended the Edinburgh conference in 1910, only twenty had been from younger mission churches in Asia, Africa, or Latin America. Remarkably, about one-half of the two hundred and forty church leaders at the Jerusalem conference represented those churches, although subsequent estimates of the number were more conservative.[31] Corey wrote:

> Here is revealed one of the great steps in progress of the last decade, being the advance toward the church as rooted in God and in the soil of its country: at once an integral part of the church universal, yet radiating its life within its own nation, alert to the problems of the community, penetrating all phases of life, kindled with missionary spirit and sharing its best with fellow churches throughout the world. In this discussion came the call of the younger churches on the field for participation in gifts and leadership from the older churches, made even more insistent because of the development of indigenous Christian life.[32]

Corey also reported that the conference discussions of "the Christian Message," centering on "the very heart of the missionary enterprise," were long and memorable.[33] Theologically liberal delegates, including Harvard University professor William E. Hocking, wanted to move the discussion on the church's relationship to non-Christian religions beyond a strict form of exclusivism and toward a more appreciative inclusivism. He would focus on relativism and secular materialism as the common foes of all religious communities. For the liberals, "world religions were viewed as possible allies in the development of a better world."[34]

Theological conservatives, including IMC chairman, John R. Mott, were dedicated to making certain that Christian uniqueness and the missionary motive were not compromised and that "the subdivision of the world into two large geographical areas–the one Christian, the other "non-Christian"–remained unchallenged."[35] As a result, according to Wolfgang Günther and Guillermo Cook, "the tensions at the conference were great," and the final report reflected these different perspectives.[36]

As Corey reported:

> There was fear on the part of some, especially the German and other continental delegations, that the recognition of the good in secular civilization and especially in the non-Christian religions, might lead to a sort of "syncretism" or a

statement made up of a mosaic of contributions from each, but the frank facing of realities only led to a more profound conviction concerning the supreme and unique place of Christ, and of his life, death and resurrection, as a redemptive act of God.[37]

Richey Hogg also writes:

William Temple drafted the unanimously accepted "Message" and incorporated in it the statement on the Christian Message prepared in 1927 at Lausanne by Faith and Order. The gospel announces God's truth: "Either it is true for all, or it is not true at all.... Christ is our motive and Christ is our end. We must give nothing less, and we can give nothing more." After acknowledging elements of truth in other major religions, Jerusalem issued a call to non-Christians to engagement—to join with Christians in a "study of Jesus Christ.[38]

Despite its strong christological emphasis, the adopted conference statement did include a more open and appreciative perspective on other religions than could have ever been contemplated at Edinburgh. In fact, utilizing "fulfillment" language that lifted up the continuity, rather than discontinuity, between Christianity and other traditions, and suggesting that the salvation, or healing, encountered most fully in Christ is also to be found even where Christ is not acknowledged, the report stated:

To non-Christians also we make our call. We rejoice to think that just because in Jesus Christ the light that lighteth every man shone forth in its full splendor, we find rays of that same light where He is unknown or even is rejected. We welcome every noble quality in non-Christian persons or systems as further proof that the Father, who sent His Son into the world, has nowhere left Himself without witness.

Thus, merely to give illustration, and making no attempt to estimate the spiritual value of other religions to their adherents, we recognize as part of the one Truth that sense of the Majesty of God and the consequent reverence in worship, which are conspicuous in Islam; the deep sympathy for the world's sorrow and unselfish search for the way of escape, which are at the heart of Buddhism; the desire for contact with Ultimate Reality conceived as spiritual, which is prominent in Hinduism; the belief in a moral order of the universe and consequent insistence of moral conduct, which are inculcated by Confucianism; the disinterested pursuit of truth and of human welfare which are often found in those who stand for secular civilization but do not accept Christ as their Lord and Saviour.[39]

Corey seemingly wanted to emphasize to Disciples readers that the conference began and ended with the central affirmation that "our message is Jesus Christ," the perfect revelation of God, while acknowledging that conference delegates had studied carefully "the weaknesses and strength in other religious systems such as Buddhism, Mohammedanism, Confucianism and Hinduism, as well as the dangers of modern secular civilization."[40] In accord with Bosch's analysis, a more balanced interpretation of the Jerusalem conference would have reported more fully the inclusivist theological stance of many delegates, which emphasized, in the manner of J. N. Farquhar's famous study, *The Crown of Hinduism,* that God was indeed active within other religions preparing the way for Christianity, something Corey failed to convey.[41]

During this period, evidence of the perspectival distance between those persons informed by evangelical and liberal paradigms for mission began to mount in issues of *World Call,* although theological confrontation was typically avoided. A. W. Fortune, pastor of Central Christian Church in Lexington, Kentucky, argued that with regard to its missionary task the church had always been certain of the basic goal—to make disciples of all nations—"but there has not always been the same interpretation of that task, and the missionaries have not all used the same methods of working." He continued:

> The first missionaries were thinking about the salvation of the heathen. In securing funds emphasis was placed on the number that were passing into perdition each moment without having heard of Christ.
>
> As the number of converts increased the missionaries began to establish churches according to the type which they had known in the homeland. Many things which had developed to meet the needs of the Occident were transplanted to the Orient regardless of whether they were best adapted to their needs. Denominational differences which had a significance in the West were taken to the East where they had no meaning.
>
> The church of our day is confronted with the same missionary task that Jesus gave to the little group of disciples, but modern conditions demand new methods. We have come to a new day in the missionary enterprise.[42]

Future mission efforts, according to Fortune, must:

(a) display consistently a Christian attitude toward non-Christian peoples, remaining genuinely sympathetic regarding their customs and ideals;
(b) create a more authentic Christian culture for ourselves, maintaining integrity between word and deed;
(c) allow the younger churches on mission fields to adapt the church to their own needs, acknowledging that we ourselves westernized what was originally an Oriental institution and that, perhaps, with their own indigenized Christian practice, they might attain a "higher type of Christianity" than we have; and
(d) recognize finally that "the church can only be firmly established in any land by those who belong to that land."[43]

Clarence Hamilton, a Disciples missionary who for many years had served on the faculty of Nanking University, responded to a question about the situation in China in the 1932 *World Call* "China Supplement":

> We are at the end of one epoch of missionary history in China as touching the relationship of the communions of the West and Chinese Christians. The Chinese have become of age and claim self-determination, and their purpose is to do away with foreign domination, political, economic, and religious. Where the missionary in the past has been organizer, director and controller of Chinese activities, the missionary of the future will be more of an advisor, friend, co-worker of the Chinese.
>
> Chinese ultimately are not anti-foreign or anti-Christian, but quite definitely anti-foreign domination. They will welcome the Western business man and representatives of Western Christianity on a basis of equal relationship and not otherwise.[44]

In concert with the proposition that a new epoch in overseas ministries was dawning, Josephine M. Stearns sought to highlight the need for interreligious understanding and cross-cultural relationships to bring "into the consciousness and conscience of the leadership of the church in America the significance of present trends and conditions in the life of the world."[45] She paraphrased E. Stanley Jones approvingly:

The final issue is between Christ and other ways of life. We want something deeper and more fundamental than issues between the systems of Christianity and Hinduism or Buddhism or Mohammedanism. Can we not sit down at the Round Table of Life and face our problems, not as Easterners or Westerners, but as men and women and see if there is a way out?[46]

How, she asked, can we understand and cooperate with people whom we have never met or whose backgrounds and circumstances we cannot really imagine? Her immediate answer was to travel globally to meet real people, establish real relationships, and move beyond the various labels by which we and others are identified. Strongly recommending, therefore, that congregations fund cross-cultural travel opportunities for their ministers, she concluded, "All who are responsible for helping to shape public opinion today should know the people and issues involved in the complex problems arising in this new post-war world-family to which we all belong."[47]

The Laymen's Inquiry

Stephen Corey recommended to readers of *World Call* John Mott's 1931 book that sought to explicate the message of the Jerusalem conference.[48] Mott justified the meeting's constructive "approach and temper" concerning non-Christian religions by words spoken by Jesus Christ—"I am come not to destroy but to fulfill" (Mt. 5:17, KJV), "My Father worketh hitherto, and I work" (Jn 5:17, KJV), and "Whoever is not against us is for us" (Mk. 9:40)—but emphasized the conference's strong affirmation of Christ as "God incarnate, the final, yet ever-unfolding, revelation of the God in whom we live and move and have our being."[49]

Jesse Bader, Donald McGavran, and others continued to articulate a more traditional "replacement model" of theological exclusivism and to emphasize personal evangelism as the central concern of Disciples missions. The more progressive "fulfillment model" of theological inclusivism that emerged at Jerusalem appeared to be moderate when compared to positions reflected in the 1932 publication of a comprehensive and controversial study of foreign missions.[50] Seven mainline Protestant denominations participated in the remarkable study funded by John D. Rockefeller Jr. They dispatched teams of fact-finders to India, Burma, China, and Japan.[51] Subsequently, a fifteen-member Commission on Appraisal chaired by William Ernest Hocking spent almost a year interviewing missionaries on those mission fields and crafting their report, largely written by Hocking.

The conclusions of the Laymen's Inquiry were controversial in two respects: its advocacy of theological pluralism, which Paul Knitter has characterized as the "mutuality model" in the theology of religions, and, second, its delineation of the temporary and permanent functions of missionaries.[52] The commission asserted that the theological outlook of Christians had been changing over the past century and attained a new stage of maturity:

> Western Christianity has in the main shifted its stress from the negative to the affirmative side of its message; it is less a religion of fear and more a religion of beneficence. It has passed through and beyond the stage of bitter conflict with the scientific consciousness of the race over details of the mode of creation, the age of the earth, the descent of man, miracle and law, to the stage of maturity in which a free religion and a free science become inseparable and complementary elements in a complete worldview. Whatever its present conception of the future life, there is little disposition to believe that sincere and aspiring seekers after God in other religions are to be damned; it has become less concerned in any land to save men from eternal punishment than from the danger of losing the supreme good.[53]

Having attained this new religious stage and recognizing the limited nature of human knowledge, Christians should look forward to real dialogical learning:

> It appears probable that the advance toward the goal [of the highest truth] may be by way of the immediate strengthening of several of the present religions of Asia, Christian and non-Christian together. The Christian who would be anxious in view of such a result displays too little confidence in the merits of his own faith. Whatever is unique in it, and necessary to the highest religious life of men can be trusted to show its value in due time and its own way. Meantime, if through growing appreciation and borrowing, the vitality of genuine religion is anywhere increased he may well rejoice in that fact. He will look forward, not to the destruction of these religions, but to their continued co-existence with Christianity, each stimulating the other in growth toward the ultimate goal, unity in the completest [sic] religious truth.... Sharing may mean spreading abroad what one has: but sharing becomes real only as it becomes mutual, running in both directions, each teaching, each learning, each with the other meeting the

unsolved problems of both.... The relation between religions must take increasingly hereafter the form of *a common search for truth.*[54]

The commissioners judged that the church was entering into a new era of ecumenical cooperation in global mission as the missionary functions and methods were appropriately changing from temporary to permanent ones. Rather than, as in the past, unilaterally sending a large number of persons overseas to engage in church planting, missionaries in the new era should assist indigenous leaders in church or society when specifically invited to do so. Rather than emphasizing the virtues of Western culture and acting so as to sever converts from their own local cultures, missionaries should seek to preserve that which is good and valuable in the converts' heritage and minimize breaks with their tradition. Rather than simply training nationals one day to replace the overseas staff, missionaries should establish specialized institutions to foster deeper cross-cultural relationships and cooperative interreligious learning.[55]

For several years after the publication of *Re-Thinking Missions,* Disciples leaders published numerous responses in *World Call.* The magazine's editors noted that the controversial study had "precipitated a major crisis in American Protestantism."[56] Editor and chief-of-staff Harold E. Fey recommended the volume by quoting the American Baptist board member, P. H. J. Lerrigo. He referred to the report as "a scintillating comet" crossing the missionary firmament, with the seven volumes of supporting materials as its "luminous tail," which, in the long run, might prove to be of even greater significance than the comet.[57]

In a front-page essay in *World Call,* the editors reported that a number of denominational mission boards were giving the instructive text intensive and sympathetic consideration, while "our own foreign department of the United Christian Missionary Society 'is in agreement with very much that has been recommended.'"[58] The editors observed:

> Since the Disciples were not represented in the communions whose laymen made this study, the report will not come before our official bodies for adoption or rejection. But there is small consolation to timid souls in that fact. The report has received such wide publicity that it is now, in a very urgent sense, the first order of business before every Christian group....

It is entirely probable that only the more forward-looking bodies will ever accept this report and unite their foreign missionary work. The real question that confronts Disciples is this: Are we capable of so mobilizing our consecration to the Great Commission that we can take a place with the communions which will in time undoubtedly accept in some form the principal recommendations of this amazingly clear, accurate and Christian report? The answer to that question will in the last analysis depend upon the answer to another: Do we have enough of Christian statesmanship in our pulpit and national leadership now to plan the wide and deep educational program which must necessarily precede that mobilization?[59]

Clarence H. Hamilton, former UCMS missionary to China and at the time professor of Christian missions at Oberlin College, contributed perhaps the most provocatively supportive essay to *World Call.* Hamilton agreed with the commissioners' conclusion that "all religions are in some sense ways to God," and that Christians could no longer naively assume that other religions "were all false; Christianity alone is truth. They have blighted the East; Christianity has saved the West. They must pass; Christianity will take their place."[60] Hamilton observed, in the face of science, secularism, and the encounter of the cultural and religious "other," all religions, including Christianity, are being compelled to reform and "to explore and restate their very best insights," each standing on "the common ground of all religion."[61] As the Laymen's report asserted, missionaries needed to study the religions around them and to associate "with whatever kindred elements there are in them."[62] Hamilton noted that it was not especially unusual for Christian missionaries in the past to try to understand the indigenous religious doctrines, rites, and institutions they encountered on the mission field. On another level, he claimed, the commissioners were calling for something much more significant and far-reaching:

While it is true that missionaries have learned much concerning traditional forms and teachings of the non-Christian religions, there has been little sustained effort to detect the essential religious meanings of these faiths and to consider in all seriousness whether in restated form they may not present something of *universal validity....* The religious Oriental is entering inevitably the common discourse of technological civilization. He, too, is learning the language of scientific discovery, international wars and economic maladjustment. Like the Occidental Christian he is asking himself, "What inner truth of my religious heritage can light the path of modern man?" It is a creative situation. Mere repetition of old sayings will not do. The answers must be given out of the travail of reformers bringing fresh messages for the times. It is the utterances of men like Gandhi and Radhakrishnan, T'ai Hsü and Hu Shih, D. T. Suzuki and Dr. Anesaki that bring forth new and significant restatement....

For association with the non-Christian religions is not figured by the report as merely a cooperation of independent organizations in forms of social work. Working together in famine, flood, earthquake or other social relief is possible and at times practiced. It may be conceived after the analogy of denominational participation in community enterprises in America. But the Laymen's proposal runs deeper. "The relation between religions must take increasingly hereafter the form of a common search for truth." Let earnest religious men of all faiths sit down together and in full mutual respect discuss their great common theme, the way of moral and spiritual guidance for modern man. Let them seek sympathetically to understand each other. Let them exchange their best and finest insights. Out of that give-and-take on the level of their deepest interest there may arise some new vision *new to all of them,* which shall be a creative discovery, "the birth of an idea which shall stir and strengthen religion in the race."[63]

Most Disciples writing in *World Call* affirmed the ecumenical emphasis of the Laymen's report and its argument about the temporary and permanent functions of missionaries. W. J. Lhamon remarked, "The book, *Re-Thinking Missions,* is receiving high praise and sharp, adverse criticism. It is a work that cannot be ignored. There are features of this *Re-Thinking* that should especially concern the Disciples of Christ and should cause them to hail it with enthusiasm.... This great work is a most notable present-day expression of Disciples attitudes."[64]

Joseph B. Hunter, former UCMS missionary to Japan, concurred, highlighting the report's perspective on evangelism, stating, "Christian evangelism in Japan and China is not against Buddhism and Shintoism but against secularism and the complete rejection of God. These religions contain many fine things and have laid a foundation upon which the Christian religion can build the Kingdom of God."[65]

Stephen Corey expressed some concern about *Re-Thinking Missions* call for the establishment of a comprehensive and unified administration over each mission field but still averred that, because of the force of the unified judgment of the commissioners from different church traditions, "There would seem to be no just ground for theological controversy with regard to the Inquiry."[66]

C. E. Lemmon noted that because of the report's critique of the whole missionary enterprise—its personnel, methods, equipment, administration, and theological underpinnings—"The older missionary leaders could scarcely have been expected to accept the document. Robert E. Speer, Secretary of the Presbyterian Board of Foreign Missions, has not concealed his opposition.[67] Stanley Jones has seemed dubious about it and accepted it with reservations."[68] Searle Bates, UCMS missionary to China, concluded:

> No one can feel that the Commission is all-wise. But it is unfortunate that emotional hostility and protective reactions are the quick response in some quarters. Certain Episcopalians throw away the Report unconsidered, because it does not maintain their traditional conception of the church; certain Presbyterians blind themselves to the merits of the study, because it does not repeat their own formulations of theology. It is easy to turn and rend the Laymen for disturbing our complacency; or to blame them for not saying just exactly what we should like to say if only we were intelligent enough to say it. But what we want is not a discordant jumble of attacks upon various portions of the Commission's work. Rather a positive utilization of all that can help us, with a welcome for the pain of new light, for the bruising that alone will make some corners of our hearts more sensitive.[69]

The Message of Madras and "Exacting Times"

Despite the positive reception of the Laymen's Inquiry in some quarters, negative reaction led ultimately to an invitation to Hendrik Kraemer, the distinguished historian of religions and neoorthodox theologian of the Dutch Reformed Church, to produce a counterpoint study for the 1938 IMC conference at Tambaram, a suburb of Madras. The resulting book embraced theological exclusivism and a replacement model in the theology of religions.[70] Kraemer emphasized a "biblical realism" that affirmed that God was mysteriously at work in the religions, but that "saving revelation" is only found in Jesus Christ, the "crisis" of all religions. That is, when viewed in relation to the saving incarnation of the Word, all religions represent human rejection of the truth. One can say that other religions prepare people for the acceptance of Christ, but it is a negative preparation, for only Christ can provide the salvation for which all people long. According to Hogg, "With his Barthian orientation, Kraemer rejected all 'natural theologies' and emphasized the gospel's 'discontinuity' from all religions. Thus emerged the 'Kraemer-Hocking debate' on Christianity's encounter with other religions."[71]

Prior to the conference, *World Call* editor George Walker Buckner Jr. gave most of the front page of the monthly issue to a discussion of the significance of Kraemer's new book, stating, "Quite apart from an official relation to the forthcoming conference…this book has vast significance for the Christian Church…. It insists that the Church must again in our day consider the whole world as its mission field."[72] Presbyterian Robert Speer also briefly described the significance of the 1928 Jerusalem conference, but not surprisingly did not even mention Hocking or the Laymen's Inquiry.[73] Church historian Stephen Neill once commented that even before the liberalism of *Re-Thinking Missions* actually had time to sink in, "the reaction against it had set in." He noted:

> A number of missionaries, mostly of continental origin, had come under the influence of the theology of Karl Barth, with its strenuous repudiation of liberalism in all its forms. Yet it has proved impossible to go back to the earlier point of view; and the kind of propaganda on behalf of missions which was acceptable in the nineteenth century now makes little appeal in the more cultivated and thoughtful circles of the Church. Western man had learned how much there was in his colonial record of which he had to be ashamed. He was much less sure than he had been of the uniqueness and finality of the Christian Gospel, and of his right to impose on the heirs of other great traditions what might prove to be, after all, no more than a western myth.[74]

In 1939, after the IMC conference near Madras, Clarence Hamilton and several other Disciples leaders contributed short related reports and articles in *World Call*, but concerns related to the coming world war, which had already begun in China, seemed to have limited responses and overshadowed new church initiatives in mission. Hamilton still claimed that ever since the Laymen's Inquiry had raised the troubling question of "whether the impact of the Church in foreign lands had been what we thought it was," the church had struggled to define the Christian message and, especially, to clarify the function of the church:

> Is it to reconstruct society, shape a civilization, bring about cultural synthesis? Is it to ameliorate suffering, spread abroad the Christian spirit, set up a Kingdom of Righteousness on earth? Or, in the face of threatening collapse, is it to save what it can of the values of civilization out of the wreckage of a ruined world? Is it, perchance, to stand in the world but not of it, uttering a word of warning and of judgment on the ways of secular life? Or is it simply to be the humble beholder of divine acts, irrupting from eternity into time, the recipient and proclaimer of a divine word not framed by man? Or yet again, is its sole and essential duty just to confront the world, through witnessing, with the revelation of God in Christ and to tell of his salvation?
>
> Questions of this type arise in Hendrik Kraemer's *The Christian Message in a Non-Christian World*.... The great point is that through all such discussion the Christian movement is bending its energies in all earnestness and devotion to understand itself and its mission afresh. Once again it re-examines its Scriptures, its history, its non-Christian environment with a view to becoming clear as to its basic motives and meaning. The process is complex and strenuous but essential to strengthening morale for the Christian task in exacting times.[75]

The "exacting times" for Disciples of Christ were to become increasingly more difficult during the terrible years of turmoil, tragedy, and global conflagration that marked World War II. The editors of *World Call* predicted accurately in 1939 that the American people would soon have to face up to "international anarchy, narrow nationalism, ugly racialism (evidenced both by America's Ku Klux Klan and Mr. Hitler's Germany), cruel individualism, class strife, and greedy lust for power, both by men and nations." They declared that in the face of disaster all people should embrace three straightforward convictions:

> That force as a method of human progress has failed utterly and will ever fail....That the interdependence of humanity is an inescapable principle of life....That the ultimate reliance of men and of nations must be upon the way of life of Jesus. No other way is comparable. It is indeed "World Chaos or

World Christianity." And it must be *world* Christianity with a World Christian Community as its burning ideal.[76]

In working toward a "world Christianity," Disciples congregations and organizations would have to deal not only with significant theological differences but with financial hardships, abandoned mission projects, severed mission relationships, and prejudice at home and abroad based on gender, race, ethnic identity, and national origin.[77] During the war years and beyond, the Disciples and all other North American denominations would have to struggle to maintain a faithful global witness while waiting upon the Spirit of God to lead them into greater measures of Christian servanthood in word and deed.

6

It's about the Conversation

GARY E. PELUSO-VERDEND

Angels need only intuit to know. And each does so alone, not in a community of inquiry, for each exhausts its own species! But we humans must reason discursively, inquire communally, converse and argue with ourselves and one another. Human knowledge could be other than it is. But this is the way it is: embodied, communal, finite, discursive.

DAVID TRACY[1]

"Come now, let us reason together, says the Lord..."

ISAIAH 1:18a (RSV)

David Tracy wrote: "There is no intellectual, cultural, political, or religious tradition of interpretation that does not ultimately live by the quality of its conversation; there is also no tradition that does not eventually have to acknowledge its own plurality and ambiguity."[2] Ecumenists will tend to agree with the first clause of this sentence. Charles Brent, founder of the Faith and Order Movement in the early 1900s, passionately believed in the method of conference as a means of moving the churches toward unity. William Adams Brown, one of the primary shapers of U.S. ecumenical thought in the first part of the twentieth century, believed in the importance of conversation because God might say something different to one person than to another.[3]

In his plenary address at the World Council's Nairobi Assembly in 1975, another Brown—Robert McAfee—reflected on Jesus' queries:

"Who do others say that I am? Who do you say that I am?" Brown asserted that the first question requires persons to listen before they speak, while the second demands that they reflect on the "I" who answers. A white African is likely to respond differently from a black African. If each is to be heard, conversation is necessary.[4] Church of the Brethren theologian Melanie May also affirmed the necessity of conversation and offered this definition: "Conversation is not an activity by which I convey my words or terms or agenda to another. Conversation is giving and receiving *my* words and *your* words until we are speaking *our* words. Conversation yields a new creation."[5]

Ecumenists, however, have been reticent to accept the second clause of David Tracy's sentence, that every tradition is fraught with plurality and ambiguity. The Orthodox, for instance, hold that the tradition in which they stand is *The* Tradition and has been faithfully preserved since apostolic times. Tradition is not ambiguous. While it allows for plural expression, it is not plural in the sense that Tracy uses the word (i.e., genuinely different possibilities of thinking and doing). Nor, of course, are the Orthodox alone in their hesitancy to embrace plurality and ambiguity within their tradition. United Methodists (my own tribe), for whom conference has an almost sacramental quality, reach to remove specks from other ecclesial eyes while great beams protrude from our own. We often fail to acknowledge the ambiguous effects of our own tradition and balk at accepting the possibility of other ways of being church.

Genuine conversation, as May wrote, involves a new creation of sorts. It involves great risk; for if one comes to understand what another is saying, one is challenged to reflect on the possibility of another way of being and doing. According to Tracy, in genuine conversation the question and not the questioners stands at the center. Participants follow the logic of the question in the search for truth similar to the way one follows the rules of a game in order to play. Conversation partners need to follow the question's logic, demands, and rhythm. They also need to be attentive, intelligent, responsible, loving, and willing to change when necessary.[6]

What would a genuine conversation among ecumenists from the United States look like? In the following fiction I attempt to imagine one. I created seven personas, each an amalgam of different real persons, mostly from the recent past. They will be brought into conversation around a vital question in ecumenical circles: the nature of the church, specifically the images and metaphors we employ when we speak about ecclesial community.

The Conversation

Participants

Richard Calvin Hooker–aged and venerable. He knew the Protestant ecumenical giants of the early to mid-twentieth century and represents their views.

Peter Niebuhr Wesley–an older middle-aged white Protestant who speaks for Methodist and some Reformed positions.

Rosemary Harkness Johnson–a younger white theologian who represents a feminist viewpoint.

Father Thomas O'Reilly–a younger white male Roman Catholic priest who knows the figures in U.S. Catholic ecumenism.

Father Nicholas Aggelopoulos–a Greek Orthodox emigrant who presents a pan-Orthodox perspective.

Martin Schmucker Weiss–a middle-aged white male Lutheran who stands for confessional traditions, especially Lutheran.

James Douglas Smith–an African American theologian who represents black traditions, mostly Protestant but also Catholic.

Gary Peluso-Verdend–the early middle-aged white male United Methodist moderator.

Peluso-Verdend–I invite you to exercise your memories of your tradition as we explore the ecumenical imagination in the U.S. We are all familiar with Paul Minear's benchmark study on images of the church in the New Testament, in which he identified some ninety-six different images.[7] We are most concerned here with images of church unity. Which images of church unity have our traditions offered in ecumenical conversations? Along with images, please include relevant anecdotes and concepts.

Hooker–I can answer for Charles Brent, William Adams Brown, and Samuel McCrea Cavert. Bishop Brent had a fertile imagination. He was more pastoral than systematic in his theology, and he used several images and concepts. He was an Anglican and held to the four points of the Lambeth Quadrilateral. He compared church unity to that of the British Commonwealth, held together by ties of personal loyalty to the throne rather than by more formal legislative ties. He liked family images: God as Father, Jesus as Son, all of us as Jesus' brothers. He envisioned all the nations of the world to be of one blood. The church's task is to draw that one family into one visible fellowship in Jesus Christ. Brent was an organicist: the church is a living *organism* rather than an *organization*. It *is* the body of Christ.

Although he once held that a federation of churches might be the unity to which Christ calls us, Brent said that he could finally stomach no other unity than organic.[8]

I think we could categorize both Brown (a professor at Union in New York City) and Cavert (a primary shaper of U.S. ecumenism in the middle of the twentieth century) as federalists. Brown might not have accepted that label, but he believed the United States began as a federal union and grew together into an organic one. That's a judgment about the U.S. I'm not sure we today could share. But Brown thought the churches could grow together in the same way that the nation had: by pursuing common tasks, by living and working side by side.[9]

Cavert greatly admired Brown, who was, after all, his theological and ecumenical mentor. Cavert believed in organic unions, meaning full structural mergers, within confessional families, but he was cool on the idea of organic unity as being the unity Christ wills. This was especially his position after the Roman Catholics opened themselves to official contact with Protestant ecumenism. He did refer to the church as the body of Christ, but he did not foresee one structural body. Cavert loved the United States' way of relating the states to one another. But he grounded his conceptions of unity in fellowship. He took from William Temple the understanding of fellowship, of unrestricted sharing in each other's lives, as the touchstone of whether or not we had the unity we seek.[10]

Wesley–I will focus on four white Protestant males: Henry Van Dusen, Robert McAfee Brown, Albert Outler, and Gerald Moede. The first two were Presbyterians, while the second two represent Methodists. All but Moede were church-oriented academics. Moede is not the theological household name that the others are, but he was instrumental in shaping the Consultation on Church Union's (COCU) theology of covenant union in the 1970s and 1980s.

Van Dusen's favorite concept of unity was conciliar, while his chosen image was familial. No one embraced the idea of councils and gushed over their potential more than Van Dusen did. As the World Council was forming, he thought it "[s]imple in structure and unpretentious in authority." The WCC was a foretaste of world community that might come about more fully one day. He also thought the National Council's birth was one of the greatest events in Christianity since the ecumenical councils of the first five centuries. My, what history does to such statements! He rejected the idea that Christ required organic union, if that meant obliteration of denominational identities, as well as any identification of the body of Christ image with one institutional body. He thought the church was faced with three basic images of unity: the body of Christ, which he thought inadequate because of its affinity with structural mergers; the community of Christians, which sounded too much like a voluntary association; and the "family of God." He embraced the last, for he believed it made room both for organic ties and choice, especially if one thinks of the church as a family of adults who have grown, matured, and recognize their interdependence rather than play out an adolescent independence or a childish dependence.[11]

I cannot remember any time when Van Dusen and Robert McAfee Brown, two fine theologians in the Reformed tradition, conversed in print; however, if they had, they would have presented an interesting argument! In the days when COCU began, Brown declared denominations had to die. Unity must be organic, and that organic unity requires the death and rebirth of the churches. Around the time of Vatican II, he declared, with Lutheran Edmund Schlink, that the only choice the churches face is between organic unity and "ecclesiastical docetism." However, in the context of the Vietnam War and his rising consciousness about the world's poor and oppressed, Brown pulled back from committing the energy and resources necessary for this kind of union. We see the change in his plenary address at the Nairobi Assembly in 1975. The Third World churches were ready to pounce on this American, but he disarmed them with a masterful address on the Jesus Christ who frees, *divides,* and unites. Ecumenism came to mean solidarity with the oppressed more than working on unity in Euro-North American categories.[12]

Albert Outler took, I think, a decidedly different view of the unity matter. He, too, advocated organic unity, but he understood it in such a way that allowed distinct denominations and confessional families to perdure. He considered it organic and not merely federal, however, for federal does not involve a shared eucharist with all the attendant conditions. Several considerations formed his stance. As with many twentieth-century Protestant ecumenists, Outler suspected the power of large institutions to stifle local and individual freedom and initiative. Very importantly, he believed that the experience of Christian community precedes doctrine, and that doctrine is disciplined reflection within an ecclesial context.

This point of view stood over against the *reine Lehre* position he thought some others (perhaps continental Lutherans?) espoused. To give an example of what the priority on community means: Outler observed that members of different denominations and communions already mingle as they attend programs and services, and occasionally commune—with or without official sanction—in a friend's church.

Sounding much like what we today are calling a practical theologian, Outler called for a new theory to reflect, and to catch up to, this practice. His conceptual way of understanding organic union was to use the analogy of orders within the Roman Catholic Church. Each order has its own head and its own distinctive witness, but each is also visibly united with the others by their communion in sacred things, by constitutional ties, and by collegial or conciliar structures. Denominations would have to die in the sense that they relinquish their absolute sovereignty, but they would also live on as orders or movements, as parts of a larger whole.[13]

Finally, United Methodist Gerald Moede advocated yet another view of organic union, this one based on the biblical concept of covenant. Moede and his COCU colleagues developed the concept of covenant communion after it was clear that COCU participating churches were not going to martyr themselves for the sake of one visible institution. Moede deftly joined the concept of covenant with organic unity and the image of the body of Christ. A covenant, initiated by God and involving persons with God and with each other, allows simultaneously for different degrees of involvement at different levels. Moede and COCU first conceived of covenanting as an interim process toward a fuller structural unity. However, between 1984 and 1988 they decided that covenant communion—in which churches recognize each other's baptisms, eucharists, and ministries, and participate in councils of oversight at various levels for mutual decision-making—is the nature of the unity we seek. The denominations would concern themselves with communion in sacred things without fussing about merging pension plans.[14]

Now some ecumenists are quite dissatisfied with what they perceive as COCU's—and Moede's—drift from a more demanding form of union. Michael Kinnamon comes to mind. His touchstone for real union is whether or not his grandmother continues to identify herself as a member of the Disciples of Christ and to worship separately from her non-Disciple neighbors. He thus prefers, with Newbigin, to see denominational identities die.[15]

Smith—We in the African American tradition have tended to see what unity is and what it requires differently from the conversation predominantly white churches have fostered. We have been a part of the ecumenical movement from the first because we, too, believe that Christ wills that his followers be one. But our interpretation of "one" has had less to do with abstract doctrine and more to do with action, especially action in solidarity with the oppressed. Our ecclesiology has tended to be a servant ecclesiology. Our preferred images express the catholicity of that service: Howard Thurman's "the Fellowship of All People" and Martin Luther King Jr.'s "Beloved Community." We distrust exalted, idealistic conceptions of the church for, in our experience, these have masked oppression.[16] Preston Williams criticized Faith and Order's language about the church being a mystery because the real mystery is that African Americans received the gospel at all![17] He did not go as far as James Cone, who declared that white churches have no legitimate claim on calling themselves "Christian,"[18] but he does underline the foundational role that racism has played in North American Christianity and the urgent need to deal with it.[19]

In addition, we have opposed organic unions understood as structural mergers because our society still lacks justice and equality. We have no assurances that the predominantly white churches will not exercise hegemony over us. No lamb in her right mind is going to dine with the wolf until she knows for certain that the wolf is not going to set the menu! This is one of the reasons the African American Methodist Churches preferred something like COCU's covenant form of unity rather than the parish-merger form. The African American style of worship cuts across denominational and confessional traditions. It took shape in slave days and when African Americans came out of the white churches. It provides a valuable context for forming our identity as African Americans, as well as a legitimate way of becoming, being, and remaining Christian. I don't see how this tradition could survive if we became a minority in a predominantly white church.[20]

Johnson–Gary, you asked about images, as well as concepts and anecdotes. While not neglecting concepts, much feminist work has been at the level of imagination. Many of us affirm, with Sallie McFague, that images and metaphors exist at a deeper level than concepts, and that concepts are the rational construction of connections between metaphors.[21]

Letty Russell and Melanie May led in trying to reimagine the nature of the unity we seek in a way that includes women's experiences, as well as in addressing the sinful trinity of racism, classism, and sexism. In opposition to strict hierarchical understandings of unity, Russell proffered images such as "rainbow spectrum" and "God's banquet of riotous variety." Listening to the world's suffering, she also heard a world groaning together. Unity is located more in solidarity with the person and story of Jesus–and with the persons to whom Jesus leads us–than in doctrinal or institutional forms.[22]

Melanie May is also concerned to break through hierarchical understandings of unity. Ecumenists have often used the image of the body of Christ to ground hierarchical understandings of authority and of ecclesial structure—and white Euro-North American males have always been privileged to represent the head! That arrangement has produced a great deal of "subjugated knowledge" that ought to be heard. May seeks not some unifying image but to listen to stories without trying to categorize them, to hear their difference from my own story without reaching for a premature and inevitably oppressive consensus.[23]

Weiss—I think many of us Lutherans would have some problems with May's formulation, Dr. Johnson, as well as with the African American tradition's sometime tendency to undervalue doctrinal agreement as an essential element of unity. Although great variety exists within the Lutheran world family, and within the North American clan of that family, our confessional agreement distinguishes us as a family. Although we are sensitive to Outler's comment about the priority of Christian community over doctrine—especially when doctrine petrifies into the seventeenth-century *reine Lehre* ilk—we would also affirm that doctrine is a constituent component of community. For all their differences, Franklin Clark Fry, Martin Marty, George Lindbeck, and William Rusch have all asserted as much.

Fry pushed for representation by confessional families in the World Council, one major reason being that there is a unity in faith that transcends all local boundaries.[24] Marty has argued that multiple confessional expressions could coexist in a worldwide family of apostolic churches that, in agreement with Outler, could be organized similarly to orders within Catholicism.[25] Lindbeck has taken a cultural-linguistic view of religion and has claimed that doctrines function in a religious community like grammar does in language.[26] Rusch argues that the New Testament canonizes a diversity of confessional stances within a common creed from which diverse structures and practices flow.[27]

Granted, each of these four understand somewhat differently what it means to be a confessional church, but all embrace the importance of confession and of dealing seriously with doctrine in any unity effort and in defining the nature of the unity we seek. This is not to say that any of these theologians downplay the importance of shared witness and solidarity with the oppressed. Marty, for one, bases his position on the need for common mission. But this work cannot be done in an intellectual vacuum. An organizational sociologist relates the story about a village that did not eat pork. One day a pig wandered into a house, and a child "playing with matches" set the house afire. The villagers discovered the now-cooked pig, ate it, and enjoyed it immensely. From that time on, anytime they wanted roast pig, they tied it in a house and burned the dwelling down! For, you see, without adequate reflection upon our experience, we may be unnecessarily burning down our homes.[28]

O'Reilly–Let me jump in here, for you have raised a point which has long concerned Catholics. In the Catholic view, Protestants–especially American Protestants–do not spend enough energy *thinking* about ecumenical issues. George Tavard complained about this often.[29] I do not disagree with Drs. Smith and Johnson. Yes, our doctrines of the church, exalting her spotlessness and her mystery, have functioned as screens for great racism and sexism. For this we need to repent, which includes changing the way we interact with non-white, non-males as well as the way we image and reason about ecclesial life. Any future form of unity will result, however, not only from solidarity with the oppressed, although that solidarity must be an element of unity. It will be the result also of much critical reflection upon our life and practice in light of our authoritative sources of scripture and tradition.

Catholic thinking has come a long way in the years since Vatican II regarding images and conceptions of unity. The image of the body of Christ no longer reigns, although it still has its proponents who support it both theologically and because of its affinities with hierarchical structures. Avery Dulles dislikes the organism image because it constricts legitimate diversity and conflict. He rejects Vatican II's reliance upon the People of God because of its exclusive tone. (Are not other peoples God's people?) His preferred model was articulated by John Paul II: "the Church as a Community of Disciples." He believes that this model provides a coherent and fruitful ordering context for images and the other five models: the church as institution, community, sacrament, herald, and servant.[30]

Dulles and Tavard have given thought to the form of a united or uniting church. Tavard thought of it as a combination of a communion of communions, with each communion holding an ecclesiology of subsistence. By that he means that each communion has its own order and polity and believes that *the* church subsists in it. But each also acknowledges that *the* church is more fully present in the communion of communions than in any *one* discrete church.[31]

Dulles prefers Willebrand's concept of a *typoi* of churches in communion with one another, meaning that a communion of communions would include more than one "type" of the church–suggesting the depth of diversity in that communion. In either case, though, the papacy is present with more than symbolic power. Such unions must include eucharistic sharing, which in turn presupposes fundamental agreement in ecclesiology.[32]

In some ways, I like the analogy between Catholic orders and a reformed role for Protestant denominations within a united church. But I cannot accept the analogy if the denominations remain un-reformed. Catholic orders differ from each other in nuances, customs, and the like. They are united in fundamentals, officially recognize hierarchies of authority (if not always in practice), and are united in the eucharist. Without similar structures for Protestant relationships, any analogy between denominations and orders is too facile.[33]

Wesley–If we are talking about un-reformed Protestantism, I agree that the analogy is too easy. But no truly ecumenically minded Protestant is content with denominational*ism*. Although many of us don't want to kill our denominations, neither do we want to live indifferently to one another.

Aggelopoulos–I have heard the presentations and discussion revolve around images and concepts: body of Christ, People of God, Community of Disciples, Family of God, Beloved Community, fellowship, federal unity, organic unity, unity in solidarity with the oppressed. When you ask about "images of unity," Gary, you ask in a way different from the way we Orthodox do. You seem to assume that one may *play* with images, interchange them, innovate, and experiment. You can, as long as we are talking only about images or metaphors. We in the Orthodox Church know that the church is not only *like* the body of Christ; it *is* the body of Christ. This is ontologically so, not only in someone's ecumenical imagination. I realize that various Faith and Order statements, including ones predating full Orthodox participation, also affirm this, but, again, with differences from the Orthodox way. We believe that each local church is fully the body of Christ, united with her Lord in the eucharist, under the presidency of a bishop who is in communion with bishops of other local churches. Local churches are not parts of the body of Christ, as Catholic and some Protestant ecclesiologies assert, but each is fully his body. Unity is manifested in the eucharist. All structures serve to undergird and protect this unity. As I am sure you are quite aware, we believe that we have maintained this structure and an unbroken unity since apostolic times. Any ecclesial body wanting to participate in Christ's body can do so only by confessing the Truth through word and sacrament as the Orthodox faithfully have.[34]

O'Reilly–Isn't it also true, Father Aggelopoulos, that the North American denominational pattern scandalizes the Orthodox churches in another way? The Orthodox ecclesiology you have outlined has room for one bishop in any one jurisdiction. That is not a problem in the Old World, where ethnic groups had their own national churches. When those groups came here, they retained their ethnic ties in substantial part through their particular expression of Orthodoxy. This retention has meant that often several Orthodox bishops claim the same geographical jurisdiction.

Aggelopoulos –You are quite right. This is a scandal, one that decreases our evangelistic effectiveness and diminishes the church's witness to uniting all peoples in the body of Christ.[35]

Peluso-Verdend–With that statement I must bring this moment of our conversation to a close. I doubt whether we have solved any problems or converted each other to "my" position. I will confess that I am not quite the same as I was when this conversation began. As I listened to each of you opine regarding our questions, I felt tugged by what you said, by the claim that your view of our Tradition made upon me. You helped me to look at what you see. Although I did not always agree with your assessments, I have again come to understand that the church would be poorer and our understandings of Christ would be diminished without each of you. I hope our conversation and our search for community in Jesus Christ will continue.

Circling Back with Fresh Eyes

*Christians Teaching Buddhist Practices
for Peace at Shalem Institute for
Spiritual Formation*

SANDRA COSTEN KUNZ

In 1973 Tilden Edwards, an Episcopal priest running the Metropolitan Ecumenical Training Center for congregational leaders in Washington, D.C., spent two months of his summer sabbatical studying meditation with Tarthang Tulku Rinpoche,[1] a Tibetan lama in the Nyingmapa tradition. Tarthang Tulku had founded Nyingma Institute in a dilapidated former fraternity house in Berkeley, California, earlier that year. Four years later Edwards published the following remembrance of this these months he spent sitting at the feet, quite literally, of a Vajrayana Buddhist teacher.

> [H]is ultimate challenge was to let go of everything. "Nothing holding anything anywhere," in mind or body—this was his repeated theme. Everything he taught was a means to that end: a great range of meditation forms, psychological and physical methods for lightening emotional attachments, philosophical concepts, disciplines for daily living, all aimed at a kind of pure iconoclasm that left nothing to cling to.[2]

...I returned from that summer feeling like someone returning from another planet. Could my experience possibly make sense to the people I work with? Could Rinpoche's approach to seeing and dealing with reality be enriching to them, or more confusing, complicating and threatening?

Soon after returning I began work with a group of clergy, religious and laity committed to explore self-clearing, self-simplifying forms of meditation and spiritual development weekly together for eight months. I received their permission to work almost exclusively for the first four months with Tibetan Buddhist approaches to relaxing, stilling and clearing the body and mind. Behind this request was my new sense of the value of stepping outside the familiar forms of our own tradition for a while into those of another more actively intuitive, contemplative tradition, and then circling back into our own with fresh eyes.[3]

This eight-month "meditation and spiritual development" group, sponsored by the Metropolitan Ecumenical Training Center, was Edwards' first attempt to circle back to his identity as a Christian teacher with the fresh eyes he had acquired as a student of Buddhism. This group led to other similar groups, which in 1978 incorporated as a separate nonprofit organization: Shalem Institute for Spiritual Formation. According to the organization's current Web site: "Shalem (pronounced Sha-LAME) is a Hebrew word related to Shalom, the familiar greeting of peace. Shalem speaks of wholeness: to be complete, full, sound. Scripture speaks of loving God with a 'lev shalem,' a whole heart."[4]

Shalem Institute's mission is to "call forth a deeper spiritual life in both person and community."[5] Edwards served as the executive director of Shalem until his retirement from that position several years ago. He is now Senior Fellow there. In 2006 Shalem's ten fulltime and many part-time teachers coordinated programs for 1384 participants. These programs included weekly meditation groups, body prayer groups, discernment groups, workshops, residential retreats, and quiet days. Academic credit for two of their two-year programs, "Spiritual Guidance" and "Leading Contemplative Groups and Retreats," is available through Washington Theological Union. The Spiritual Guidance program offers training in "the ancient Christian practice of spiritual direction reclaimed, explored and disciplined for our time" for "those called to the ministry of one-on-one spiritual guidance."[6]

Although Shalem is very forthright about its use of non-Christian Eastern religious practices, Edwards maintains that he has always seen

Shalem as "a Christian center."[7] This chapter looks at the careful and intentional use of religious practices and teaching techniques that Edwards and other Shalem leaders learned from Buddhist teachers. I will examine how borrowing the traditional practices of these religious "others" has affected these Christians' sense of identity and rootedness within their original religious communities, and how it has changed their practice within their own tradition, particularly practices aimed, at least in part, on promoting reconciliation and peace.

Reconciliation has been an ongoing thread in Edwards' career. He has drawn together amazingly disparate groups across racial, class, denominational, and religious lines. Peacemaking has been a theme woven through many of Shalem's programs. Edwards has stated that, although he would never make a direct causal connection between any particular Buddhist practice and the resolution of any particular conflict, his immersion in Buddhist practice has given him a broader array of skillful means for teaching Christians how to become more responsive and less reactive in conflictual situations with all types of "others." In other words, it has helped him teach Christians to act in ways that more clearly embody Jesus' teachings about self-sacrifice and reconciliation with enemies.[8] I will examine the specific practices and other overall emphases of Nyingmapa Buddhism that have been used at Shalem to address the intrapersonal and interpersonal dynamics underlying conflict.

The Metropolitan Ecumenical Training Center's Contemplative Groups and Shalem's Early Years

During his 1973 sabbatical, Edwards immediately began integrating Buddhist meditation practices with Christian meditation upon scripture. He wrote:

> After an average day of twelve hours of meditation...lecture, and dialogue...I saved just enough energy to open the Gospels and read for a while each day. Part of this was a defensive reaction: I didn't want to lose my own spiritual lineage. Part of my motivation was open concern: I wanted to see what would happen in a daily dialogue between Jesus and Gautama, between the Christ and the Buddha. Would they clash or coincide?
>
> I was amazed to find how many of the difficult sayings of Jesus began to appear freshly lucid—what it means to "lose your life to find it"....[9]

Before returning to Washington, Edwards spent his last week of this sabbatical on a silent Ignatian retreat at a Jesuit center in

Wernersville, Pennsylvania. He devoted a great deal of time to reading works by Christian contemplatives: Eckhardt, John of the Cross, Teresa of Avila, Rusbroek, Tauler, the author of *The Cloud of Unknowing*, and others. He commented later, "I was struck many times by the similarity of their descriptions of their 'enlightened' awareness to those of Tarthang Rinpoche's and certain Buddhist texts."[10]

Gerald May, a psychiatrist who had left the church as a young adult and was doing regular Buddhist practice, attended the first retreat of the first METC meditation group Edwards started upon his return to Washington. May was for many years Director of Spiritual Guidance at Shalem and a Senior Fellow when he died in April 2005. He describes this first Buddhist-Christian retreat that Edwards led:

> It was very rich.... I was impressed with the beauty and impact of Tibetan chants and visualizations, and amazed at how some of the physical postures and breathing exercises helped to clear my mind. But most of all I was struck by how "Christian" it all seemed. Here was this group of people, most of them Roman Catholic, Episcopal, or other Christian clergy and laity, meeting at a Roman Catholic retreat center, doing yoga and chanting Sanskrit syllables at one moment and sharing the eucharist the next. At meals, after a very Protestant-sounding grace, there was a very Buddhist sort of silence in which everyone was "mindful," watching hands moving, feeling mouth chewing, sensing the meal. Then the Jesus prayer, silently, in time with breathing, in the afternoon.[11]

Soon other Metropolitan Ecumenical Training Center groups focused on developing "contemplative presence" were formed. In 1975–1977 METC received a two-year grant from the Lilly Endowment, Inc., for "research into the state of spiritual development in the contemporary world."[12] Quaker sociologist Parker Palmer, then director of Pendle Hill Study Center near Philadelphia, helped design the research model, which involved interviewing "different modern spiritual leaders,"[13] including Episcopalians James Fenhagen, Alan Jones, Morton Kelsey, and Graham Pulkingham; Jesuits Donald Foree and Dick Hunt; Trappist Thomas Keating; rabbis Lawrence Kushner and Zalman Schachter; Quaker Douglas Steere; Korean Zen master Seung Sahn Soen-Sa; and Japanese Zen master Joshu Sasaki Roshi.[14] When Shalem incorporated, its first board included James Forbes (an African American homiletics professor at Union Seminary who recently retired as pastor of Riverside Church in New York), Conrad

Hoover (pastor of Church of the Savior in Washington, D.C.) and Joanna Macy (an eco-feminist scholar who has written books on relationships between Buddhism, ecology, and systems theory).[15]

Spaciousness, Interconnectedness, and Peacemaking: Buddhist Imagery Breathing Fresh Air into Christian Doctrine

In 1996 I asked Edwards how much Shalem's programs were still incorporating influences from Nyingma Institute. He replied that Tibetan influence was implicit in many programs but was seen most explicitly in the use of certain particular meditation practices and the use of Kum Nye, Tarthang Tulku's name for the vigorous exercises he put together, which appear to draw heavily upon hatha yoga and qigong. Many of Shalem's programs open with Kum Nye or some other movement exercise. For years Isabella Bates, who spent many weeks at Nyingma Institute, taught a body prayer class that met for two hours a week for thirty-six weeks, using Tarthang Tulku's book *Kum Nye Relaxation* as its text.[16] "Some of the analytical meditation practices have also endured," Edwards maintained, "the stuff that deals with thoughts–and the space between thoughts–and the observer of thoughts–and the observer of the observer of thoughts."[17] One particular practice of this sort is watching the flow of one's thoughts and counting these thoughts as they change. Noting that the Tibetan language includes twenty-eight words for various states of consciousness, he maintained that Tibetan psychology and epistemology are intertwined because they have developed tools for precise and detailed description of "first hand attention to mind and its experience"[18] in a way Western scholarship has rarely attempted.

Six months before the fall of the World Trade Center towers, I interviewed Edwards and May, both of whom adamantly and unequivocally identified themselves as Christians. During the interviews I asked each of them two questions:

1. What specific practices, which they had learned from Buddhist teachers, had they, as Christians, found personally helpful in situations involving some sort of conflict?
2. Had any other participants in Shalem programs ever told them about noticing a correlation between particular Buddhist practices and an increased ability to act in ways that promoted reconciliation?

Edwards and May were extremely hesitant to make any direct connection between mastering any particular practice used by

Buddhists and acting in a reconciling manner in a hostile situation. May pointed out that when deep, genuine reconciliation happens there seems to be "non-achievement-like quality" operative. "Christians say 'God does it.' Buddhists say 'the situation's true nature is realized.' Either way it's not an accomplishment.... I don't hear people saying, 'I pulled it off'...or, 'Now I've learned how to do this.' They instead describe something like grace, gift, happening–serendipity."[19] Speaking to the question of why one should then bother with the practices in the first place, May speculated:

> What I can say is that people catch the idea that this has something to do with being really present in a situation–and being responsive rather than reactive–being in a position to have some space to choose what kind of response might be best, or, in a Christian context, to turn to God for guidance. In a Buddhist context it would be to perceive the situation correctly as it is–and out of that perception rises compassion.[20]

When asked about the relationship between these practices and peacemaking, he replied:

> There's nothing magic about the practice itself that I've been able to ascertain. I'm fond of telling about the Japanese Ninja assassins who trained with the same sort of meditation practices as Zen masters, but their context was to get to be good assassins for their warlord.... They became completely, wonderfully efficient–they developed this pervasive awareness and responsiveness and all that. But the context wasn't exactly what most people would call loving.[21]

Edwards and May noted that this element of context seems crucial in learning how to be a reconciling influence in conflict. May explained:

> In one sense it's the practice, but maybe more so than that is the kind of context or teaching around the practice. So, for example, the Dalai Lama gives those teachings about *Mahamudra* or *Dzogchen*. And there's practices involved there, meditation practices. But what he says about it is: "This is meant to facilitate compassion–compassion and warm feeling." He encourages the cultivation of that compassion not only towards everything and everyone–but towards one's self. And he communicates, then, this whole atmosphere of

gentleness, willingness, and openness. A lot of the Tibetans do that, and they carry a lot of authority with it because of what's happened to their country. So it's not just what they say, but to some extent who they are and what they symbolize or represent in their capacity to have a certain *freedom* with how they've been wronged.[22]

This capacity for "having a certain freedom" with how one has been wronged is certainly fundamental not only to Tibetan Buddhism, as the Dalai Lama teaches it, but to the Buddha's teachings as they are presented in his earliest sermons recorded in the Pali canon. It is also fundamental to Jesus' insistence in the gospels that both God and human beings have the capacity to forgive in a way that changes the direction and outcome of past harmful actions. The Christian doctrine of the resurrection of the crucified God insists that the love that molded the cosmos includes the particularity of "a certain freedom with how one has been wronged." It shows God's freedom and love as, ultimately, triumphant over all wrong. If we take God's creation and sustenance of the universe seriously, we must see this love as the context, ultimately, for any action, be it violent or reconciling. The New Testament writings proclaim that this "freedom with how one has been wronged" is transformative. Mahayana Buddhism in all of its forms also teaches that gaining a "certain freedom" from the chain of conditioned, selfish, vengeful responses brings transformative power.

Edwards noted that even people who have followed a discipline of regular meditation practice for a very long time still tend to emphasize, when recalling specific moments of "discovering" a reconciling way to act, not so much what they've learned from *doing* the practice over time, but what they learned when they were first *introduced* to the practice. They remember the cosmology—that is, the overall vision of the universe within which the practice was situated. Edwards observed that, in crises calling for reconciliation, "What seems to come to them is, often, simply single words, words like 'compassion,' or 'freedom,' or 'spaciousness.'"[23]

I was struck how often Edwards and May resorted to spatial imagery when connecting Buddhist practice and peacemaking. They often used words that, when used literally, describe the spatial relationships between various things: words such as *disconnected* or *integrated–disengaged* or *engaged–tightness* or *looseness–shutdown* or *open–squashed* or *expansive–spacious* or *cramped.* Perhaps one way to think of the relationship between the "cosmological context" within which a religious practice is taught, and the disciplined "doing" of that practice, is that "doing the practice" is, at least in part, time dedicated to reenvisioning the cosmos in terms of the spatial imagery with which the practice was taught. I'll present some examples from Edwards' and May's ponderings.

Both Edwards and May concurred that discovering an increased "sense of spaciousness" is often mentioned when long-time participants at Shalem describe particular "graced moments" of finding loving ways to respond to conflict. May explained, "They've got this notion going deeper and deeper in their minds—so that it becomes part of who they are—that a compassionate response *is* an option—that the *space* between the stimulus and the response is an option."[24]

Here is an example of how this sense of spaciousness might be applied in a conflict situation. Suppose a contemplative practice (perhaps a practice focused upon noticing and trying to expand the spaces between one's thoughts) is taught within the context of an image of a cosmos that includes bountiful resources of time and space for discovering a compassionate response. Might this not make it more likely—when one stumbles into an argument with a colleague—that one might discover a sliver of time and space between the stimulus of a criticism and one's usual, conditioned response of a clever, but cynical, riposte?

The cosmological imagery one uses both in constructing one's context in the big sense (i.e., how one views the cosmos as a whole) and how one views one's context in the little sense (i.e., the microcosm of each passing moment) is fundamental for how one experiences life. The practices Shalem has adopted from Nyingmapa Buddhism seem to be oriented toward changing the way one goes about the integrated task of taking in, sorting, screening, and constructing meaning out of sensory data—changing: (a) the way one constructs one's self-identity and the world's identity, and (b) the way one construes the relationality between self and world—that is, the way one constructs the relationship between "self" and "other."[25]

Put another way, this shift involves a change in the way one perceives the relationships between the various elements in one's perceptual field. This field might be as broad as taking in the full sensory sweep of a summer night (or of a political protest turning violent) or as narrow as focusing upon the subtle changes in one's own inhalations. Both Edwards and May spoke repeatedly about this perceptual change, insisting that one notices (paradoxically) both an "increased spaciousness" separating the various particular elements in one's attention, and a "closer interconnectedness" joining these elements. The paradox lies in the fact that this perceptual shift seems to involve both seeing the elements in one's perceptual field as being more individual, more distant, and more free in their unique particularity, and yet more connected, close, and similar in their common unity within the perceptual gestalt. The key element in this perceptual shift seems to lie in how one construes the fundamental cosmic relationality between things–the space that both keeps things apart and connects them together.[26] Edwards put it simply. "It's about love. It's about compassion. You discover that what's there in the space is love."[27]

Is Shalem Really Christian?

Shalem's use of Buddhist spatial imagery and Buddhist practices has certainly raised questions about the organization's identity as Christian in the minds of other Christians. In 1996 Edwards recounted an experience of Emma Lou Benignus, a seminary professor. She "was leading a Shalem workshop for a group of clergy. She had them do a simple breathing exercise. Afterward, one of the members left in great huff exclaiming: 'Breathing isn't Christian!'"[28]

Part of what seems to have happened in both Edwards' and May's experiences of circling back to a strengthened identity as Christians–with fresh eyes that see a greater spaciousness for nonviolent responses in conflictual situations–is that they have transferred spatial imagery–imagery that they began to use in Buddhist contexts– back into their original Christian context. This imagery grows organically out of Tibetan Buddhist cosmology. Buddhist practices are informed by, and reinforce, a Buddhist view of reality. Some aspects of this Vajrayana cosmology are, I have become convinced, absolutely irreconcilable with aspects of the cosmology implicit, and sometimes explicit, in the Old and New Testaments out of which much of Christian doctrine has historically developed. But Tibetan Buddhist spatial orientation may help Euro-Americans retrieve some aspects of Hebrew cosmologies that post-Enlightenment Euro-American perceptual grids have screened out.[29] I think it is important to investigate how Edwards and May have been able to integrate this Buddhist spatial imagery into teaching peacemaking to Christians in ways that mesh with Christian doctrine rooted in biblically derived images.

Part of the answer is, I suspect, that this spatial imagery, which portrays all things in the cosmos as being simultaneously held apart in their unique particularity and held together in their fundamental unity, is one of the real areas of commonality between Buddhist cosmologies and the cosmologies of the biblical authors. This commonality is apparent, I contend, however much Buddhist and Christian *explanations* for the nature of this compassionate basis of all relationality do, in fact, differ. The Bible certainly contains images of grace-filled spaciousness. As Edwards pointed out, "One of the Hebrew roots in the name *Yeshua,* Jesus' name in Hebrew, is associated with both salvation and spaciousness,"[30]—that is, with having enough room in a tight situation to find a way out.

Biblical images of spaciousness—and graciousness—have not, however, always been the particular images that have been foregrounded when some Christian traditions have squeezed the Old and New Testaments through the interpretive grid of their dominant culture at that time. In the United States in the twenty-first century, Christian congregations have been tempted to perceive the Bible through the interpretive grid of competitive, dualistic, Western post-Enlightenment individualism. The result of these selective interpretations of the biblical text (and as good postmoderns we now all know that all readings of any text are inherently selective) is that some twenty-first–century North American churches have ended up with a canon-within-the-canon of Christian scripture that rarely foregrounds these images of spaciousness. As a result, the hermeneutics of some North American Christians too often fail to apply consistently the New Testament images of the possibility for a space for forgiveness between violent action and violent response. Part of what has happened to Edwards and May is, I think, that exposure to Buddhist images of spaciousness spurred them to reclaim premodern and non-Western ways of interpreting the Christian scriptures. Some Buddhist spatial images call to mind the more organic imagery often used by non-Western Christian theologians, ranging from second-century Syrians to twenty-first–century Copts. Both are examples of Christians whose churches do not tend to interpret the Bible through a somewhat jurisprudence-oriented Latin mindset.

Conclusion

Why have so many Christians in the United States often ignored the teachings about alternatives to violence in the New Testament? Why have so many North American churches ignored the Christian contemplative tradition? When I posed these questions to Edwards and May, both differentiated between "popular religion," which uses institutional power in a way that supports the status quo, and "spirituality," which, when it encounters the status quo using power violently, looks for spaces in which to find an alternative to violence. Given the fuzzy way in which the term "spirituality" is used in much current popular North American religion, I seriously question the clarity and long-term helpfulness of popular religion/spirituality dichotomies.[31] I also think that Edwards' and May's differentiations here fail (totally unintentionally, I am sure) to give enough credit to popular religion in the United States, especially the popular religions of many of the American poor. I've witnessed startlingly spacious acts of freedom undertaken in "popular" religious communities, even those that seem quite conformed to some of the violence of the American status quo.

Despite my critiques of Edwards' and May's popular religion/spirituality differentiation, I agree with them that if one looks at the global picture, one can indeed find people who identify themselves as Christians—and people who identify themselves as Buddhists—whose sense of self is strongly tied to violent defense of their religion's institutional grip upon the status quo. Both Buddhist and Christian traditions of contemplative spirituality challenge the practice of rooting one's sense of self in anything as narrow as membership in a religious group. When trying to fathom the ways in which Christians and Buddhists have condoned violence, I think a more useful differentiation might be one between:

a. religious practices that tend to shore up a sense of self over against "the other,"
b. religious practices aimed at losing the self, or at least relaxing the individualistic self's constant competition with "the other."

Gerald May has died since he and Edwards so graciously conversed with me about the ways Shalem has taught Buddhist practices, and how this instruction has helped Shalem's participants foster reconciliation in contexts of conflict. Edwards and other long-time leaders of Shalem, while still contributing in vital ways through teaching and other leadership roles, are no longer as involved as they had been in the past in the day-to-day oversight of the institute. The current organization has inherited a rich legacy of trust that the God Jesus called Father sowed seeds of wisdom in all cultural traditions. Based on this trust, Shalem continues to explore Buddhist teachings and practices in the light of the good news of Jesus and to teach them to Christians wanting to follow Jesus' way of nonviolence more fully.

I conclude with two hopes for Shalem and for all the points of contact between Buddhist and Christian traditions in North America.[32] The first is that the relationships developing among Buddhists and Christians in the United States may be *spacious* enough so we may encourage each other to preserve the unique wisdom within our radically different heritages, and may be *interconnected* enough so that we may recall that each tradition arose out of the teachings of a reformer who challenged a religious status quo that was oppressing the poor. At the heart of both traditions is the call to lose one's self, or as Edwards puts it, "no longer rest satisfied with an identity exclusively defined by biology, personality, gender, family, culture, nation-state, or even institutional religion."[33] My second hope is that North American Buddhist and Christian contemplatives will remember that the texts and practices of most "spiritual" contemplative traditions of "spaciousness" have been preserved and transmitted via the narrow confines of "religious" institutions. This transmission, so full of hope for peace, has continued in spite of the fact that both Buddhist and Christian institutions have, at times, seriously compromised the very teachings they claimed to promote.[34] Christian and Buddhist scriptures and contemplative practices appear to be not only more spacious, but more durable than any culture-bound wineskins into which they are poured.

8

Labyrinth Walking as a Prelude to Spiritually Based Conversation

MADY FRASER

Entering into conversation concerning sacred beliefs and their underlying spiritual values is more than an intellectual exercise. Our lives are grounded in faith—however we may define it—and faith is an activity of the whole person, not simply the mind. Spiritually based conversation is the sharing of the stories of our faith and our lives. If these conversations are to be fruitful, by bringing about a holistic understanding of and communal relationship with one another, it is important to first make a connection with one another as human beings, as companions on the journey of life.

I believe a ritual prelude, which can take conversation partners beneath the surface of religious trappings and ego consciousness, will bring greater openness and understanding to spiritually based conversations. Often, the doctrines, the polity, the rites, and rituals of particular religious or faith perspectives get in the way of opening ourselves to the humanity we share with our conversation partners. Only as we claim our common humanity can we truly listen to the hearts, as well as the minds, of others and hear the meaning their faith tradition provides for them and to the world.

I am proposing that those committed to spiritually based conversation set aside an hour to walk a labyrinth together prior to the beginning of their conversation. A labyrinth walk has the potential to lead to an atmosphere of hope, humility, and hospitality greater than if the conversants simply gather at the table from their individual contexts.

A labyrinth walk is a contemplative walk. "Contemplation means withdrawing attention from outward, objective, particular, and temporal concerns, and refocusing on inward, subjective, general and even eternal realities.... Contemplation is not just an intellectual activity. It is also a moral and a devotional matter."[1] A labyrinth walk, a ritual walk of contemplation, may bring its practitioners to the center of their beings and lead them to a more universal point of view. This viewpoint places individuals into a position of entertaining broader ways of perceiving, experiencing, and–together–imagining a world of peaceful coexistence and appreciation for a wide variety of faith traditions and spiritual realities.

The Labyrinth

Hermann Kern (1941–1985), a lawyer and art historian, produced the most comprehensive existing collection of information on the labyrinth. Kern states, "What is probably the first mention of a labyrinth appears on a small Mycenaean clay tablet found at Knossos, dating from ca. 1400 BCE."[2] This reference to the labyrinth is tied to the Cretan legend of "Ariadne's thread." Ariadne's love, Theseus, was sent into the palace, Knossos, as a sacrifice to the half-bull, half-human Minotaur, which resided at the center of the labyrinthine structure within. As he entered the palace, Ariadne gave Theseus the end of a red thread with which to mark his path as he found his way to the Minotaur's lair. Rather than becoming a meal for the Minotaur, Theseus was able to slay the monster and find his way out of the palace. Ariadne's thread, the path Theseus followed to the center of the maze and out again, is the unicursal path of the labyrinth. The labyrinth may have originated as a dance that acted out the myth.[3] "The dance paths were probably marked on the dance surface fairly early on, therefore, the two manifestations, the dance and the graphic version, coincided with one another."[4]

Examples of this design have been found in Europe, India, Java, Sumatra, and the United States of America, specifically in the states of New Mexico and Arizona, where it is related to the Hopi tribe of Native Americans.[5] The labyrinth design found in all of these locations is similar to that shown in Figure 1, the path of which is often referred to as the "thread of Ariadne."[6] At one time common knowledge claimed the labyrinth arose in various parts of the world from primal human knowledge, partly because of its similarity to the shape of the human brain and intestines. Kern's research concludes that rather than springing up in various parts of the world at the same time, the labyrinth, originating in Minoan Crete, was transmitted from culture to culture through "migration and borrowing."[7] Each new culture, finding the concept meaningful, appropriated the labyrinth for its own uses.

Figure 1. The earliest labyrinth design.

According to Kern, only two transformations of the labyrinth design were significant, "the 'Roman quadrata'[8] (Figure 2) and the Christianization of both the design and the concept in the ninth and ten centuries."[9] Within the context of the Roman Catholic Church, the figures first appeared in manuscripts and later were enlarged and drawn on the floors of churches.[10]

Figure 2

Dedicated in 1260, the currently most recognizable labyrinth design can be found on the floor of Chartres Cathedral in France (Figure 3). The labyrinth "takes up the entire width of the nave; since the floor was not covered by chairs until the nineteenth century; pilgrims entering from the west portal would have understood the invitation it offered: to walk into the labyrinth at the entrance and advance to the center, instead of simply walking over it to reach the altar."[11] The Middle Ages (ca. eleventh through fifteenth centuries) was the height of the use of labyrinths by Christians. During this period the church had a particular openness to the use of many images and symbols.

Figure 3

After the invention of the maze during the Renaissance, (ca. fourteenth to seventeenth centuries), the use of labyrinths died out or became secularized. The labyrinth "was no longer understood as the carrier of a clear message of faith."[12] The concept of the maze still has a strong influence in Western cultures and their individualistic and dualistic ways of thinking. The designation of a design as a labyrinth, as opposed to a maze, fits the following criteria:

- The design of a labyrinth fills the interior space of a circle, polygon, or rectangle with a very circuitous path.
- The path continually changes direction, folding or switching back on itself.
- There is only one entrance to a labyrinth. A maze can have more than one.
- The design is unicursal, having only one path. A maze has several paths that intersect each other.

- There are no dead ends on the labyrinth path, as in a maze, and the inward path always ends at the center of the design.
- The path repeatedly leads past the center before reaching the center.
- The way in is the way out—the walker follows the same path out from the center of the design.
- The labyrinth is a metaphor for a communal state of mind, as opposed to the individualistic state of mind related to the maze. Labyrinth walkers, with their individual perspectives, move together on one path as they grow spiritually together.
- The labyrinth is symbolic of orientation, rather than the dis-orientation of the maze. It is holistic, cohesive.
- Labyrinths are ancient and conceived within community, a symbol of unity. Mazes focus on fragmentation and deception.[13]

Kern, in celebrating the renewed interest in labyrinths as early as the 1980s, believes it is partly because "labyrinths are shrouded in mystery.... This might be interpreted as criticism of the current world, as representing a rejection of an entirely rational way of life, which splinters human existence into a thousand individual pieces."[14] Those interested in labyrinths often see them as a path to moving away from extreme rationality to a more balanced and interconnected perspective on life. "The notion of hopelessly going astray is only conceivable against a backdrop of certainty, order, and orientation, and as a search for unity and wholeness.... Since the labyrinth is a symbol of wholeness, offering one clear path, it is a very topical figure."[15]

One interpretation of the labyrinth correlates with the "embodiment of initiation rites."[16] The interior area of the labyrinth, defined by the outer edges, is isolated from the outer world and requires a level of maturity to enter. Walking the path requires physical dexterity and communal adaptability. It is filled with "the maximum number of twists and turns,"[17] making it a journey of patience and physical effort to reach the center. The path also has the potential to bring frustration to the walker as it approaches, then leads away from the center.[18]

The ego-centered perspective with which the average individual enters the path while walking toward the center of the labyrinth, loosens up during the inward journey. Judgment, based on the assumption that the definition of what is good and what is bad depends on what supports personal needs and desires, evolves toward the idea that good and bad relate to the greater whole. In the center the walker is alone with the opportunity to open the self to the Divine, to discover new awareness connected with the ancient realities of creation, to be touched by the needs of the greater whole. As the walker leaves the center, a 180-degree turn is made, facilitating the individual to be further distanced from the perspective with which he or she entered the labyrinth, marking a new beginning, a rebirth into a more communal mindset. Walking from the center, wandering the path in reverse, the individual takes on a new perspective. The outward path is a reorientation, a transforming movement toward a new way of being in relationship to the community and to the world.[19]

The Labyrinth: Metaphor for the Spiritual Journey

The concept that the walk to the center and out again along the circuitous path brings the walker to a new, more open perspective, is what speaks to its use by many Christian, as well as non-Christian, communities today. As the labyrinth is embraced as a form of prayer or connection with the universe, remember, "It was a community—not an individual—that saw and recognized itself in the labyrinth."[20] Community is where spirituality lives and works through all creation, particularly human beings.

Human spirituality is the metaphorical breath of God[21] that made the creature, formed from the dust of the earth, a living being. Spirituality connects humans with all life and is the basis of human relationship with all creation. Spirituality brings depth and meaning to belief systems, connecting them with the mystery of the Divine.

Spiritual practices, disciplines, or rituals are forms of prayer, ways of opening the human spirit to commune with the Divine. They facilitate the opening of the human spirit to the mystery of God's being and to what it means to be human beings living in community—whether it is a community of three or the community of the world.

Spiritual practices influence beliefs regarding the ways humans define the holy, God, the universe, and the meaning of life on earth. In turn, these beliefs about the Divine influence human willingness to be vulnerable to and enter into the mystery of relationship with God, with other human beings in community, and with all creation.

The labyrinth is a tool for contemplative prayer, a spiritual discipline for drawing the attention of the labyrinth walker away from the stresses of daily life toward inward, subjective, and eternal realities. Entering into this prayer walk can enhance the possibility of being addressed by the holy, bringing the human focus inward to subjective, general, and eternal realities. It is a spiritual walk, a walk that provides opportunity for individuals, whether walking alone or with others, with openness and intention to unite with the community of life by being guided toward a new openness and a new wholeness. The spiritual journey to the center and back enables entering into the ambiguity of mystery that brings balance of mind and spirit.

Signs of change in the world that Kern may have observed before his death are reflected in three shifts in perspective, among a growing number of people, regarding what it means to live on earth as human beings. One is an evolving "ecological intelligence...a new way of thinking about ourselves in the world, how we relate to the earth, to nature, to all of created reality. It removes us from our supposed 'center of the universe' and, as people of faith, brings us to the awe and wonder of poetic and prayerful response."[22] A second shift is a move from individualistic thinking to communal thinking, particularly manifested as a greater openness to the validity and celebration of differences–the many as one. The third is a growing desire of people to create mental, emotional, physical, and spiritual space in which all live equitably and justly on earth.

These shifts of perspective by people who embrace ecological intelligence, who believe the many are one, and who desire equality and justice cannot be limited to any group currently defined in the world. Neither do those who hold these values in common begin with common viewpoints regarding their own belief systems. What is shared in common is a simple human yearning, "a yearning within us and between us in the most important relationships of our lives...as an entire earth community."[23] This longing is not new, it "is an ancient longing and a perennial wisdom. All the great spiritual traditions of humanity have pointed in their distinct ways to the Oneness from which we come and the Oneness that we long for."[24]

The emergence of the labyrinth in the past twenty-five years as a metaphorical spiritual journey is symbolic of the growing awareness of the ancient human yearning for relationship with all creation. As that yearning is primal and ancient, so is the labyrinth. Part of the beauty of the labyrinth is that it belongs to everyone. No particular cultural or faith tradition can lay claim to it as exclusively their own.

"A labyrinth is not a maze...designed for us to lose our way; a labyrinth is designed for us to find our way."[25] The three stages of pilgrimage to the soul in the labyrinth are characterized by the folk saying, "The way in, is the way out." The single path twists and turns, leading into and away from the center. As a person enters and begins to walk the labyrinth path, the mind quiets and the body releases the stresses of the everyday world. By the time the walker arrives at the center, breathing deepens and the individual becomes more open to the Spirit, listening for the greatest desires of the universe. Leaving the center and returning to the beginning, along the same path, is a process of incarnating desires of the holy within the human spirit.

The labyrinth walk is a union of the wholeness and holiness of creation, bringing together the physical movement of the human body and the essence of human be-ing, the spirit, by engaging both sides of the brain, re-forming the chemical pathways, and bringing individual walkers toward their centeredness in creation.[26] For those who are intentional, the labyrinth walk is an experience of coming to the understanding that each one who is walking comes to the journey reflecting her or his own belief system and spirituality. Walking the labyrinth is a coming together of the individual and the communal. Each person enters the labyrinth in her or his own time, walking at a comfortable pace, passing those who may be moving more slowly, encountering—and perhaps interacting with—those who are moving in the opposite direction. The labyrinth is a symbol of living in a world focused on all-encompassing "relationship grounded in trust and love, in contrast to a world of fragmentation based on fear with hard-edged, exclusive boundaries."[27]

Hope, Humility, and Hospitality

Labyrinth walking, as a prelude to spiritually based conversation, is the concept of using this form of contemplative prayer to bring a focus of all-encompassing relationship, grounded in trust and love, to that conversation. "Learning to work together and celebrate our differences is hard work. It needs introspection and discernment; it demands action on the individual and collective level. This is the mission of the labyrinth as it reenters our world."[28] Making the time to practice this communal spiritual discipline together, before taking seats at the table, provides opportunity for individuals, involved in conversation regarding their faith and spirituality, to quiet themselves into silence, bringing a more balanced heart and mind. "All words come out of silence. Words that have a depth, resonance, healing, and challenge to them are words loaded with ascetic silence...[a silence in which individuals] risk themselves in the interior space [of their being]."[29] The labyrinth walk is the embodiment of initiation to spiritually based conversation. Within this context I image the three movements of the labyrinth journey as hope, humility, and hospitality.

Entering the first stage of a labyrinth walk, as prelude for spiritually based conversation, is stepping out in hope. Beatrice Bruteau speaks of "radical optimism,"[30] hope that believes in and has confidence that a world united in life-giving community is possible. Beginning with hope gives conversation partners a creative attitude for finding new ways of drawing near to one another, for listening to and relating with one another as traveling companions on the journey of life. Hope that is radical optimism leads to "the roots of our being.... [Without hope] we will not have the will and the energy and the earnestness and the perseverance and the courage to engage the present [world] crisis unless we believe that we can preserve our lives and our values."[31] Hope taps the imagination. It fills the heart and mind with a belief that the dream of a world based in trust and love can come into being, in spite of the greed and despair that surrounds us. "The imagination is powerful, and therefore it is important. We *live* out of our imaginations. We may think or wish that we lived out of our intellect and will, but...the *proximate* cause of our behavior is the imagination."[32]

The first stage of the labyrinth walk, the stage of hope, takes the conversation partners to the center, the place of humility, where the Divine awaits discourse. Humility is an attitude of the heart that "recognizes that no person loves or does any good without the help of God.... Humility itself is countercultural.... It wreaks havoc with all individualistic values.... It calls for renunciation of all deep attachments to what the world holds dear."[33] An attitude of humility opens the labyrinth walker to the universal and the eternal, enlarging the perspective of the self from being the center of the universe to being a single aspect of the universe. Humility allows for the union of the finite and the infinite, expanding the awareness of the role of humanity in the cosmic order. Entering into dialogue with God from an attitude of humility opens spiritual conversation partners to greater attentiveness to the dreams and desires of the Divine for creation. It expands the consciousness of the walkers into the reality that the love of the Divine is expressed in and through the human.

Making the turn from the center of the labyrinth, with an attitude of hope and humility, to enter the winding pathway going in the opposite direction clothes the conversation partners in hospitality. Defining hospitality, Henri Nouwen writes:

> Hospitality...means the creation of a free space where the stranger can enter and become a friend.... Hospitality is not to change people, but to offer them space where change can take place. It is not to bring men and women over to our side, but to offer freedom not disturbed by dividing lines.... [It is] the liberation of the fearful hearts so that words can find roots and bear ample fruit...[and the freedom where people can] sing their own songs, speak their own languages, dance their own dances.[34]

Hospitality is being the host: creating safe space for others. It is being the guest: receiving the hospitality of others. It is being the one who seeks out and welcomes the stranger: greeting the Divine in every human being and all creation. For those entering into spiritually based conversation, hospitality is listening with an open mind and heart. It is receiving the offerings of others without judgment. Hospitality is recognizing the Divine in the personhood and the faith of those with whom they are in conversation.

Conclusion

Entering into conversation concerning sacred beliefs and their underlying spiritual values is an exercise of hope, humility, and hospitality. Walking the labyrinth, as a prelude to spiritually based conversation, can facilitate those involved to come to the table with hope that reimagines the future of the world united in life-giving community. A journey through the labyrinth can bring conversation partners to the table as persons with an attitude of humility, allowing for the union of the infinite and the finite in every human being. Labyrinth walking can transform spiritual conversation partners into true practitioners of hospitality: hosts, guests, and seekers of strangers who listen, receive, and recognize the Divine in one another.

9

"Tell Me What You Want, What You Really, Really Want"

Desire, Vocation, and Gifts for Service

DUANE R. BIDWELL

Sometimes it seems like everyone in the developed world recognizes the above line from "Wannabe," a pop song by the British group the Spice Girls. The song describes the importance of friendship and sacrifice in a love relationship.[1] It describes the way two people sometimes flirt when romantically attracted. A certain resonance rings out between "Tell me what you want" and the process of discerning Christian vocation and gifts for service. Both ask us to identify, articulate, and explore our strongest desires and then to listen to another respond. Followers of Jesus who want to clarify God's call can benefit greatly from clarifying and naming their desires, offering those desires honestly to God, and listening to what God stirs up in response. The dialogical process of naming, offering, and listening creates an environment in which people can understand more clearly the particular ways they are called to serve in the world and identify the gifts God has provided for that purpose.

It might strike some as odd or even troublesome to give desire such prominence in vocational discernment. But the Holy One often acts in and through our desires. By clarifying what we want, we can hear more clearly God's invitation to meaningful work—work that witnesses to reality's "secret abundance"[2] right here, right now. Desire belongs at the center of vocational discernment because God responds continually and constantly to our deepest wants,[3] sending consolation when our desires fit God's intentions and leading us away from desires that don't fit divine priorities. Attending to God's consoling movements in our hearts and lives allows us to confirm or convert our desires; in the process of confirmation and conversion we can clarify our vocational call and gifts for service.

It is important that the twenty-first–century church attend to vocation and call in new ways. Mainline Protestant denominations are seeking to maintain mission and ministries despite shrinking membership, and the Roman Catholic Church has embraced new forms of lay leadership that move beyond a predominately clerical paradigm for ministry.[4] Vocational discernment is increasingly important for all Christians. This chapter suggests that the classical Protestant distinction between "inner call" and "outer call" is inadequate; it fails to capture the complex interrelationship among desire, vocation, and gifts for service that shapes the experiences of contemporary Christians, and it privileges individual and intrapsychic dimensions of vocation when, in fact, the social and communal dimensions often precede a sense of personal call and giftedness.

Desire and Mary of Magdala

Mary of Magdala offers one way of understanding the relationship between desire, call, and gifts for Christian service. After all, it is desire that leads Mary to the tomb on that first Easter morning;[5] she wants Jesus desperately–desperately enough to risk her life by publicly identifying herself as a friend of this criminal who was tortured to death by the Roman Empire. We might even say that Mary's heart is aflame with desire for God. In response to her desire, Mary receives the spiritual gift of clear vision, a consoling ability to recognize the Holy Lover she seeks.

Here is the story of Mary's visit to the tomb as told in John 20:1, 11–18:

> Early in the morning on the first day of the week, while it was still dark, Mary of Magdala came to the tomb. She saw that the stone had been rolled away from the entrance....
>
> She stood weeping beside the tomb. Even as she wept, she stooped to peer inside, and there she saw two angels in dazzling robes....
>
> They asked her, "Why are you weeping?"

She answered them, "Because they have taken away my Rabbi, and I don't know where they have put the body."

No sooner had she said this than she turned around and caught sight of Jesus standing there, but she didn't know it was Jesus. He asked her, "Why are you weeping? For whom are you looking?"

She supposed it was the gardener, so she said, "Please, if you're the one who carried Jesus away, tell me where you've laid the body and I will take it away."

Jesus said to her, "Mary!"

She turned to him and said, "Rabboni"–which means "Teacher."

Jesus then said, "Don't hold on to me, for I have not yet ascended to Abba God. Rather, go to the sisters and brothers and tell them, 'I'm ascending to my Abba and to your Abba, my God and your God!'"

Mary of Magdala went to the disciples. "I have seen the Teacher!" she announced. Then she reported what the savior had said to her.[6]

By understanding and acting on her desire for Jesus, Mary receives the gift of vision; it allows her to recognize the Holy One who came into the world to seduce us away from an economy of scarcity, hierarchy, and dominance to a life so abundant that our grateful response is to give it away.[7] When she recognizes him, this lover of hers (and ours), Mary clings to him out of her desire. His response is to say: "Don't hold on to me... [Rather,] go to the sisters and brothers and tell them...."

In that moment–"Don't hold on to me.... Go...and tell them"– Jesus gives Mary the vocation of proclamation and the spiritual gifts necessary to succeed at it. This anonymous Near Eastern woman becomes the world's first preacher of the good news of Christ Jesus, the first evangelist of Christian faith–a vocation rooted in her desire and empowered by a gift she receives in the process of acting on it. You might say that what Mary wanted preceded both her call and the gifts that made her capable of responding effectively to it.

Desire in Dominant Discourse and the Christian Traditions

Most of us are unaccustomed to thinking about desire as a key to hearing God's voice and discovering the gifts of the Spirit expressed through our lives. We have internalized a deeply ambivalent attitude toward desire, an attitude that marks the dominant discourses of

North America and other North Atlantic settings. On one hand, the worldwide market economy celebrates desire as something good and natural, and the economy thrives by creating and stimulating appetites that are perceived as good, legitimate, and healthful despite their cost in terms of human lives and damage to the environment.[8] From this perspective human beings are considered to be primarily consumers, and any desire is legitimate to the extent that the market sustains it.[9] On the other hand, these cultures also host a discourse that positions desire, especially sexual desire, as a part of corrupt human nature. From this perspective, what humans want stands in opposition to God; our desire must be controlled, eradicated, or properly channeled to avoid sin, often narrowly understood as a moral transgression.

The church has contributed to this ambivalence by viewing desire negatively, as something associated with sexuality[10] that is necessary to restrain or from which to escape. But the church has not always interpreted desire as negative, suspect, or even primarily sexual. In the Middle Ages, for example, Thomas Aquinas asserted that God's grace could work *through* human desire to incorporate a person into the body of Christ—that is, to bring a person to salvation even if that person did not profess Christ.[11] In the Reformed tributary of the Christian traditions, John Calvin understood union with Christ as a joining of divine and human wills[12]—that is, a shared desire between God and humanity in which the creature was oriented toward the goals of the Creator. More recently, pastoral theologian John Blevins[13] has turned to the apophatic theology of Pseudo-Dionysius to reclaim desire as an essential dimension of our relationships with God and each other. Blevins understands desire as a life-giving aspect of Christian ministry; it motivates the actions we take as friends of Jesus to exercise our spiritual gifts on behalf of God and to anticipate and reflect[14] in this world God's ultimate dreams for the cosmos. In this sense, what Blevins proposes is similar to what we see happening in the story of Mary of Magdala as she encounters Jesus outside the tomb on Easter morning.

Note how the story unfolds: Mary's desire leads her to seek Jesus, and God responds by revealing the resurrected Christ to her. God affirms Mary's desire through consolation; her heart is aflame with desire for God, and she is given the gift of a particular type of sight that allows her to see Jesus. But when her desire causes Mary to cling to Jesus—to "hold on" to him in a form of relating that isn't a priority for God at that moment—Jesus responds by *reordering* Mary's desire. He directs her away from himself and toward the community where she is to proclaim the mystery and reality of the resurrection—the marvelous fact that a dead man is yet alive—and the ascension of that same man to a majestic new life with God.

The shift in Mary's desires—from wanting something that accords with God's desires, to wanting something for herself that doesn't quite fit God's dream, to hearing and acting on God's desire in the moment—illustrates a consistent theme in Christian spiritual traditions: our desires must be rightly ordered—that is, brought into congruence with God's desires. Each of us encounters disordered desires on a daily basis; every marketing message that imposes itself on us in our consumptionist-consumerist culture seeks to stir up and direct our desires in ways not usually consistent with what God wants. Yet God actively converts desires by reordering them toward divine intentions. We can trust that God acts through our spiritual practices and spiritual communities—indeed, through every dimension of our lives—either to confirm the desires we experience that are consistent with God's intentions or to redirect disordered desires toward the vision that God has for us and for creation. By paying attention to God's movement in our lives, we can sense how God is responding to our desires. Noticing what we "really, really want"—desires that are more oriented toward God than toward the empire of conventional wisdom—is a key to the discernment process.

Scripture can help us assess whether our desires are rightly ordered. In the first letter to the church at Corinth, the apostle Paul suggests two criteria for discerning whether human desires are "on target." First, are people using their spiritual gifts to serve the community rather than to serve themselves (1 Cor. 12:7)? Second, do people acknowledge God, and not themselves, as the source, object, and goal of their gifts for service (1 Cor. 12:4–11)? Rightly ordered desires refuse to participate in exploitive human power; rather, they motivate people to enter deeply into the sufferings of a particular context, responding to God willingly by serving others in public ways (see Phil. 2:5–11). In discerning rightly ordered desire, it is important to remember that we are elected, called, and gifted for service in the world, not for privilege.

Contemporary Experiences of Desire, Gifts, and Service

Much literature about spiritual gifts and vocation harbors the unspoken assumption that if we identify our gifts, we'll know what to do with them[15]—that spiritual gifts point toward vocation. Although this assumption is, to my knowledge, untested, many resources have been allocated to helping church members "discern" their spiritual gifts through pen-and-paper inventories and online assessments.

Desire rarely enters into these conversations. When it does, the validity of a desire is predicated on the presence of the gifts necessary to achieve it. Assumptions such as these offer wonderfully linear ways of understanding the relationship among desire, gifts, and call. But reality is rarely linear, and the experiences of faithful contemporary people contradict these ways of thinking.

As I began to consider the interplay of desire, gifts, and vocation, I invited a convenience sample of fifty thoughtful people to respond in writing for seven minutes to a particular question[16] about the topic. Of those fifty who were invited, sixteen people actually responded: men and women ranging in age from their thirties to their seventies. Professionally, they were employed as physicians, teachers, psychologists, administrative assistants, ministers, musicians, managers, and lobbyists. All were white, most were college-educated, and the majority had graduate degrees. Fourteen belonged to or were shaped by liberal Protestant traditions, one was Catholic, and one had grown up in a fundamental, evangelical tradition. Using a qualitative research method called grounded theory, I analyzed their written responses to identify patterns, themes, and shared understandings in the documents they submitted. The goal was not to produce "scientifically valid knowledge," but to create a description of the relationship among desire, vocation, and gifts for service that fits and accounts for the ways that people make sense of their experiences of these elements of life.

People did not write, of course, of generic or disembodied notions of "vocation," "desire," and "gifts for service." They wrote from the specificity of their own jobs, families, and spiritual lives. They described the joy of discovering unknown gifts and interests, the internal struggle when paid work did not fit their sense of call, and the often-unfilled yearning to engage in work that served God and creation in meaningful ways.

In general, the written responses suggested a complex, ambiguous, and nonlinear relationship among desire, gifts, and vocation. Five common themes emerged: a conflation of "work" with "vocation;" a yearning for congruence among the three elements; a privileging of vocation over gifts and desires; an emphasis on social process; and an awareness of stewardship as a proper response to gifts, desire, and vocation. Each theme is discussed briefly below.

Conflating "Job" and "Vocation"

Nearly all respondents noted tensions between what they do every day to pay the bills (work) and the dreams that God has called and gifted them to make real in the world (vocation). A musician in his forties, employed by day in the telecommunications industry, wrote that his desire—to make music—and gifts had always been aligned. But his desire and vocation were at odds for a long time because he "used to equate 'vocation' with 'primary source of income.'" The quandary presented itself every time he met a new acquaintance:

> During the course of conversation, the question, "So, what do you do?" is raised fairly frequently…. Well, I think about, talk about, write, and play music. I do these things more than I do other things, even the nonmusical activities that get me a paycheck. I now interpret vocation, or "what do you do," literally. I have begun identifying and introducing myself as the one thing I have always desired to "be." "I'm a musician," I say.[17]

Respondents wrote of finding ways in which their paid work could serve their larger or "truer" vocations, which were often expressed in existential, creative, or religious terms. This process of bringing vocation to bear on their jobs entailed discovering how spiritual gifts and desires could be expressed in particular settings to serve God and others. "The position that I fill helps me to live out more fully my greater calling…" wrote a program administrator in a human services organization. "God has been good to me, allowing me to find a place in which my desires and gifts can be lived out in my vocational calling."

Opening themselves to serve God, no matter where they were employed, seemed to create opportunities for respondents to use gifts in new ways, to satisfy desires for meaningful work, and to develop new gifts that expanded their senses of vocation. An administrative assistant at a hospital wrote:

> Once I opened myself up to be used, I have had opportunity after opportunity to use my gifts of mercy, hospitality, and generosity of spirit to reach others. I am very satisfied with my "paying" vocation, which is working every day with patients who are often suffering from post-traumatic stress disorder,… lonely because they are estranged from their families, or… scared because they are at the end of their life. In the last year or so, several younger patients have been placed in my path who are recovering from substance abuse…. I've entered into relationship with many of them—listening to them, promising to pray for them, and truly becoming a friend to some. I thank God every day that I can make a difference

in their lives if I remain open to really "see" their needs and respond.... I am grateful to know that God calls everyone to various forms of service and that it is not just a pastor's job. I now pray that I will recognize the person who crosses my path today that needs to see God's love. Most importantly, "God does not call the equipped. He equips the called!" That is comforting to me.

People were aware that they continued to discern gifts and desires in the midst of their paying jobs; identifying one's vocation is not a once-and-for-all process. "It may be in the crucible of work," wrote a denominational executive nearing retirement,

> that our self-appreciation of gifts finally is clarified. While interested in the political role of my position, I had no idea I would like and be reasonably good at the detail of its administrative responsibilities. Or, in the midst of that, discover that I had a penchant for, a "gift," if you will, for a wider systems view of denominational matters. So...my "line" would probably start with vocation; hit gifts; discover desire.

Desire, in the written statements, has a tendency to stretch a person's gifts, to pull him or her beyond a particular vocation in ways that suggest God is asking something new. Only by engaging in particular service in the world, it seems, do people tend to awaken particular desires or discover particular gifts and then develop a desire to use them. This suggests that we have to get our hands dirty if we want to enter fully into the lifelong process of responding to God's invitations and making manifest the dreams and gifts that get "caught" in the web of who we are. New gifts emerge when we honor rightly ordered desires, and desires seem more connected than gifts to God's call to a particular form of service.

Creating a match between vocation and employment, however, can be problematic—especially when a particular job seems to limit the gifts or passions that a person brings to the position. "My desire is to serve in relationship, and I believe that's a good fit with my gifts for service," wrote an academic in his fifties:

> [But] I have never seen myself as a particularly warm or public person; I'm more of an outgoing introvert. So, there is a tension between some of what I see as my gifts for service and my vocation as a professor, which requires me to be more public in my service than is sometimes comfortable....

Sometimes the tension among all of these makes it difficult to be hopeful regarding the optimal application of my gifts.... I *do* feel called to teach, but teach-in-relationship, which is not easy in my current paid position.

Yearning for Congruence

A yearning for greater alignment between the three elements was a common theme in the written statements. A psychotherapist-turned-academic, for example, wrote of his strong vocational ambivalence:

The relationship among my desire, my gifts, and my vocation is a complex one.... At times I have felt compelled to serve or work in a particular way, like when I practiced psychotherapy. I felt this was a calling, something for which I had been given gifts to use for God's or humanity's service.... [T]his often felt like a burden. I have felt more freedom, in some ways, not working in the field of my "calling" than I was [feeling] when intensely working...in the field of healing. Perhaps my true calling is doing what I am doing now, and the sense of burden I felt practicing psychotherapy was a result of being "off my path." But I don't think so.

Respondents were aware that multiple desires and multiple vocations can manifest in a single life. People wrote of honoring different desires and vocations at various times, with gifts for service seeming to follow whichever desire or vocation they chose to privilege for a particular season of life. A retired minister wrote of her frustration prior to ordination, when she was "just" a wife and mother. Serving as a pastor seemed to allow her "true" gifts and vocation to emerge. When she retired, she found this perception changing. "[A]mazingly, at this age," she wrote, "I now embrace that first vocation of mothering as the most important thing I ever did—and the modeling to my children and my grandchildren and my great-grandchildren of striving to be all that God created them to be is the utmost value in my life." In retirement, she has a sense of "returning" to her original vocation with new insight into its value and importance.

Privileging Vocation over Gifts and Desires

While affirming that gifts, desires, and vocation do not fall into a linear, progressive, or developmental relationship, most participants nonetheless privileged "vocation" over gifts and desires. "My desire is not always in tune with God's will," wrote a minister in her mid-fifties.

If I use my gifts without any awareness of my vocation, they become just another commodity. But if I understand my vocation to be a baptized daughter of God, then I have a framework within which to understand my desires and fulfill those which are in accord with my vocation, as well as a grounded understanding of "my" gifts and from whence they come. Vocation is that which holds our desires and our gifts in healthy tension.

She continued:

The image I keep coming up with in my head is a triangle... the kind of triangle that you rack up pool balls with.... Maybe it's not such a bad image after all—perhaps these are the three things that cordon together all the various pool balls of your life, without which they would be free to be scattered by the first opposing force. As long as the elements are contained by desire, gifts, and vocation, they can be held in recognizable shape.

A minister nearing retirement also understood vocation as bringing order to his gifts and desires. But he suggested that the three could not be separated:

"Desire" is what I want to do. My "gifts for service" is what I can do. My "vocation in the world" is what God calls me to do, or perhaps what creation needs me to do. I may want to do a myriad of things for which I am not gifted, but when it gets down to it, I know that what I really want to do is what I can do.... All three parts bring wholeness. Take away any one part and there is brokenness.

Discerning Gifts, Vocation, and Desire as Social Process

The written statements often referenced the influence of family, friends, mentors, and congregations on self-understandings and vocational choices. Discernment of gifts, desires, and vocation is not an "inner event" or negotiation between God and an individual. Rather, the identification, clarification, and discernment of desires, gifts, and vocation occur through social processes; we discover what we want, what we can offer, and ways to serve through relationship and in conversation with others. This is not always a simple or affirming process; history, geography, and social location can shape us in ways that fail to honor our particular gifts and vocations, and sometimes we have to overcome social influence, or find a new community of discourse, to respond faithfully to God's call. One respondent wrote:

> [F]or some of us "desires" in our younger years may come less from self-appreciation and more from what others have told us we'd be good at—or what our admired role models did.... Gifts, the self-appreciation of gifts, the discovery of gifts, are sliding-scale values hugely affected by other persons' views and comments.... So one task...is the discovery and refining, lifelong, of desire.

The retired female pastor wrote poignantly about the influence of family and social context on vocation:

> [M]y mother clearly understood herself as needing to "earn her space" on this earth.... I was her only daughter; of course, I absorbed that precious bit of information that, as a woman and as a Christian, my role was that of Martha.... Home was to be kept, family fed, neighbors and relatives cared for...with any spare energy focused on church.... My struggle came, however, with my gifts. I was invited to "bring the message" during a Youth Sunday at church. It felt right. But when I approached my pastor about maybe I could become a minister, I was literally patted on my head and told that little girls didn't get to be preachers. But if I wanted to serve Jesus, God, and the church, I should maybe marry a minister. I looked at the current crop of would-be ministers and decided the church would have to get along without me. One marriage and five children later, I realized a sense of envy, frustration, even hurt, as I watched those inadequate guys become inadequate ministers, leaders in the church, many of them acclaimed by the community, for doing what I knew darned well I could have done at least as good if not better.

As a whole, however, respondents indicated that social context clarifies God's call in and on our lives more often than it deforms it. They also suggested that communal affirmation of gifts and call often preceded a sense of "inner call." This challenges the classical Protestant emphasis on the primacy of "inner call," which is secondarily affirmed by the community through an "outer call."

Stewardship of Gifts, Desire, and Call

A final theme underscores an important theological point: the gifts that the Spirit calls forth from an individual do not belong to that person–they are God's gifts to the community, and the individual *and the community* are the stewards of those particular gifts. As Christians, we are accountable to each other, to Christ, and to scripture for how we use our gifts, how we respond to our vocational calls, and how we order our desires. Our community is responsible for helping keep our desires ordered toward the praxis of God in the world. Respondents most often voiced this as an intention that their work and gifts serve others; for some, it was connected to a sense of compassion. "I find it important to follow my heartbreak," wrote the psychotherapist-turned-academic. "By this I mean finding where I am most compassionate in serving humanity and the world to bring about greater global healing and change.... It is about finding a particular issue (human rights, sexual abuse, poverty, environmental issues, animal rights, etc.) to become radically active in ameliorating."

Service to God and to others served many respondents as twin criteria for discerning whether they had accurately heard God's call. "Desire, gifts for service, and vocation, for me, all begin in the same place that is at the very core of who I am: made by God, commissioned by God, and equipped for service by God," wrote a second-career pastor in her late thirties. "It is that central core that urges me to serve God and neighbor.... If I can be arms, feet, eyes, ears of Christ to another, then I will have answered God's call on my life." Likewise, a Catholic physician who practices medicine and teaches at a medical school had a clear sense that his vocation is inextricably bound with his desire to serve others and to connect in relationship:

> As a doctor, I have the opportunity to touch the lives of my patients and their families in a compassionate, caring, and ongoing relationship. In my role as a teacher of medicine, I purposefully engage my students in the elements of medicine beyond an actual disease and its treatment. I always say that after awhile, the medicine is the easy part. The challenge is dealing with the complex psychosocial aspects of care. Those are the pieces that must fit together to help the patient and the family, and in the end they remind me of the gratitude I have at being willing to listen and tackle the issues rather than ignore them. Engaging students in this process is eye-opening and quite powerful as they begin to understand the value of the patient-doctor relationship to both sides.

That we are accountable to community for the ways in which we engage our gifts, desires, and vocations can fly in the face of our individualistic culture, the ethical discourse of North America, and the value that North Atlantic societies place on personal agency, self-determination, and personal accountability for the use of resources. Communal discernment and communal accountability are two of the countercultural dimensions of Christian faith. But they are dimensions that were present from the very beginning: when Jesus reordered the desire of Mary of Magdala, telling her to let go of him and go and tell her brothers and sisters, he not only gave her the gift of proclamation; he was also sending her back to her friends to submit her experience to their discernment.

This brings us back where we began: the value of telling others about our deepest desires and listening for the movement of Spirit either to confirm the direction of our desire as congruent with the praxis of God or to nudge us toward desires that help make God's dreams a reality.

Toward a Theory of Desire, Vocation, and Gifts for Service

If, from this small study, I were to advance a tentative theory of the relationship between desire, vocation, and gifts for service, it would be this: these elements of Christian life might best be illustrated as a Venn diagram, three circles that overlap to a greater or lesser degree. "Vocation" would be the largest of the circles, outlined with a bold line; this indicates its primacy as a norm by which desires and gifts for service are to be evaluated and qualified. Gifts and desires that do not "fit" with one's call cannot overlap with the circle of "vocation." In a perfect situation, the smaller circles of "gifts" and "desires" would be entirely contained within the circle of "vocation." However, I suspect the best we can hope for is significant overlap among the three, an overlap that is never static, but rather shifts on an ongoing basis.

The primacy of "vocation" in this model does not render unimportant the smaller circles of "desire" and "gifts for service." These two elements often serve as the entry to serious reflection on one's vocation. They help determine the "fit" of a particular job with God's call to an individual or community, and they can be indicators of God's confirmation or conversion of a particular understanding of call. In addition, attending to gifts and desires can help us assess whether vocation is shifting in unexpected ways. All three circles should be understood to be located in the broader field of biblical and theological understandings of God's desires and purposes for the world, which provide the norms by which understands of vocation, gifts, and desires are to be evaluated.

Implications for Ministry

From my perspective, this chapter has three primary implications for ministry.

First, it suggests that congregations need to focus less attention on identifying spiritual gifts and more on helping people identify and articulate their desires and connect those desires to their vocations.

Second, the chapter suggests that seminaries and divinity schools need to teach new pastors the skills of individual and corporate discernment that are vested in the Christian spiritual traditions. Attending to desire, call, and gifts requires careful attention to the inner movements of consolation and desolation, and few Protestant seminarians formally learn these practices and the principles that govern them.

Finally, individual Christians might profit more from asking, "How do my desires fit God's desires at this point in my life?" rather than asking, "What is my purpose in this life now and forever?" Vocation, gifts, and desires shift over our lifetimes, and they are best discerned and negotiated in a lively and attentive relationship with God and community for a particular context and season of life.

10

Ties That Bind Too Tightly

A Reflection on Relinquishment and Self-differentiation in Women's Leadership

NANCY CLAIRE PITTMAN

"Blest be the tie that binds," is the first line of the old hymn about the bonds of Christian community.[1] Much of the literature on women's leadership echoes that sentiment. In recent years, a spate of books has been published that celebrate the abilities of women to create ties and weave webs of connection within and among social units, whether those abilities are rooted in psychology, women's experience, socio-cultural expectations, or self-consciously chosen feminist theology and ethics.

Katherine Rhodes Henderson writes of a feminist ethic of connection: "For the women interviewed for the book, living a seamless life means trying to pull things together, link disparate parts, transcend boundaries, make connections—in short, to seek and value interrelationship."[2]

Susan Willhauck and Jacqulyn Thorpe prescribe a style of leadership built around the metaphor of a spider's web over against the hierarchical models that have dominated our understandings of church for centuries. They claim that women pastors have been discovering "a caring, connectional weblike leadership" that gives them opportunity to move away from older top-down models of church organization.[3] This move allows power to be shared and all persons, even and especially those at the margins, to be included in leadership.

These and other books and articles present important and useful tools for understanding ways in which women typically lead in congregations and institutions of care. Yet they present models of leadership that all of us, women and men, can appropriate and utilize in our ministries. A danger lurks under the surface—a danger that in all this connection and relationship women in leadership might lose not only a vision of what God is calling them to be and do beyond the demands of immediate relationships, but also the capacity and energy to keep these webs and ties vibrant. In other words, sometimes we must disconnect as much as connect.

One of my earliest mentors was a woman pastor who was well respected by her peers. She remarked that she felt as though too many people had somehow attached their umbilical cords to her and now were sucking the life out of her. To shift the metaphor, she had become enmeshed in a web of relationships and connections, all in an attempt to build the very networks described in the literature mentioned above. Ironically, she had become, not the spider carefully weaving webs of life, but the fly in the web.

As women enter pastoral ministry in increasing numbers, and as the issue of women's leadership continues to be discussed, we might consider a caution even as we embrace nonhierarchical models of leadership. In this essay I am suggesting that we listen to two Jewish rabbis from very different cultures and eras, about what they have to say about ties that bind too tightly. On the one hand, Jesus of Nazareth, a Jewish rabbi in the first century C.E., urged his followers to relinquish those family commitments that kept them from being faithful to the gospel he preached. On the other hand, Edwin Friedman, a Jewish rabbi of the twentieth century, taught ministers and rabbis to lead their churches and synagogues with self-differentiation. I would argue that in their work we find a useful, corrective reminder that even as we weave ties that bind and spin webs that bring people together, we as leaders learn to practice certain forms of detachment that keep us focused on the primary tasks God has given us and balanced among the many claims of our lives.

A Challenge to Relinquish:
Jesus and the Family in the Gospel of Matthew

"Do not think that I have come to bring peace to the earth;
I have not come to bring peace but a sword.

"For I have come to set a man against his father, / and a daughter against her mother, / and a daughter-in-law against her mother-in-law; / and one's foes will be members of one's own household.

"Whoever loves father or mother more than me is not worthy of me; and whoever loves son or daughter more than me is not worthy of me; and whoever does not take up the cross and follow me is not worthy of me. Those who find their life will lose it, and those who lose their life for my sake will find it." (Mt. 10:34–39; see also parallel in Lk. 12:49–53 and 14:26)

While he was still speaking to the crowds, his mother and his brothers were standing outside, wanting to speak to him. Someone told him, "Look, your mother and your brothers are standing outside, wanting to speak to you." But to the one who had told him this, Jesus replied, "Who is my mother, and who are my brothers?" And pointing to his disciples, he said "Here are my mother and my brothers! For whoever does the will of my Father in heaven is my brother and sister and mother" (Mt. 12:46–50; see also parallels in Mk. 3:31–35 and Lk. 8:19–21).

In these two passages, we encounter some of the most uncomfortable words uttered by the Matthean Jesus. First, he exhorts his disciples to sever family ties; then he acts out the exhortation with his own family. In other words, he is demanding the relinquishment of some of the most basic and valued social ties in his time, and in ours, a relinquishment that will ultimately further the aims of his mission.

The first text follows a series of warnings about the faithlessness of the people the disciples will encounter and instructions to be courageous and faithful regardless of the dangers. Jesus portrays himself and his mission in a profoundly negative way: "Do not think I have come to bring peace to the earth," he declares. The phrase "to the earth" stands in opposition to the reign of heaven, in which Jesus does bring peace. In particular, this peace that Jesus claims not to bring is acted out as dissension in the family.[4] To make this point, Jesus paraphrases Micah 7:6: "...for the son treats the father with contempt, / the daughter rises up against her mother, / the daughter-in-law against her mother-in-law; / your enemies are members of your own household." The context of these words in Micah signifies a situation of total corruption and faithlessness on the part of the people chosen by God. The Matthean Jesus loosens these words from the Micah setting and turns them around—now the enmity among family members is a sign of faithfulness to the Messiah. This meaning is confirmed in Matthew 10:37: "Whoever loves father or mother more than me is not worthy of me; and whoever loves son or daughter more than me is not worthy of me."

In the second passage, Matthew 12:46–50, Jesus acts out this challenge to relinquish kinship ties. This time he is talking to the crowds, presumably inside a building or enclosure; Jesus' family is outside. The location is more than simply geographical—it is also theological. The biological family stands outside the theological household of God. When someone brings this uncomfortable situation to Jesus' attention, he looks around and asks rhetorically, "Who is my mother, and who are my brothers?" Then he answers his own question, "Here are my mother and my brothers! For whoever does the will of my Father in heaven is my brother and sister and mother." His biological siblings and his own mother wait outside, never to be invited in and given a place in Jesus' new family, at least as Matthew tells us in this incident.

This sociohistorical milieu of the gospel of Matthew yields additional clues for understanding the nature of this relinquishment. Scholars generally agree that the gospel of Matthew was produced in 80–100 C.E., a time when the fledging Christian movement was separating itself from its native home in first-century Judaism. The author of this gospel was attempting to produce an authoritative account of the teachings and events of Jesus' life in an intense conversation, even debate, with the rabbinic Judaism that was taking shape in the aftermath of the destruction of the Jewish temple.[5] Thus, the text is permeated with religious conflict and a self-righteous sense of persecution as Jews confessing Jesus to be the Messiah began to separate themselves from the synagogues of the ancient Near East. Some of those Jewish Christians may have had to leave their biological families to make that confession and join the new religious household constituted by the followers of Jesus. In this situation, these words mirror the circumstances of their own churches and reinforce their decision to relinquish their families to follow Jesus.

Our understanding of the relinquishment Jesus is urging is not complete until we also look at the social and cultural expectations of family of the first century. According to Jerome Neyrey, "the most important institution in antiquity was the family, which conveyed to its members their personal identity and social standing."[6] This standing could be one of honor or of shame, depending upon how well each member lived in accordance with socially approved norms and mores. If one member stepped beyond these boundaries, the entire family was dishonored. If one member rejected the family, he or she rejected the shared blood that coursed through their veins, consequently bringing great shame upon all kinsmen and kinswomen.

When Jesus tells his disciples that they must not love their parents or children more than they love him, he is advocating an action that would be considered quite dishonorable among their peers. When he repudiates his own mother and brothers in favor of the persons gathered around him, he himself acts shamefully. His family, in their efforts to see Jesus, seems also to shame him in turn in order to force him to act with honor. After all, they come not to listen to him, as his disciples do, but to speak to him, the act of speaking carrying higher weight and honor than listening.[7] Jesus persists in rejecting their claim upon him, thereby returning dishonor for dishonor.[8] Then he bestows honor upon the members of his new family, calling them "brother and sister and mother" and placing them in a familial relationship with himself and his Father in heaven, who is, after all, the most honorable One of all.

The point of these passages is this: Jesus, in word and action, challenges his disciples to relinquish familial attachments in favor of a new attachment to himself, his mission, and his God. He calls them to cut these too tightly bound ties so that they might participate in the new family of God, the kin-dom of God.[9] The radicality of this call still echoes today as we wrestle with these texts. Although in modern North American culture we do not frame relationships in explicit terms of honor and shame as in the ancient Near East, we are still shaped by embedded norms that suggest that women ought to take care of their families first; that women ought to put the needs of their families first; that women ought to seek out their families' approval first. Often these relational ties are extended to ecclesial communities, referring to themselves as families, in which women leaders are implicitly invested with roles of mother and sister and all the nurturing, care-giving, self-sacrificing responsibilities such roles imply.

For some women, Jesus' call to act against these kinds of bonds comes as a near-impossible challenge, and they meet it with anger: How can Jesus ask followers to act against, even to sever, such natural and appropriate ties? For others, it is good news: family cords, biological or ecclesial, that bind and strangle can at last be cut as they seek first the things of God that lead not just to the well-being of a single family, or a single community, but to all creation. As women seek their own leadership styles and begin to negotiate the more tangled webs of family relationships that permeate biological families, churches, and synagogues, the Matthean Jesus' words bring both challenge and comfort. A Jewish rabbi of the twentieth century provides another view of this corrective to the effort to build communities with nonhierarchical forms of leadership.

A Call for Self-differentiation:
Friedman and Family Systems Theory

"The basic concept of leadership through self-differentiation is this: If a leader will take primary responsibility for his or her own position as 'head' and work to define his or her own goals and self, while *staying in touch* with the rest of the organism, there is a more than reasonable chance that the body will follow."[10]

In recent years, few people have exercised as much influence in the literature of church leadership as has Edwin H. Friedman (1932–1996), an ordained rabbi, family therapist, and leadership trainer. His fundamental insight that ecclesial communities not only call themselves families but function like families has drawn attention throughout North America. Pastors and rabbis continue to use his work in understanding the internal workings of their congregations and synagogues. Although Friedman provided a number of conceptual tools drawn from the family systems theory of Murray Bowen in understanding congregational dynamics, none have proven more durable and useful than that of self-differentiation.

A brief overview of Friedman's work as it applies to congregational life provides context. Friedman theorized that human relational systems are full of free-floating anxiety that will attach to issues and people, sometimes with little rhyme or reason, causing individuals and the system itself to respond, often in very unhealthy ways.[11] This is true because groups of people of any size function like cells do in an organism–they are individual, but at the same time they are integrally related to other cells. When one cell changes, for better or worse, the whole organism must adjust and change, either for its own good or for ill.

Friedman further postulated that someone, usually the leader of a group, must develop a nonanxious presence in the face of the anxiety that permeates a system so that others can be infected, not by this rampant anxiety, but by the calm of the leader. This nonanxious presence, he said, requires self-differentiation: "the capacity...to define...life's goals and values apart from surrounding togetherness pressures, to say 'I' when others are demanding 'you' and 'we.'"[12] A self-differentiated person actively works to cultivate her (or his) own ideas, beliefs, goals, and values, whether or not they are the same as those with whom she is in relationship. She also vigorously separates her self-perceptions from the perceptions of her held by others around her, refusing to take on their expectations and understandings of her role in any given situation. At the same time, it is essential that a self-differentiated individual remain in touch with the other members of the organism—that she knows what others are thinking and feeling, that she is aware of the anxiety, chronic or acute, that is infecting the system at any given moment, and that she is able to respond to needs and concerns as opposed to reacting to them.

This process of self-differentiation may seem on the surface to be similar to various concepts of self-actualization in which the development, health, and well-being of the self becomes the goal of life. In notes for his final book, *A Failure of Nerve: Leadership in the Age of the Quick Fix,* which was published posthumously, Friedman wrote, "Differentiation…is not to be equated…with similar-sounding ideas such as individuation, autonomy or independence. First of all, it has less to do with a person's behavior than with his or her emotional being. Second, there is a sense of connectedness to the concept that prevents the mere gaining of distance, leaving, or cutting off as ways to achieve it." [13] For Friedman, self-differentiation in any one individual's life can and should be beneficial to the entire system. Thus, even as an individual seeks her own identity and well-being in the process of self-differentiation, such a process cannot help but be ultimately useful to the whole system. In Friedman's view, both the health of the whole organism—be it family, church, or synagogue—as well as that of the individual remains central to his work.

Although Friedman himself did not provide explicit theological content to his understanding of self-differentiation, this last point leads me to suggest two brief reflections about the theological significance of his work from a Christian standpoint. First, the system in Friedman's thought, or—to shift slightly to the apostle Paul's language—the *body* is never left behind. Considerations for its health and well-being, including his prescriptions for leadership and self-differentiation, are the focus of his theory and practice. In a Christian context, the community of the faithful is the primary unit through which the purposes of God might be fulfilled. Its mission is to model, in an imperfect way to be sure, the kin-dom of God to which Jesus pointed and to offer its gifts and blessings to all humankind. This mission, however, cannot even begin to be accomplished without attention to the internal well-being of the whole community and its members.

Second, claimed Friedman, for this well-being to occur, the individual's needs, desires, concerns cannot be absorbed into some kind of monolithic collective. To express this in Christian terms, the individual herself is a child of God who bears the *imago Dei,* the image of God. As Leroy T. Howe explains, "Theologically construed, the capacity for self-differentiation is the capacity to be the persons God intends us to be, sharing with all human beings a common destiny to care for the earth on our creator's behalf."[14] He continues, "Just as God differentiates his own divine nature from, but in relationship with, all that is other than himself...human beings are created with both the capacity and the calling to differentiate themselves as distinctive individuals even as they remain connected and contributory to the larger family which is humankind itself."[15]

Herein, then, lies a significant connection to Jesus' challenge to relinquish one's family for the creation of the kin-dom of God. Jesus summons believers to life beyond the confines of family arrangements and kinship groups, offering them opportunity to look beyond their own horizons, conditioned by socio-cultural obligations, to God's horizons. Friedman's summons to pursue self-differentiation also has a goal of reaching beyond the needs and concerns of those who are threatening to keep us as individuals and communities from becoming the persons and churches that God intends us to be. We are called to be in relationship with others, to be sure, but not in attachments that bind too tightly and are not beneficial for ecclesial communities or for God's entire creation.

Some years ago, Valerie Saiving, an early Anglo feminist, suggested that the temptations to sin that women face are not "pride" or "will-to-power," which male theologians so often have suggested as the primary human temptations. She argued instead that women's temptations take the form of "dependence on others for one's own self-definition; tolerance at the expense of standards of excellence...in short, underdevelopment or negation of the self."[16] These temptations, she said, were rooted in the expectations of the maternal role, which must be countered in some way.

> A mother who rejoices in her maternal role—and most mothers do most of the time—knows the profound experience of self-transcending love. But she knows, too, that it is not the whole meaning of life. For she learns not only that it is impossible to sustain a perpetual I-Thou relationship but that the attempt to do so can be deadly. The moments, hours, and days of self-giving must be balanced by moments, hours, and days of withdrawal into, and enrichment of, her individual selfhood if she is to remain a whole person. She learns, too, that a woman can give too much of herself, so that nothing

remains of her own uniqueness; she can become merely an emptiness, almost a zero, without value to herself, to her fellow men [*sic*], or perhaps, even to God.[17]

Saiving's words help me summarize the argument of this essay: in building webs of connectivity and relationality in our communities, in bringing together individuals in ties that join us to one another and to the work of God in the world, women must be cautious about webs that entrap so firmly and ties that bind so tightly that we cannot free ourselves or others. The two Jewish rabbis whose words we have considered here supply correctives to otherwise useful models for developing nonhierarchical models of leadership. As women continue to assume positions of authority and power in ecclesial communities, as we continue to seek ordination and serve as pastors, we will bring with us new models for organizing communities and developing opportunities for all to participate. My hope is that we might also incorporate practices drawn from the wisdom of Jesus and the understanding of Friedman to keep us from being bound too tightly to these communities and free us to work toward the kindom of God.

11

Does Constructive Theology Matter?

What Political Candidates Can Teach Ministry Students about Theology and Pastoral Leadership

JOSEPH A. BESSLER

For many ministry students the discipline of constructive theology—as they encounter it in seminary or divinity school—remains disconnected from the practice of ministerial leadership. For some, theology, with its more technical, abstract vocabulary, can seem at once too formalistic and detached from the real-life concerns of ordinary people and too intellectually distant and complex for the minister himself or herself to access quickly as a resource for pastoral guidance and leadership. Yet even those who love the subject matter and the nuanced discussions of theological method tend not to think about theology when they engage in practices of ministerial leadership and pastoral care. While it is something of a truism that behind this disconnect lies the curricular distinction between theoretical and practical disciplines, I believe that the retrieval of *leadership* as a goal for students in Master of Divinity and Doctor of Ministry programs requires that theological schools and faculties attend more seriously to helping students make the connection between the discipline of theology and the practices of ministerial leadership.

My essay demonstrates the importance of theology for ministerial leadership by showing how political candidates attend, in disciplined ways, to a set of topics that overlap significantly with the basic topics of constructive theology.[1] First, showing how political candidates interpret these topics as a way of presenting a coherent image of themselves as political leaders, I then suggest what pastors and teachers of pastors can learn from the rhetorical work of political candidates, even as I point to the necessity of Christian leaders remaining faithful to the distinctiveness of the Christian gospel.

Basic Topics of Political Leadership

Imagine that you want to run for political office. It could be a local or a state-level race, but let's say you want to run for President of the United States. Let us also assume—since we are imagining anyway—that you have wonderful credentials from a life of public service as well as solid financial backers; money will not be a serious problem. To be successful in the election, you must offer a more coherent and convincing interpretation of five fundamental topics than your opponent. If you cannot interpret these topics persuasively and with real conviction, you will not succeed (unless your opponent does an even poorer job than you). In addition, because, as a candidate, you cannot be reinventing yourself at every turn in the campaign, these fundamental issues (one could even think of them as meta-issues) need to be thought through as carefully and as strategically as possible, before launching the campaign itself. Here are the five topics:

1. *Interpretation of the creative and enduring goodness of America.* You have to interpret and embody the creative and enduring goodness of America and its people. If voters do not believe that a candidate ultimately believes in the goodness of the people and represents them and their deepest interests, they will not support the candidacy.

2. *The crises requiring leadership.* You have to diagnose the crises or challenges that threaten the inherent goodness in the American people in the present and near future. In other words, you need to convey the urgency of your candidacy.

3. *Yourself as leader and key policy proposals.* You have to offer yourself, your leadership, and your policy proposals as a corrective to those current challenges. Your leadership will restore continuity with the creative goodness of the people and will tap into the moral and creative reservoir of the people's goodness for the sake of a courageous and hopeful future.

4. *The importance of joining together.* Recognizing that you cannot accomplish the needed changes alone, you must invite others to join with you in creating the conditions for a new spirit in the nation as, together, it faces the difficult and dangerous time ahead. Imagine a candidacy without supporters expressing faith in the message—a campaign going nowhere.

5. *A vision of the nation's future.* You have to offer a vision of the future that is achievable for the nation if it works together in support of you and your policies. That vision of the future, of a renewed and prosperous nation, is crucial and further intensifies what is at issue in topic three: if you and your policies will not make a substantial difference in improving the nation's future, why should anyone bother voting for you?

Neither you, nor anyone else, has the single way to interpret these five topics successfully. Candidates will do so in a variety of ways depending on their personal background and professional credentials, their political affiliation, and the kinds of issues and concerns shaping the context of the election itself. What *is* crucial is that candidates do so in a systematic and coherent way, because all of these five areas, or topics, are mutually interdependent. How each of these categories is interpreted shapes the interpretation of the remaining four categories.

Political candidates need to have thought through these meta-issues in a consistent and coherent way—not simply as a single academic exercise, but as a way of approaching virtually every policy question that comes before them. Time and again, a candidate has to return to these basic interpretations as core guidelines for framing issues that come up in the course of the campaign. In Barack Obama's March 18, 2008, speech on race in Philadelphia, for example, he had to respond to video clips of his pastor, the Rev. Jeremiah Wright, saying, "God damn America," in a sermon. Those clips created a crisis for the Obama campaign to which he had to respond.

Obama's address opens (1) by citing a phrase from America's great founding document, the U.S. Constitution, "a more perfect union."[2] Affirming the profound goodness of the U.S. Constitution, he quickly moves (2) to note the fall, the "original sin of slavery" that wounded both the Constitution itself and that divided Americans from each other on the basis of race; he continues (3) by speaking honestly about the ambiguities and difficulties of race in America for both blacks and whites, and identifying his candidacy and campaign as uniquely able to help America "come together"; and (4) encourages his listeners and supporters to come together in honest conversation to heal America: "When we come together there is no issue we cannot solve." He concludes (5) by holding open a future vision of an America moving toward the Constitution's goal of a "more perfect union."

How did Obama deal specifically with Wright? By rejecting Wright's words as offensive, but also, in keeping with his analysis of ambiguity, by affirming the basic goodness of the man who had been his pastor for twenty years and meant much to him. Balancing ambiguities, black and white, Obama also dealt with offensive comments by his white grandmother in the same way.

As one sees in the example of the Obama speech, a candidate must interpret these categories coherently not only to represent one's candidacy most forcefully but also to defend oneself from political attacks—in this case, the attempt to discredit Obama's fitness for office by virtue of his longtime association with Wright. Virtually all of an opponent's attacks will be directed at a candidate's interpretation of these topics—to raise doubts and suspicions about the moral integrity of the candidate and the legitimacy of his or her candidacy. When Ronald Reagan accused Jimmy Carter of saying that the American people suffered from a "malaise," he argued that Carter had lost touch with the enduring goodness and dignity of the American people. That argument goes to topic one, above.

Senator Ted Kennedy's disastrous 1979 interview with CBS correspondent Roger Mudd, in which Kennedy offered no compelling argument for his candidacy, left him open to the disparaging accusation that he presumed he was entitled to the office, seeking coronation just for being a Kennedy. Kennedy's failure to give a sense of urgency to his campaign resulted in a serious self-inflicted wound in an already difficult uphill battle to unseat President Carter as the presumed Democratic nominee.

When, in the 1984 Democratic primary contest, Senator Gary Hart was making inroads against former Vice President Walter Mondale by touting the importance of a leadership of new ideas, Mondale finally responded with the words from a popular fast-food restaurant commercial, "Where's the beef?" Mondale argued effectively that all of Hart's "new ideas" were not new at all, undercutting Hart's interpretation of topic three.

In his 1992 address, Bill Clinton shaped his discussion of a renewed American community, providing a marvelous example of how to interpret topic four:

> Tonight, every one of you knows deep in your heart that we are too divided. It is time to heal America. And so we

must say to every American: Look beyond the stereotypes that blind us. We need each other–all of us–we need each other. We don't have a person to waste, and yet for too long politicians have told the most of us that are doing all right that what's really wrong with America is the rest of us–"them." Them–the minorities. Them–the liberals. Them–the poor. Them–the homeless. Them–the people with disabilities. Them–the gays.

We've gotten to where we've nearly "them'ed" ourselves to death: Them, and them, and them. But, this is America. There is no "them." There is only "us." One nation, under God, indivisible, with liberty and justice for all. That–*That,* is our Pledge of Allegiance, and that's what the New Covenant is all about.[3]

When, during the 1992 campaign, George H. W. Bush said he didn't "get the vision thing," Clinton quoted back to him a passage from Proverbs: "Where there is no vision, the people perish" (29:18, KJV). Bush, he said, had lost touch with the most fundamental moorings of American government, the vision of the American Dream–achievable for all Americans–a strong criticism of Bush's failure to interpret topic five. For his part, Bush never seemed to recognize the damage Clinton had inflicted. With respect to both presenting and defending oneself and one's candidacy, therefore, successfully interpreting these five categories is a significant mark of one's capacity for leadership.

The Political Use of Christian Theological Structures

The five fundamental topics, or meta-issues, that shape the questions of political leadership and a political theology of the nation overlap significantly with five basic topics of Christian theology: (1) the inherent created goodness of the human person and human culture; (2) the estrangement from that created goodness, frequently discussed in terms of "the Fall," which haunts our individual and collective histories; (3) the redemption of our individual and collective existence by an heroic and selfless redeemer who calls us from the old to the new, from failure to renewal, from despair to hope; (4) the formation of the beloved community in faith, empowered by grace to be a transformative presence in the world; and (5) the vision of the *telos* or goal of a transformed creation, when God will establish a "new heaven and a new earth" and be "all in all."[4]

The task of theologians and pastors–over the centuries–has been to *interpret* these topics of the Christian narrative from within their own historical and cultural contexts. Just as we have no single political interpretation to the topics discussed above, we have no single theological interpretation of these key topics in Christian theology. How is one, for example, to understand the created and distinctive goodness of the human creature? Does the sense of the *imago Dei* lie in the idea of a rational soul, as many have argued? Does it lie in our capacity for language, or in our unique capacity to be response-able to our world, or in our capacity and task as interpreters? Or, as some have suggested in an ecologically stressed time, is the concept of the *Imago Dei* itself part of the problem—elevating human existence hierarchically above the rest of creation? Just as theologians have interpreted this topic of created goodness in multiple ways—similar to and yet different from one another—so have they interpreted the other topics of sin, christology, faith-and-grace, the church (or ecclesiology), and the end of all things (or eschatology). What makes for a coherent theology is recognizing, first, that the interpretation of these topics always occurs in conjunction with the interpretation of one's own cultural and historical context, and, second, that how one interprets one topic shapes the way one interprets the others. Coherence, of course, in both politics and theology is no proof of the adequacy of one's position. Nonetheless, the coherence of one's self-presentation does function as an intellectual, if not moral, threshold, as any politician or theologian accused of "flip-flopping" or "equivocation" can testify.

Religion in Politics

Accepting for the moment an analogical relation between these two structures of fundamental, interconnected topics—one political, the other theological—one might ask whether we have any reason to assume that American political candidates are drawing intentionally upon the structure of Christian theology as a resource for shaping their own political visions of America? The answer, I believe, is clearly no *and* yes.

A candidate running for public office may not be *explicitly* aware or fully conscious of drawing upon the architectural topics of Christian theology in framing her or his candidacy. Nonetheless, the marks of intentionality are present. Consider: in anything like a major statewide or national election a candidate cannot possibly meet all potential voters personally (with the possible exception of the Iowa caucuses). The challenge for the candidate is how best to convince voters that he or she shares their deep and abiding values as persons and citizens.

Invoking the language or themes of the dominant religious tradition can reassure audiences that one is in touch with their principles, interests, and commitments.[5]

Because one cannot simply quote biblical themes, however, lest one sound too much like a minister (a particular challenge for former Arkansas governor and former Baptist minister Mike Huckabee in the 2008 Republican primaries), utilizing the narrative structure of Christian theology to interpret those basic topics functions as an effective unconscious, or subliminal, mode of persuasion. Moreover, as one can see in the following analysis of two convention addresses, some markers of Christian discourse are simply too obvious to be unintentional if one assumes any skill at all in the speechwriting process.[6]

Most often, it is the implied christology of a speech that first alerts the listener that religious categories are being invoked: Bill Clinton in 1992 announcing the "new covenant" between the American people and their government, or Bob Dole in 1996 encouraging both those in the convention hall and throughout America to "follow me," or George Bush in 2000 calling for a "new beginning," or John Kerry in 2004 intoning both military and messianic language to describe the thrust of his campaign, "Help is on the way."[7]

While the language of these challengers is distinctly messianic, one finds here as well something of a realized eschatology in the language of "Help is on the way!" or, "It won't be long now!" or, "Without a vision the people perish!" The new leader is already in the midst of the people and ready to lead them in reclaiming America from the current administration, which has inevitably fouled things up and soiled the inherent goodness of the nation.

A closer look at the 1992 nomination acceptance speech by Bill Clinton and the 2000 nomination acceptance speech by George Bush will show how the entire architecture of both speeches is informed by the sequential and analogical interpretation of the basic Christian topics.[8] The point of such theological borrowing, however, is not the construction of an explicitly Christian theology but the construction of a persuasive American political theology—or vision of the nation.[9]

Clinton, 1992

Clinton's discussion of his "new-covenant" proposal does not occur until the middle of his speech. He opens the speech by interpreting the inherent goodness of the American people and identifying himself with that goodness:

And so, in the name of all those who do the work, pay the taxes, raise the kids, and play by the rules, in the name of the hardworking Americans who make up our forgotten middle class, I proudly accept your nomination for President of the United States. I am a product of that middle class, and when I am President, you will be forgotten no more.

As Clinton introduces himself to the nation, he describes his own middle-class background and the "values" he learned from key figures in his life. Beginning with "I never knew my father," Clinton told stories about his single-parent mother's hard work and sacrifice, his grandfather's fairness and respect for all hard-working people, and his wife, Hillary's, concern with America's children. These were the stories, he said, that shaped him, but more than that, he said, they were America's stories. Taking up stories that dealt with America's families, with race, and with the nation's children, Clinton connected the shared values of the "American Dream" and its commitment to reward "hard work" to his own policy commitments.

It is possible, however, that the American dream of rewarding hard work can be ignored or forgotten. That's the "sin" of the Reagan-Bush years, according to Clinton: "But the folks of Washington turn the American ethic on its head. For too long those who play by the rules and keep the faith have gotten the shaft, and those who cut corners and cut deals have been rewarded."

In case his listeners had missed the subtle shift from inherent goodness to this second topic of critique, Clinton invoked the language of "the Fall": "Our country is falling behind." Echoing the Christian tradition's sense of sin as bondage, Clinton added: "The President is caught in the grip of a failed economic theory. We have gone from 1st to 13th in the world in wages since Reagan and Bush have been in office…. Our country has fallen so far so fast that just a few months ago the Japanese Prime Minister actually said he felt sympathy for the United States."

Clinton goes on to criticize President Bush, not as an "evil" president, but as one who lacked the will to fight the special interests. "A president ought to be a force for progress. But right now I know how President Lincoln felt when General McClellan wouldn't attack in the Civil War. He asked him, 'If you're not going to use your army, may I borrow it?' And so I say: 'George Bush, if you won't use your power to help America, step aside—I will.'" Clinton went on to list other major battles Bush didn't have the will to fight.

He won't take on the big insurance companies…. He won't… implement the recommendations of his own commission on

AIDS.... He won't streamline the federal government.... He won't break the stranglehold the special interests have on our elections.... He won't give mothers and fathers the simple chance to take some time off from work when a baby is born or a parent is sick.... He won't take the lead in protecting the economy...and he won't guarantee a woman's right to choose." To all of these, and other failures of will, Clinton responded: "I will."

President Bush's moral failure according to Clinton was not simply personal in scope. Instead, Bush's failure of political leadership was indicative of a systemic problem, a breakdown in the most basic priorities of government. Hence, the third move of the speech.

Clinton called his plan for a "new approach to government," one that "puts people first," a "New Covenant"—a "solemn agreement between the people and their government not simply on what each of us can take but what all of us must give to our nation." This New Covenant was what Clinton, as a messianic challenger, offered the nation—a plan that sought to expand John Kennedy's "Ask not..." rhetoric from 1961 into a contemporary moral framework of governance.

To further explain what he meant by the New Covenant, Clinton turned to a trinity of terms. "We offer opportunity. We demand responsibility. We will build an American community again." In the ensuing paragraphs, Clinton goes on to discuss the need to expand job, educational, and health care opportunities, and to deal with taxes and welfare. Following are several paragraphs; notice, in particular, the play between "opportunity" and "responsibility."

> That's what the New Covenant is all about. An America in which the doors of colleges are thrown open once again to the sons and daughters of stenographers and steelworkers. We'll say: Everybody can borrow the money to go to college. But you must do your part. You must pay it back from your paychecks or, better yet, by going back home and serving your communities....
>
> That's what the New Covenant is all about. An America where we end welfare as we know it. We will say to those on welfare: You will have and you deserve the opportunity through training and education, through child care and medical coverage, to liberate yourself. But then, when you can, you must work, because welfare should be a second chance, not a way of life....

After laying out these and similar proposals calling for a balance of opportunity and responsibility on the part of government, businesses, and ordinary people, Clinton intones a shift to the fourth move of his speech. "But the New Covenant is about more than opportunities and responsibilities for you and your families. It's also about our common community." Analogous to the theological discussion of the church as a new community, he turns to the passage on "healing" America, which I included above in my discussion of the basic topics. Virtually on cue, he mentions the importance of renewed faith:

> We can renew our faith in each other and in ourselves. We can restore our sense of unity and community…. But I can't do this alone—no President can. We must do it together. It won't be easy and it won't be quick. We didn't get into this mess overnight, and we won't get out of it overnight. But we can do it—with commitment, creativity, diversity, and drive!

The renewal of faith in one another and in America—"We can seize this moment, make it exciting and energizing and heroic to be American again"—opens onto the final, eschatological moment in the speech: his invocation of the future.

> I want every person in this hall and every person in this land to reach out and join us in a great new adventure, to chart a bold new future….
>
> Somewhere at this very moment a child is being born in America. Let it be our cause to give that child a happy home, a healthy family, and a hopeful future. Let it be our cause to see that that child has a chance to live to the fullest of her God-given capacities.
>
> Let it—let it be our cause to see that child grow up strong and secure, braced by her challenges but never struggling alone, with family and friends and a faith that, in America, no one is left out; no one is left behind. Let it be—let it be our cause that when this child is able, she gives something back to her children, her community, and her country.
>
> Let it be our cause that we give this child a country that is coming together, not coming apart, a country of boundless hopes and endless dreams, a country that once again lifts its people and inspires the world. Let that be our cause, our commitment, and our New Covenant.

Clinton concluded by invoking the primary eschatological virtue: "I end tonight where it all began for me. I still believe in a place called Hope. God bless you, and God Bless America."

Bush, 2000

One need not stop with Clinton's convention address. While space doesn't allow me to trace in detail the similar set of moves in George W. Bush's 2000 address, it is relatively easy to sketch the broad outline.[10] For Bush, America's enduring capacity for greatness[11] (first move) has been tarnished by the Clinton administration's sloth (second move): "For eight years, the Clinton/Gore administration has coasted through prosperity. And the path of least resistance is always downhill." If his audience didn't catch the "fall" imagery in that sentence, Bush added more. "Our current president embodied the potential of a generation. So many talents. So much charm. Such great skill. But, in the end, to what end? So much promise, to no great purpose." Using the background of the Lewinsky sex scandal, Bush turns Clinton's rhetorical gifts against him, reminding the nation of Clinton's capacity for evasion and self-centeredness.

Urging Americans to reject Gore after two terms of the Clinton administration, Bush moves toward his own messianic appeal. "This is not a time for third chances; it is a time for new beginnings. The rising generations of this country have our own appointment with greatness.... Greatness is found when American character and American courage overcome American challenges."

How is Bush an exemplar of America's greatness? By being the opposite of the rhetorically gifted Bill Clinton.

> When Lewis Morris of New York was about to sign the Declaration of Independence, his brother advised against it, warning he would lose all his property.
>
> Morris, a plain-spoken Founder, responded.... "Damn the consequences, give me the pen." That is the eloquence of American action....
>
> Tonight, in this hall, we resolve to be, not the party of repose, but the party of reform. We will write, not footnotes, but chapters in the American story.

Later, at the close of a long section detailing his intentions to act decisively, yet with compassion, and on principle, Bush adds:

> And to lead this nation to a responsibility era, a president himself must be responsible.

And so, when I put my hand on the Bible, I will swear to not only uphold the laws of our land, I will swear to uphold the honor and dignity of the office to which I have been elected, so help me God.

I believe the presidency—the final point of decision in the American government—was made for great purposes....

I do not need to take your pulse before I know my own mind. I do not reinvent myself at every turn. I am not running in borrowed clothes. When I act, you will know my reasons.... When I speak, you will know my heart.

From this point, Bush speaks his "credo," a set of faith statements that has the feel of a country-western song intoning his affirmation of the American creed.

I believe in tolerance, not in spite of my faith, but because of it.

I believe in a God who calls us, not to judge our neighbors, but to love them.

I believe in grace, because I have seen it.... In peace, because I have felt it.... In forgiveness, because I have needed it.

I believe true leadership is a process of addition, not an act of division. I will not attack a part of this country, because I want to lead the whole of it.

Drawing the country into the process of renewal, he reiterates his christological theme:

My fellow citizens, we can begin again. After all of the shouting, and all of the scandal. After all of the bitterness and broken faith. We can begin again.

From this point, he turns to the eschatological theme of, "It won't be long now," pointing to an imminent return of American greatness.

I believe America is ready for a new beginning.

My friend, the artist Tom Lea of El Paso, captured the way I feel about our great land. He and his wife, he said, "Live on the east side of the mountain.... It is the sunrise side, not the sunset side. It is the side to see the day that is coming... not the side to see the day that is gone."

Americans live on the sunrise side of mountain. The night is passing. And we are ready for the day to come. Thank you. And God bless you.

Both Clinton and Bush used their interpretation of the five theologically shaped topics to frame not only the key issues facing the nation but also to frame themselves as moral leaders. To be sure, one need not look only at convention addresses to find this pattern; one can look to virtually any significant or defining speech of a candidate, as we did with Obama's speech on race, above.

Challenge to Ministry Students, Ordained Clergy, and Theological Faculties

Studying the analogical connection between political and theological discourse may encourage both teachers and learners to recover the deep connection between the rhetorical tasks of pastoral leadership and the work of constructive theology in at least four ways.

First, simply noticing the rhetorical discipline of political candidates as they draw on, and interpret, a set of interconnected topics that overlaps significantly with the basic interconnected topics of Christian theology—and noticing that they do so precisely to present themselves as moral and responsible leaders of the nation—can help ministry students recognize the importance of constructive theology for their own roles as pastoral leaders.

Second, by attending to the different ways Clinton and Bush, Obama, McCain, and others interpret this set of topics—and by analyzing their reasons for doing so—ministry students can see that *how* one interprets the fundamental topics of Christian theology—the issue of theological method—really does matter. Thus, a comparative rhetorical analysis of political speeches can help students better appreciate the kinds of questions involved in thinking through others', and their own, theological methods. There is a world of difference between the words and the work of Martin Luther King Jr. and of Kirbyjon Caldwell, between William Sloane Coffin Jr. and Jerry Falwell. The differences between them are not simply rhetorical, but theological.

Third, as one recognizes more clearly how political speeches draw upon theological themes and structures, one also recognizes that candidates' "political theologies" are not authentic Christian theologies. Students may find themselves asking with a shock of recognition: To what extent have these political theologies displaced more authentic Christian models of reflection within the life of Christian congregations?

Do not many congregants—and perhaps the students themselves—tend to view disputes in the congregation, and even other church members, in terms of a liberal-conservative axis derived from current political orthodoxies? Thus, analyzing the political theologies of presidential candidates can move students to ask critical questions about which kinds of discourse *really* shape the "religious" attitudes and beliefs of the American public, including themselves and members of their congregation. The emergence of this reflexive mode of critical questioning in students can further enable them to pursue even more deeply the question of how to interpret the heart of the Christian gospel for our time and place.

Finally, and closely related to the preceding point, because any authentic understanding of Christian theology must extend far beyond the national and economic interests of the American government and its people, ministry students can learn that they have a prophetic obligation as leaders of Christian communities. As it requires both theological clarity and courage, however, to speak forcefully when either candidates or elected officials veil unjust policies behind a facade of Christian belief, students can also learn that serious attention to the work of constructive theology—as a discourse of ministerial leadership—is essential to their own moral authority and integrity as pastors.

12

Deep and New

Earth-centered Ecumenism

ELIZABETH BOX PRICE

"The primary sacred community is the universe itself."

THOMAS BERRY, *Evening Thoughts*

Educators and leaders of the religions of the world are beginning to take seriously the findings of science that present a view of the origins and unfolding of the universe and the findings that the environment of the planet is at risk. During this last century scientific observations have led science to construct a story of an emerging universe over 13.5 billion years.[1] At the same time, observations have revealed that the Earth is experiencing destruction of multiple species and habitat due to carbon emissions that provoke radical climate change. This new scientific cosmology raises questions about the place of humans in it, especially regarding the place of humans in the cosmological context and the role of humans in the environmental crisis. "If scientific cosmology gives us an understanding of the origins and unfolding of the universe, the story of cosmology gives us a sense of our place in the universe. If we are so radically affecting the story by extinguishing other life forms and destroying our own nest, what does this imply about our religious sensibilities or our sense of the sacred?"[2]

Since both education and religion claim life interpretation at an ultimate level and provide some guidance about the future, they have a significant role to play in making known what is happening to the world in which we live, how it functions, and how the human fits into the larger community. This includes the place humans fulfill in the story of an unfolding universe and in the context of a historical sequence of physical and cultural developments.[3]

Role of Religions in the Environmental Crises

Religions of the world have been quite late in addressing the environmental crisis. This is not due to a lack of information about what is happening to the Earth. Descriptions and studies about the state of the environment abound and have been highly publicized in scholarship and the public media.[4] Evidence of climate change is experienced around the globe, modifying weather patterns that affect life in many concrete ways–such as hurricanes, flooding, drought, famine, and various extremes. Information is abundant about how carbon emissions are altering life on our globe: the effect of technology, the rapid extinction of numerous species, genetically modified organisms, deforestation, desertification, destruction of the ozone layer, melting of the polar ice caps, the depletion of oxygen, and increased global warming.

With so much information about a problem of such magnitude, what has contributed to the late involvement of religions in responding? An initial response might be that if religions could be more informed about the state of our planet, they would readily take positive action, especially since humans will be greatly affected. In exploring this question the literature discusses many possibilities; among them are a primary emphasis on personal salvation, a focus on divine-human relations resulting in an anthropocentric ethics, the devaluing of the material world resulting in a search for otherworldly rewards, and the surrender of nature theologies to scientific cosmologies.[5]

The underlying problem is one of cosmology, both scientific and cultural. Cosmology is a view of the world, both perception and conception, that assumes how the world came to be and our relationship to all beings and reality. Cosmology is the story of the way we structure reality. We have more than one story that calls for our allegiance and impacts our consciousness: our particular creation story from our religious tradition, and the scientific story of the universe.[6]

Even with these deterrents to involvement, religions have much to contribute and need to be examined in light of the current crisis.

> ...religions help to shape our attitudes toward nature in both conscious and unconscious ways. Religions provide basic

interpretive stories of who we are, what nature is, where we have come from, and where we are going. This comprises a worldview of a society. Religions also suggest how we should treat other humans and how we should relate to nature. These values make up the ethical orientation of a society. Religions thus generate worldviews and ethics which underlie fundamental attitudes and values of different cultures and societies.[7]

An important component of the environmental crises is ethical and spiritual.[8] Religions of the world have a very important role to play that has not been met by responses from other institutions and initiatives already involved for some time.

> Despite their lateness in addressing the crisis, religions are beginning to respond in remarkably creative ways. They are not only rethinking their theologies but are also reorienting their sustainable practices and long-term environmental commitments. In so doing, the very nature of religion and of ethics is being challenged and changed. This is true because the reexamination of other worldviews created by religious beliefs and practices may be critical to our recovery of sufficiently comprehensive cosmologies, broad conceptual frameworks, and effective environmental ethics for the twenty-first century.[9]

The World Council of Churches has had a group working on environmental issues for several decades, especially since the early 1970s.[10] The 1983 Vancouver (B.C.) Assembly of the World Council of Churches declaration on the integrity of creation was a milestone. More recently a project of the WCC has been the Ecumenical Water Network. We have evidence of interreligious activity and cooperation by the world's religions in sharing a concern for the common good of the planet. Mary Evelyn Tucker points out that leaders and laity of the world's religions have been present to focus on the environment at international conferences such as the Global Forum of Spiritual and Parliamentary Leaders meeting in Oxford (1988), Moscow (1990), Rio de Janeiro (1992), Kyoto (1993) plus the Parliament of World Religions in Chicago (1993), and Capetown (1999). These were followed by the Millennium World Peace Summit of Religious and Spiritual Leaders at the United Nations (2001). In addition, multiple international interreligious projects such as the Forum on Religion and Ecology, the Alliance of Religion and Conservation, and the World Faiths Development Dialogue plus the National Religious

Partnership for the Environment and the Zimbabwean Institute of
Religious Research and Ecological Conservation are in operation.[11]
The response of religions has been not only a beginning rethinking
of theology but also a reorienting of sustainable practices and long-
term environmental commitments.[12] Religions are also beginning
to examine and identify their specific characteristics that are both
transformative and constraining in light of the environmental crisis.

> A series of conferences on religions of the world and ecology
> took place under the supervision of the Harvard University
> Center for the Study of World Religions during the late '90s.
> Recognizing both the promises and problems of religions, the
> conferences acknowledged that they are still key shapers of
> people's world views and values. The project identified ideas
> and practices from the religions of the world that support a
> sustainable environmental future.[13]

This project is a major tool for the dialogue. But, how possible is
it? How will the ecumenical dialogue be affected? Will the diversity
among the religions regarding this issue be too great?

Effect of Earth-centered Focus on the Ecumenical Dialogue

The more deeply religious communities can connect with the
needs of the planet, the more they will find themselves ecumenically
connected. A threatened planet can be a common gathering point
for the dialogue among the religious communities.

> This is what I mean by the image of deep ecumenicity: the
> more the religions of the world can ground themselves in this
> earth the more deeply they can connect with the nature and
> the needs of this planet, the more they will find themselves
> interconnected. The more deeply religious persons become
> ecologically attuned, the more effectively they will become
> ecumenically connected.[14]

One earth is home for the many religions that make up the
ecumenical dialogue. The Greek word, *oikos,* is translated into English
as "house," "household," or "home," and is the root word for *ecology,
economy,* and *ecumenism.* The world's religions share a common world
house, a common home. This home is now threatened by climate
change that is affected to a large degree by human activity and
choice. This is an issue that affects all. Religions of the world will
find themselves more deeply connected when they are engaged in
concern for the survival of the natural world.

Knitter suggests several reasons why an interreligious dialogue is not only necessary but also possible. Diversity is key here, not unanimity or common ground, but a diversity in which it is impossible to reduce diverse truths and beliefs. What is held in common is life on one planet and the state of being of that one planet, gathering the religious communities together on the "common ground of our threatened earth."[15] He is convinced that the state of the natural world of our planet is a problem that affects everyone on the planet, making the saving of the earth a great collective project in which individual ethical discourses can be linked.[16]

Knitter does not propose a single world view or a unified global ethic. He is convinced that religions have an essential part to play in the discussion of environmental solutions for at least two reasons. First, he argues that there is the need for an ecological ethic to rest upon a foundation of a spiritual vision of life:

> Our relationship with the beings of the earth—animate and inanimate, sentient and insentient—has to be more than an instrumental relationship; it must also become... an interpersonal relationship.... To perceive and feel and affirm our interpersonal relationship with rocks and plants and animals is to feel that which connects them with us and grounds their value and sacrality. It is to feel what some religious persons would want to symbolize as "Spirit" or "Tao" or "Dharma" or "Buddha-nature" or "Wakan-Tanka"—that which *grounds* everything and *connects* everything and indeed makes us family. If environmentalists are concluding that in order to protect the earth we have to love it, religious persons are suggesting that they can help in fostering such love.[17]

The second reason that religions have an essential part to play in the discussion of environmental solutions is that although utilitarian individualism (a public philosophy that measures well-being in terms of production and consumption) pervades economic and political life across most of the globe, religions have a countercultural vision that is diametrically opposed to this view. "To question growthism is to take a thoroughly, and often lonely, counterculture stance...and what is needed, is not just that each religious congregation assemble its environmental prophets and lobbyists; we need a joining of ranks, a common front built on common ground, for an interreligious prophetic voice and lobby!"[18]

To move from an anthropocentric understanding to a biocentric understanding of the world and humanity's place in it is a shift that is a religious one. It involves a decentering of ourselves and recentering around a greater reality. "Now we need somehow to discover an old formula: that the tribe, or nature, or God, or most likely some amalgam of the three, is at the center of things. In such a world it becomes possible to imagine certain limits, to imagine fulfilling our unique ability as a species to limit ourselves."[19] It is this kind of essential awareness that religions may be indispensable to provide.

> A case can be made that all the living religious communities...
> are inherently and essentially antianthropocentric. In the
> multiple and vast forms of religious experience, we can
> find this movement away from self-centeredness to Reality-
> centeredness in an awareness that whatever our true selves
> are, they can be realized only in a decentered relationship
> with other selves. Traditionally, these other selves have
> been the human Other and, for most traditions, the Divine
> Other. Today, religious communities are recognizing the
> "Other" must also include the earth Other. One cannot
> truly be Other-centered or Reality-centered unless one is
> life-centered, biocentric.[20]

Life is what all religions share; life on this planet is the context out of which it is shared. This is a message that all religions have the capacity to discover since it comes from the heart of religious experience, and the religious community has the capacity to deliver it.

This interreligious conversation can best begin with ethics, an ethical focus on earth, and with the question of moral praxis, not the question of belief, but rather the question of how we act together for the earth. It is this earth ethic that brings the religious community closer together and strengthens the ecumenical dialogue. The ecumenical dialogue has focused on unanimity, then diversity, of the human community, but now is challenged to expand the diversity to embrace the diversity of life in the earth community.

The role of the world's religions is to participate in a "simultaneous bifocal recognition of our cosmological context and our environmental crisis."[21] This means that, while we are beginning to come to terms with the scientific story of the origins and unfolding of the universe, we also are learning of the rapid destruction of species and habitats around the globe. Religions are challenged to "re-vision our role as citizens of the universe and to reinvent our niche as members of the Earth Community."[22] This means looking anew at our sense of the sacred.

Can religions situate their stories within the universe story? Can they re-vision human history within Earth history? Can the religions open up their traditions to embrace the planet as home and hearth? Can religions re-evoke and encourage the deep sense of wonder that ignites the human imagination in the face of nature's beauty?... The environmental crisis calls the religions of the world to respond by finding their voice within the larger Earth Community.[23]

Experimentation and Exploration

If the world's religions are to renew a sense of the sacred, there will be a need for experimentation and exploration of multiple forms that take into account the depths of religious traditions. One such example is the work and leadership of Matthew Fox as found in creation spirituality.

Spirituality for Earth-centered Ecumenism

Fox calls for a deep ecumenism in which religions practice together the presence of God. Deep ecumenism goes to the core of religious traditions to find the spirituality that is there. Religions of the world are called to participate in spirituality that is basic to and is found in all, a universal spirituality. This moves to a level deeper than dogmas, history, and theological arguments, to a level of experiencing mystery and wonder in common rather than the old focus on distinction and division. He believes that "in their core and depth we do not encounter many different religions so much as one experience that is expressed variously and with great diversity and color flowing in the name of different traditions and cultures."[24] This is based on mystic Meister Eckhart's idea that God is a great underground river from which many wells draw. The wells represent many traditions, such as Buddhist, Sufi, Christian, Native American, Jewish, Goddess, Islamic, Celtic. In the depth of the wells is the common water.

The reality of interconnection is at the heart of what he means by deep ecumenism. By this he does not mean "syncretism," the fusing of many religions together, but identifying what is common in their essential being. He quotes Father Bede Griffiths: "We have, of course, to guard against syncretism of any kind, but this only means that we have to learn to discriminate within each tradition between that which belongs to the universal religious tradition of mankind and that which belongs to its own limited and particular point of view."[25] For Fox the realization that we have a cosmology in common is essential because it is about the whole. This worldview can move religions on beyond interfaith dialogues or theological position papers, and into the depths of shared prayer and shared celebration and shared social action and compassion.

Though diversity is the reality of the world's religions, Fox acknowledges and pleads for a sifting through and discovery of a common source for essential spirituality. This supports a cosmology that recognizes all religions as part of one sacred community.

> Will the world's religions assist in the further development of the human spirit as they have throughout their long, unfolding journey to the present? If religions are vessels for nurturing the sense of the sacred, surely they will continue to respond to the sacred that is manifest in the wonder of life and in its continuity.[26]

As religions begin to contribute to the emergence of a broader cosmological orientation and environmental ethic, they can move away from the central anthropocentric focus to include the concerns regarding the cosmos. If a gap remains between ideas and practice and between forming ideas and translating ideas into practice among knowing, learning, and acting, how is this gap to be overcome? What will it take to stir the deep passions for environmental transformation?

Theological Education for Environmental Transformation

A main characteristic of religions is to inspire and inform the individual conscience. A deep sense of connection to a vast universe process has potential to open our imagination to sacredness and beauty; a deep feeling of connection is essential. The telling of the Universe Story by Berry and Swimme[27] has already been most successful in generating such an effect. There have also been practical programs by religious communities such as the National Council of Churches' Global Climate Change Campaign in conjunction with the Coalition for the Environment and Jewish Life. Also, the Episcopal Power and Light Project has made a public impact in creating enthusiasm for how religious communities can participate in renewable energy.[28]

Though Christianity has historically shown little interest in the new cosmology, opting to live out of the Hebrew story of creation, some seminaries within Christianity are beginning to offer this possibility in the curriculum to students and leaders of churches. Though it is still difficult to find a theological education institution that has an adequate program on creation, seminaries and divinity schools of the United States and Canada have given some attention to environmentalism and ecology through course offerings. These courses, for the most part, have been offered from the perspectives of theology and spirituality, practical theology, and in connection with globalization issues. Very little has been done to generate courses that develop expertise for teaching and learning that engages the imagination in discovering a cosmological vision.

When courses are offered by the field of Christian religious education, the focus has been on stewardship of the natural world in accord with a Doctrine of Creation, but rarely inclusive of the perspective of a theology of Nature. These courses generate some enthusiasm, but initial practices in advocacy, lifestyle, and interest tend to wane.

However, Christian religious education knows about the power of myth and how the internalization of narratives and stories affects values, attitudes, and behaviors. These cultural narratives transmitted from generation to generation form values that can be changed through new narratives.[29] Seminary curricula across diverse fields need to engage educators in the new cosmology and to relate the story being composed by the new cosmology to the Hebrew stories of creation while discerning implications for Christian ministry and discipleship. Some religious educators are beginning to understand the need for methodologies that promote embodied knowledge of the story being composed by the new cosmology in relation to the traditional stories of creation and human identity. These methodologies reflect the dynamics of the universe as known in the new cosmological consciousness rather than a mechanistic dualism of cause and effect that values mind over body, rationality over intuition, and spirit over matter.

A course with these aims, "Christian Nurture and the New Cosmology,"[30] is being taught at an ecumenically oriented seminary in the Midwest, Phillips Theological Seminary, and is a curriculum requirement for some of the seminary's degree programs. The course is designed to enable theological students to become informed of conversations occurring between science and religion; to consider a constructive partnership especially concerning cosmology and perceptions of the universe; and to discern how these conversations may be incorporated into the education of faith communities. The acclaimed course[31] has been very successful in helping students to form a learning community in which they become aware of cosmology and its new story, imagine and integrate a relationship between Christian stories and the scientific cosmic story, discern how both these stories may be intentionally incorporated into the education of faith communities, use tools for creating curriculum, and generate methodologies for transformative learning.

This course is intentional not only in content about the new cosmology but also in process. The course embodies the implications of the current cosmology for education. It seeks to engage processes and methods that are congruent with the way the world works especially as revealed by self-organizing systems, quantum physics, biology, and chaos theory.[32] For example, rather than isolating and promoting competition among students, processes encourage a community of interdependent learners. Group and self-directed projects are encouraged with the expectation that students will learn interdependently from each other through the formation of a supportive community of learning. Liturgy, litany, and ritual that focus on themes and concepts from extensive assigned reading integrate the new cosmology and scripture from Genesis, Psalms, Isaiah, and Romans[33] in which silence, paying attention, meditation, dance, poetry, art, role play, drama, and music are prepared and participated in together. An example is the *Cosmic Walk,* from the Genesis Farm Earth Literacy curriculum, which engages students in entering and walking the story of the universe as a sacramental reality using movement, music, reflection, and aspects of a labyrinth and stations to relate the specific events over a 13.5 billion year spiral.

Multiple and connected ways of knowing are acknowledged– including conceptual, experiential, participative, and reflective. The course methodology focuses on seeing (as well as hearing) and incorporating an "attention epistemology,"[34] coupled with confluent education processes engaging cognitive and affective dimensions and "multiple intelligences"[35] and implementing further dimensions of somatic or bodily learning and conative (the will to act) learning. It practices partnership[36] as the model of teaching/learning recognizing collaboration between the roles of teachers and learners. The varieties of processes used in the course are designed to enable students to name their own questions and insights and to integrate their ways of knowing.

> Partnership process is an integrated teaching style or peda-
> gogy that honors students as whole individuals with diverse
> learning styles. It focuses not only on cognitive or intellectual
> learning but also on affective or emotional learning. It
> recognizes the additional dimensions of somatic or bodily
> learning and conative learning…the will to act…. It cultivates

less linear, more intuitive, contextualized and holistic ways of learning.[37]

Partnership teaching also relies on nonverbal experiences through art and music, drama and poetry, contact with nature, and above all, play...the conceptual play of mature minds exploring rich possibilities in our selves and our world.[38]

Crucial to the entire course is the bodily way of appropriating what we have come to know through scientific discoveries that involve aesthetic and affective components. The methods were designed "to enable persons to transcend the split modern condition of experiencing the world one way, while knowing the truth of the world is otherwise."[39]

For example, through a simple guided exercise at sunset, the class enters the experience of the Earth "rolling over" rather than the "sun setting." Also, an exercise of stargazing encourages an imaginal shift in consciousness. During a field trip on a starry night, class members stretch out on their tarps and imagine themselves as they are at that moment, held tightly to the Earth only by gravity itself, and though looking up, are asked to shift perspective and look *down* into the universe! Through the imaginative power of the senses, and the courage for re-education, subjectivity is and can be transformed, entering into a visceral knowledge of the new cosmology.

Spatial learning is engaged especially in the choice of place and space in which the class meets: a log cabin retreat center on a wooded hill. While the academic classroom was designed as a space that encourages a dominance of the mind, the class setting encourages interconnected learning through the mind, senses, bodily experiences, and "paying attention" to the natural world, relating and integrating a "sense of place."

This course demonstrates the kinds of methods that can create a new consciousness for theological students and persons in local communities of faith that can transform practice. It engages processes that can change hearts and the commitment of will. The processes used by the course activate a partnership of learning through embodied knowing, conceptual imaging, visceral experience, and somatic learning. It provides sensory stimulus and imaginal concepts that shift perception. The course forms a community of learners that develop a shared consciousness regarding cultural narratives and myths that can impact attitudes and values. The course explores how these may be changed by new narratives appropriate for sustainable and flourishing ways of living. This learning community embraces a new vision of what our role and place can be in the universe—a vision of illumined hope and the will to act.[40]

Conclusion

Conclusions drawn and lessons learned from the implementation and practice of this course could lead seminaries to consider offering similar courses. Consideration should be made of how the introduction of such a course into the curriculum affects other courses across the curriculum. Even further, seminaries need to consider the integration of Christian stories and the new cosmology as an organizing principle for curriculum design in both content and process.

Educators and leaders of the religions of the world must take seriously the new cosmology and the findings of science that present a view of the origins and the unfolding of the universe, as well as the findings that the environment of the planet is at risk. It is time that religions make central the Earth and the human relationship to Earth. It is time to give significant energy and contributions regarding the planetary crisis. When the ecumenical venture can evoke wonder and a sense of the sacred in the story of the universe and embrace the new cosmology, it will be not only deep, but *new*.

Notes

Introduction

[1]Anthony L. Dunnavant, *Restructure: Four Historical Ideals in the Campbell-Stone Movement and the Development of the Polity of the Christian Church (Disciples of Christ),* American University Studies, Series 7, vol. 85, Theology and Religion (New York: Peter Lang, 1993), 5–6.

[2]M. Eugene Boring, *Disciples and the Bible: A History of Disciples Biblical Interpretation in North America* (St. Louis: Chalice Press, 1997), 3.

[3]Ibid., 20.

[4]Ronald E. Osborn, "The Disciples Mind," in *Chalice Hymnal,* ed. Daniel B. Merrick (St. Louis: Chalice Press, 1995), 553.

[5]S. Morris Eames, *The Philosophy of Alexander Campbell* (Bethany, W.V.: Bethany College, 1966), 20.

[6]Alexander Campbell, "Common Schools," *Millennial Harbinger* 3, no. 8 (August 1853): 439.

[7]D. Duane Cummins, *The Disciples Colleges: A History* (St. Louis: CBP Press, 1987), xiv.

[8]Alexander Campbell, *Popular Lectures and Addresses* (St. Louis: John Burns, 1861), 291.

[9]The educational principles were gleaned from various issues of the *Millennial Harbinger* reflecting Campbell's numerous writings on education over the years. See also Cummins, *The Disciples Colleges: A History,* and John M. Imbler, *Beyond Buffalo: Alexander Campbell on Education for Ministry. Footnotes to Disciples History,* no. 8 (Nashville: Disciples of Christ Historical Society, 1992).

[10]*Declaration and Address by Thomas Campbell and Last Will and Testament of the Springfield Presbytery by Barton W. Stone and Others* (St. Louis: Mission Messenger, 1978), 17.

[11]Ibid., 44.

[12]Ibid.

[13]Alexander Campbell, "Church Organization," *Millennial Harbinger* 7, no. 2 (February 1843): 83.

[14]Ibid., 83.

[15]Ibid., 84.

[16]This Council was re-formed and expanded as the National Council of the Churches of Christ in the U.S.A. in 1950, with participation by a variety of Protestant denominations and Orthodox churches.

[17]The name was changed from Oklahoma Christian University to Phillips University in 1912 as a fitting memorial to its chief benefactor T.W. Phillips, a noted Disciples lay leader and philanthropist.

[18]*Bulletin of Oklahoma Christian University,* Prospectus Number, May 1, 1907 (Enid, Okla.): 15–16.

[19]Ibid., 15.

[20]Minutes of the College of the Bible faculty, Enid, Okla., February 5, 1951.

[21]*Yearbook and Directory 1990 Christian Church (Disciples of Christ)* (Indianapolis: Office of General Minister and President, 1990), 259.

[22]Ibid.

[23]Christian Churches Together comprises six Christian families–Evangelical, Pentecostals, Roman Catholic, Orthodox, Racial/Ethnic, and Historic Protestant– representing approximately forty different denominations and fellowship groups. A

dozen church bodies currently are in the process of determining participation or sit as observers. In addition to specific faith communities, a number of organizations such as Bread for the World and Habitat for Humanity are also participants.

²⁴Consistent with Salvation Army regulations, his mother lost her rank when she married his father, who was a government employee.

²⁵The College of the Bible in Glen Iris, an Australian Church of Christ seminary, at that time was classified as a Seminary Associate with the Christian Church (Disciples of Christ) in the United States and Canada through the Division of Higher Education (now Higher Education and Leadership Ministries). It still maintains connections with the North American church and its affiliated theological education institutions.

²⁶William Tabbernee in discussion with the author, Tulsa, Okla., October 17, 2007.

²⁷Ibid.

Chapter 1: The Ecumenical Paradox in Three Linguistic Strategies

¹Paul Ricouer, *Interpretation Theory: Discourse and the Surplus of Meaning* (Fort Worth, Tex.: The Texas Christian University Press, 1976), 55. For a fuller discussion see chapter 3 and Paul Ricouer, *The Rule of Metaphor: Multi-Disciplinary Studies of the Creation of Meaning in Language*, trans. Robert Czerny (Toronto: University of Toronto Press, 1977).

²Note another use of "symbol," as in mathematical or chemical symbols, in which the strategy is to communicate by narrowing down to one, and only one, signification.

³Martin Luther is purported to have made this declaration in April, 1521 during his defense at the first Diet of Worms. Some scholars question the historicity of the specific words, but the classic biography of Martin Luther by Roland H. Bainton is entitled *Here I Stand: A Life of Martin Luther* (Nashville: Abingdon-Cokesbury Press, 1950). See pages 180–86, and especially 184 on the first Diet of Worms. A paperback edition of *Here I Stand* was released by Plume Books (New York) in 1995, and Hendrickson Publishers (Peabody, Mass.) plans to release a hardback edition in 2009.

⁴Dom Helder Camara, *A Thousand Reasons for Living* (London: Darton, Longman and Todd, 1986), 40.

⁵Wolfhart Pannenberg, *Theology and the Philosophy of Science*, trans. Francis McDonagh (Philadelphia: The Westminster Press, 1976).

⁶Wolfhart Pannenberg, *The Church*, trans. Keith Crim (Philadelphia: The Westminster Press, 1983), 23–35.

⁷Ibid., 24.

⁸Ibid.

⁹Ibid., 27.

¹⁰See chapter 8.

¹¹Ibid., 33–35.

¹²Cf. the groundbreaking Faith and Order Paper No. 111, *Baptism, Eucharist and Ministry* (Geneva: World Council of Churches, 1982).

¹³Pannenberg, *The Church*, 35.

¹⁴Ibid., 151.

¹⁵Ibid. See also Wolfhart Pannenberg, *Theology of the Kingdom of God* (Philadelphia: The Westminster Press, 1975), chap. 2.

¹⁶Pannenberg, *The Church*, 153.

¹⁷Ibid.

¹⁸Cf. Wolfhart Pannenberg, *Human Nature, Election, and History* (Philadelphia: The Westminster Press, 1977), chap. 4.

¹⁹The Phoenix Affirmations are available in both summary and full version on the Crosswalk America Web site: www.crosswalkamerica.org.

[20]The Eight Points are available, and a discussion guide is also available, on the Web site of the Center for Progressive Christianity: www.tcpc.org.

[21]Eric Elnes, *The Phoenix Affirmations: A New Vision for the Future of Christianity* (San Francisco: Jossey-Bass, 2006).

[22]Eric Elnes, *Asphalt Jesus: Finding a New Christian Faith Along the Highways of America* (San Francisco: Jossey-Bass, 2007).

[23]Scott Griessel, producer, *The Asphalt Gospel* (Scottsdale, Ariz.: Crosswalk America, 2006).

[24]Peter Steinfels, "Praying for Christian Unity, When Diversity Has Been the Answer," *The New York Times,* January 19, 2008.

Chapter 2: "Give Me Thy Hand"

[1]The institution was at that time named Northeast Louisiana University.

[2]Jim is a Kentucky native and graduated from Asbury College. He sought a liberal corrective in his seminary work and attended the Disciples of Christ's College of the Bible in Lexington, Kentucky (now Lexington Theological Seminary). He later earned an M.A. in evangelism at Scarritt College in Nashville, Tennessee. He was ordained in the Kentucky Annual Conference, and in 1969 was seeking a new job because his civil rights activism had harmed his career. Jim affiliated with the Louisiana Annual Conference and remains a retired elder in full connection there. He continued civil rights advocacy at ULM, and the Hicks Award is based in part on that, along with his pioneering ministry with the gay and lesbian community. These significant aspects of his career are beyond the scope of this essay, which focuses on ecumenical and interfaith activity.

[3]His reasoning includes an implicit assumption that attendance–even coerced attendance–in Christian worship is more likely to lead to conversion to Christianity than serious conversation and sustained observation fostered through relationship-building. This is a privileging of one particular kind of experience over both reason and other kinds of personal experience that deserves exploration.

[4]Schubert Ogden, *Is There Only One True Religion or Are There Many?* (Dallas: SMU Press, 1992).

[5]John Wesley, "The Character of a Methodist," in *The Works of John Wesley*, ed. Thomas Jackson (London: Wesleyan Conference Office, 1872), reproduced at http://new.gbgm-umc.org/umhistory/wesley/character accessed March 25, 2009.

[6]John B. Cobb Jr., *Grace & Responsibility: A Wesleyan Theology for Today* (Nashville: Abingdon Press, 1995), 142.

[7]"The Articles of Religion of the Methodist Church," *The Book of Discipline of the United Methodist Church* (Nashville: United Methodist Publishing House, 2004), 59–65.

[8]Charles M. Wood and Ellen Blue, *Attentive to God: Thinking Theologically in Ministry* (Nashville: Abingdon Press, 2008), 10.

[9]Print coverage in the local black-owned newspapers made it clear that my gender was only a secondary issue. Their headlines heralded the appointment not of a "woman pastor" but rather of a "white pastor" to the historic congregation.

[10]A white friend of mine who hadn't attended church in years visited worship on campus one Sunday and began attending regularly. "When I saw a dark-skinned guy with a pony tail wearing lime green walking shorts taking up the collection, I knew I had found a spiritual home," she said. She later learned that he was Hindu and inquired why he chose to attend Christian worship. He told her that for him, Krishna and Christ were identical. As a Christian theologian, I can find quite a number of things to dispute in that assertion, but I cannot argue with his confidence that the deity Christians worship can also be present in other forms of worship.

[11]The judge did have to dismiss a juror who wouldn't change his "innocent" vote to get a conviction. Since all the alternates had already been used, Edwards was convicted by only eleven jurors. There was a sense in Louisiana that while this was

apparently legal, it really wasn't quite sporting, so many of us wound up believing that although he was probably guilty, he also probably shouldn't be in jail. Political life in Louisiana is nothing if not complex.

Chapter 3: Seeking Wholeness

[1]The full identity statement is "We are Disciples of Christ, a movement for wholeness in a fragmented world. As part of the one body of Christ, we welcome all to the Lord's Table as God has welcomed us." The statement may be accessed online at the Web site of the Office of the General Minister and President of the Christian Church (Disciples of Christ) in the United States and Canada, http://www.disciples.org/AboutTheDisciples/tabid/67/Default.aspx.

[2]Richard H. Lowery, *Sabbath and Jubilee* (St. Louis: Chalice Press, 2000), 85–87.

[3]The word *bara'* carries the secondary meaning "to be fat." Fatness is often associated in biblical tradition with prosperity. Thus in Pharaoh's famous dream (Gen. 41:2–20), seven "fat" cows (the adjective is a variant of *bara'*) symbolize seven years of bumper crops. Oil, the liquid fat of olives, is poured over the head of the newly elected king, a ritual prayer for prosperity and peace in the coming reign (1 Sam. 10:1). See Gen. 41:2, 4, 5, 7, 18, 20; Judg. 3:17; 1 Sam 2:29; 1 Kings 5:3; Ps. 73:4; Ezek. 34:3, 20; Hab. 1:16; Zech. 11:6; and Dan. 1:15.

[4]In the Babylonian *Enuma Elish*, for example, heaven and earth are sculpted from the dismembered corpse of the vanquished deity Tiamat. Humans, made from clay mixed with the shed blood of Tiamat's consort/general, are created to do the tedious work of keeping the world running—dredging canals, supplying the tables of the gods, etc.—so the gods can take it easy. See W. G. Lambert, S. B. Parker, *Enuma Elihs: The Babylonian Epic of Creation* (London: Oxford University Press, 1966); Alexander Heidel, *The Babylonian Genesis: The Story of Creation* (Chicago: University of Chicago Press, 1963).

[5]A cohortative clause ("let us…"), followed immediately by a clause that begins with a nonconverted imperfect verb ("and they will…"), normally expresses purpose or result. See Ronald J. Williams, *Hebrew Syntax: An Outline*, 2d ed. (Toronto: University of Toronto Press, 1976), paragraph 187, p. 35. Thomas O. Lambdin, *Introduction to Biblical Hebrew* (New York: Charles Scribner's Sons, 1971), 119. Scripture translations in this chapter are my own.

[6]There have been a substantial number of challenges in recent years to the existence and dating of the literary sources of the Pentateuch identified in the classical formulation of the Documentary Hypothesis. See Ernest W. Nicholson, *The Pentateuch in the Twentieth Century: The Legacy of Julius Wellhausen* (London and New York: Oxford University Press, 2003) for a good overview of the major challenges. See also John Van Seters, *The Edited Bible: The Curious History of the "Editor" in Biblical Criticism* (Winona Lake, Ind.: Eisenbrauns, 2006); Anthony Campbell and Mark A. O'Brien, *Rethinking the Pentateuch: Prolegomena to the Theology of Ancient Israel* (Louisville: Westminster John Knox Press, 2005); and Rolf Rendtdorff, *The Problem of the Process of Transmission in the Pentateuch, Journal for the Study of the Old Testament* Supplement 89 (1990).

[7]*qaniti*, a pun on the name Cain.

[8]Stephanie Dalley, *Myths from Mesopotamia: Creation, the Flood, Gilgamesh, and Others* (Oxford and New York: Oxford University Press, 1989 [paperback: 1991]); William W. Hallo and K. Lawson Younger, eds., *The Context of Scripture*, vol. 1 of *Canonical Compositions from the Biblical World* (Leiden, New York, Köln: Brill, 1997).

Chapter 4: The Idealization of Christian Origins in Acts of the Apostles

[1]Eusebius' history of the church became definitive for later generations. Ron Cameron notes, "Eusebius' decision to base his history on Luke's Acts of the Apostles was a fateful one. Biblical scholarship is still living with that legacy." ("Alternate

Beginnings–Different Ends: Eusebius, Thomas, and the Construction of Christian Origins," in *Religious Propaganda and Missionary Competition in the New Testament World: Essays Honoring Dieter Georgi,* ed. Lukas Bormann, Kelly Del Tredici, and Angela Standhartinger [Leiden: E. J. Brill, 1994], 507).

[2]The Stone-Campbell movement has been especially susceptible to the influence of Acts since Acts often functioned as a "canon-within-the-canon" for early Stone-Campbell leaders from Alexander Campbell to J. W. McGarvey; on this see M. Eugene Boring, *Disciples and the Bible* (St. Louis: Chalice Press, 1997), 69–72, 127, 248.

[3]J. A. Fitzmyer, *The Acts of the Apostles,* Anchor Bible 31 (New York: Doubleday, 1998), 51–55, has a good review of the discussion. Some have proposed an early date, in the 60s; others, a late date, ca. 100–130. Fitzmyer prefers ca. 80–85 because: "There is no good reason to oppose that date, even if there is no real proof for it" (54). He is satisfied with that shaky reasoning because "in the long run, it is a matter of little concern when or where Luke-Acts was composed, since the interpretation of it, especially of Acts, depends little on its date or place of composition" (55). He is wrong on both counts; we have good reasons to oppose the date in the 80s, and the date does matter.

[4]Richard Pervo, *Dating Acts: Between the Evangelists and the Apologists* (Santa Rosa, Calif.: Polebridge Press, 2006). Joseph Tyson has surveyed the lack of scholarly research behind the consensus date for Acts in *Marcion and Luke-Acts: A Defining Struggle* (Columbia: University of South Carolina Press, 2006), 1–3; see his earlier article, "The Date of Acts: A Reconsideration," *Forum* 5, no.1 (Spring 2002): 33–35. Pervo has noted the same point in *Dating Acts,* 4–5; see his earlier article, "Meet Right–and Our Bounden Duty: Community Meetings in Acts," *Forum* 4, no. 1 (Spring 2001): 45–62.

[5]Pervo, *Dating Acts,* 346.

[6]Tyson joins those scholars who have argued for an early date for the preaching of Marcion: "We probably will not be far off if we conclude that Marcion's views were known, at least in part and in some locations, as early as 115–120 C.E." (31). Pervo acknowledges the possibility of the influence of the Marcion controversy on the writing of Acts, but does not emphasize it to the extent that Tyson does (*Dating Acts,* 330–31).

[7]Recently extensively argued by Colin J. Hemer, *The Book of Acts in the Setting of Hellenistic History* (Winona Lake, Ind.: Eisenbrauns, 1990), 308–34. See also F. F. Bruce, *The Book of Acts,* NICNT, revised edition (Grand Rapids: Eerdmans, 1988), 7; Ben Witherington III, *The Acts of the Apostles: A Socio-Rhetorical Commentary* (Grand Rapids: Eerdmans, 1998), 51–60.

[8]See especially Pervo, *Dating Acts,* 51–147. Pervo acknowledges his debt to the work of several scholars who have been arguing for the use of Paul by Acts, most especially William O. Walker ("Acts and the Pauline Corpus Reconsidered," *JSNT* 24 [1985]: 3–23; "Acts and the Pauline Corpus Revisited: Peter's Speech at the Jerusalem Conference," in *Literary Studies in Luke-Acts,* festschrift for Joseph B. Tyson [Macon, Ga.: Mercer University Press, 1998], 77–86).

[9]See Pervo, *Dating Acts,* 109–11, for analysis of these texts.

[10]See, for example, Luke T. Johnson, "Where we can check him on details, Luke's factual accuracy in the latter part of Acts is impressive" (*The Acts of the Apostles,* Sacra Pagina 5 [Collegeville, Minn.: Liturgical Press, 1992], 5). Gerd Luedemann bases his assessment of the sources of Acts on the view that Acts did not use Paul's letters; see *The Acts of the Apostles: What Really Happened in the Earliest Days of the Church* (Amherst, N.Y.: Prometheus Books, 2005), 17–18, where he dismisses recent arguments for the use of Paul's letters by the author of Acts.

[11]This is central to Pervo's argument in *Dating Acts,* thus the subtitle of his book, *Between the Evangelists and the Apologists;* see especially chapter 8, "Acts as a Writing of the First Decades of the Second Century," 309–42.

¹²This is the presupposition, for example, of the series of studies edited by Bruce Winter, et al., *The Book of Acts in its First Century Setting*, 5 vols. (Grand Rapids: Eerdmans, 1993–96) and of Hemer, *The Book of Acts.*

¹³A number of recent studies have deconstructed Acts' story of the origin of the church in Jerusalem, among which see: Christopher R. Matthews, "Acts and the History of the Jerusalem Church," Merrill P. Miller, "Antioch, Paul, and Jerusalem: Diaspora Myths of Origins in the Homeland," Dennis E. Smith, "What Do We Really Know about the Jerusalem Church? Christian Origins in Jerusalem According to Acts and Paul," all in *Redescribing Christian Origins*, SBL Symposium Series 28, ed. Ron Cameron and Merrill P. Miller (Atlanta: Society of Biblical Literature, 2004), 159–75, 177–235, 237–52; Richard I. Pervo, "My Happy Home: The Role of Jerusalem in Acts 1–7," Dennis E. Smith, "Was There a Jerusalem Church? Christian Origins According to Acts and Paul," both in *Forum* 3, no. 1 (Spring 2000): 31–55, 57–74; Milton Moreland, "The Jerusalem Community in Acts: Mythmaking and the Sociorhetorical Functions of a Lukan Setting," in *Contextualizing Acts: Lukan Narrative and Greco-Roman Discourse*, SBL Symposium Series 20, ed. Todd Penner and Caroline Vander Stichele, (Atlanta: Society of Biblical Literature, 2003), 285–310.

¹⁴For a review of the discussion, see Joseph B. Tyson, "From History to Rhetoric and Back: Assessing New Trends in Acts Studies," in *Contextualizing Acts,* 23–42. The classic presentation of Acts as a "historical novel," in the tradition of Greco-Roman novels, is that of Richard Pervo, *Profit with Delight: The Literary Genre of the Acts of the Apostles* (Philadelphia: Fortress Press, 1987).

¹⁵Joseph Tyson, "Acts: A Myth of Christian Origins," a paper presented to the Acts Seminar at the meeting of the Westar Institute, Santa Rosa, Calif., October 18–21, 2006. See also his comments in Tyson, "From History to Rhetoric and Back," 36.

¹⁶As examples, Tyson references classic studies by Jean Danielou and Henri Marrou (*The First Six Hundred Years* [London: Darton, Longman and Todd, 1978]) and by W. H. C. Frend (*The Rise of Christianity* [Philadelphia: Fortress Press, 1984]). Among current historians of early Christianity, William Tabbernee stands apart as one who is paying attention to new research on Acts and beginning to assess its significance; see Tabbernee, *Early Christianity in Contexts* (Grand Rapids, Mich.: Baker Academic, forthcoming 2010).

¹⁷See most recently John Dominic Crossan and Jonathan Reed, who present a substantive critique of Acts as a historical resource, yet feel compelled to use it nevertheless. Their method is as follows: "[It] must be done according to whether Luke disagrees with Paul (omit it), whether Luke adds to Paul but within his own rather than Paul's theology (bracket it), and whether Luke adds to Paul but within Paul's rather than Luke's own theology (keep it)" (105). This method makes sense only because it is based on an assumption that Luke did not use the letters of Paul. See *In Search of Paul: How Jesus' Apostle Opposed Rome's Empire with God's Kingdom* (San Francisco: HarperSanFrancisco, 2004), esp. 13–41.

¹⁸See also the conclusion of Marianne Palmer Bonz: "Luke's use of supernatural beings as a narrative device employed at critical junctures to shape the direction and further the movement of the plot finds its closest parallel in Greek and Roman epic. Originally introduced by Homer, supernatural interaction with the central characters of the narrative remained a signature characteristic of the epic genre" (*The Past as Legacy: Luke-Acts and Ancient Epic* [Minneapolis: Fortress Press, 2000], 164). Works produced within the epic genre tended to function as "myths of origins" for the cultures within which they were embedded (192–93). While Bonz argues for the influence of Virgil on the writing of Acts, Dennis R. MacDonald has argued for the influence of Homer; see *Does the New Testament Imitate Homer? Four Cases from the Acts of the Apostles* (New Haven: Yale University Press, 2003).

¹⁹This is clearly an exaggeration, as scholars often point out. But attempts to set a more reasonable number for the first church in Jerusalem still miss the main problem, namely that this is a fictional account that assumes a "big bang" beginning. One does not deal with the problem by revising the statistics. See also L. Michael White, "The

Pentecost Event: Lukan Redaction and Themes in Acts 2," *Forum* 3, no. 1 (Spring 2000): 75–103.

[20]C. K. Barrett, *Acts*, ICC, 2 vols. (Edinburgh: T&T Clark, 1994), 1: 161; Fitzmyer, *The Acts of the Apostles*, 268; Johnson, *The Acts of the Apostles*, 61.

[21]Walker, "Acts and the Pauline Corpus Revisited," 3–23. See also Walker, "Acts and the Pauline Corpus Reconsidered: Peter's Speech at the Jerusalem Conference."

[22]Note that the speech Peter gives in Acts 15:7–11 references the earlier story in Acts. Clearly it is a reference internal to Luke's story, which is presented for the benefit of the reader of Acts.

[23]The purpose was to "'rehabilitate' Paul in the minds of those Christians who, for whatever reason, look upon him with suspicion," and to do so by tying him closely to Peter (Walker, "Acts and the Pauline Corpus Revisited," 85).

[24]See Pervo, "Meet Right–And Our Bounden Duty": 45–62.

[25]Ibid., 60.

[26]The back stories of the births of John and Jesus promote the theme that both of them came from pious stock (Luke 1:1–2:52). The story of the conversion of Cornelius in Acts 10:1–11:18 plays off the theme that Peter is an observant Jew who would never eat unclean food (10:9–16). Paul was a persecutor of the early Christian movement (8:1–3, 9:1–2), regularly began his preaching in the local synagogue (13:5, 14; 14:1; 17:2, 17; 18:4; 19:8), and, when pressed, participated in Jewish ritual activities (16:3; 21:26).

[27]See Tyson, "Christian Self-Definition and Anti-Judaism in the Second Century: Marcion, Acts, and Justin." Paper presented to the Acts Seminar, Santa Rosa, Calif., March 8–9, 2008.

[28]See, e.g., Acts 4:1–3; 5:17–42; 6:8–8:3; 9:23–25; 12:1–5; 13:44–52; 14:2, 19–20; 17:3–9, 13–15; 18:5–17; 21:27–23:35.

[29]On anti-Judaism in Acts, see Joseph B. Tyson, *Images of Judaism in Luke-Acts* (Columbia: University of South Carolina Press, 1992); Richard I. Pervo, "The Gates Have Been Closed (Acts 21:30): The Jews in Acts," paper presented to the Acts Seminar, Santa Rosa, Calif., October 22–23, 2004; id., *Dating Acts*, 345–46.

[30]Burton L. Mack, *Who Wrote the New Testament? The Making of the Christian Myth* (San Francisco: HarperSanFrancisco, 1995), 47.

[31]Ibid., 43–73.

[32]Ibid., 75–96.

[33]The study of Christian origins has received new emphasis in the last couple of decades especially by means of newly formed research seminars. The SBL Seminar on Ancient Myths and Modern Theories of Christian Origins ran from 1992 to 2002 and published its first volume of collected papers and conclusions in: Ron Cameron and Merrill P. Miller, eds., *Redescribing Christian Origins*, SBL Symposium Series 28 (Atlanta: Society of Biblical Literature, 2004). As an outgrowth of that seminar, the SBL Redescribing Early Christianity Group was formed and is still active. Another new seminar has been formed under the auspices of the Westar Institute as the Jesus Seminar on Christian Origins.

Chapter 5: Clippings from *World Call*

[1]Paul F. Knitter, *Introducing Theologies of Religions* (Maryknoll, N. Y.: Orbis Books, 2002), 63. For the purposes of this paper I will define theological exclusivism as the view that "no salvation exists apart from the atoning action of the triune God known in the life, death, and resurrection of Jesus Christ and that no spiritual community other than the Christian church is a God-inspired mediator of saving grace" (cf. Don A. Pittman, et al., *Ministry and Theology in Global Perspective: Contemporary Challenges for the Church* [Grand Rapids: Eerdmans, 1996], 55). Theological inclusivism refers to the view that Christians must hold together in tension two equally binding convictions: (a) the universal will of God to save, or more specifically the operation of the healing grace of God everywhere, including in and through non-Christian traditions, and (b) "the uniqueness of the manifestation of the grace of God in Christ, which makes a

universal claim as the final way of salvation." (See Alan Race, *Christians and Religious Pluralism* [London: SCM Press, 1983], 38.)

[2]Mark G. Toulouse, *Joined in Discipleship: The Shaping of Contemporary Disciples Identity,* rev. ed. (St. Louis: Chalice Press, 1997), 189–217. See also Don A. Pittman and Paul A. Williams, "Mission and Evangelism: Continuing Debates and Contemporary Interpretations," in *Interpreting Disciples: Practical Theology in the Discipleis of Christ,* ed. L. Dale Richesin and Larry D. Bouchard (Fort Worth: Texas Christian University Press, 1987), 206–47.

[3]See Mark G. Toulouse, "Disciples Theology: Revisiting the History to 1960" (unpublished manuscript, 2006).

[4]See Kenneth Scott Latourette, *The Great Century, A.D. 1800–A.D. 1914, Europe and the United States of America,* vol. 4, *A History of the Expansion of Christianity* (New York: Harper & Brothers, 1941).

[5]William Richey Hogg, "The Rise of Protestant Missionary Concern, 1517–1914," in *The Theology of the Christian Mission,* ed. Gerald H. Anderson (New York: McGraw-Hill, 1961), 95–111.

[6]Stephen Neill, *A History of Christian Missions* (Baltimore: Penguin Books, 1964), 454. Please note that while using inclusive language to write this paper, I have not reconstructed the non-inclusive language used in historic conference reports or the writings of other individuals.

[7]See John R. Mott, *The Evangelization of the World in This Generation* (New York: Student Volunteer Movement for Foreign Missions, 1904).

[8]David J. Bosch, *Transforming Mission: Paradigm Shifts in Theology of Mission* (Maryknoll, N.Y.: Orbis Books, 1991), 298 and 301.

[9]"The World Call," *World Call* 1, no. 1 (January 1919): 3.

[10]Stephen J. Corey, "The Foreign Fields and Post-War Conditions," *World Call* 1, no. 1 (January 1919): 8–9.

[11]"The High Noon of Missionary Opportunity: A Symposium," *World Call* 2, no. 3 (March 1920): 37–39.

[12]Cynthia Pearl Maus, "Americanization Calls to the Youth of the Church," *World Call* 1, no. 11 (November 1919): 26.

[13]See *World Mission Conference, 1910, Report of Commission I: Carrying the Gospel to All the Non-Christian World* (New York: Fleming H. Revell Co., 1910), 362. Excerpted in "Findings of the Commission, Edinburgh 1910," in *Classics of Christian Missions,* ed. Francis M. DuBose (Nashville: Broadman Press, 1979), 329–37.

[14]See DuBose, *Classics of Christian Missions,* 330.

[15]Jesse M. Bader, "Won to Win," *World Call* 2, no. 3 (March 1920): 42.

[16]Elimelech Korn, "From Judaism to Christianity," *World Call* 4, no. 9 (August 1922): 30–34.

[17]See, for example, photograph of "The New Day in Tibet: Lee Gway Gwan Baptizes Thirty-one," *World Call* 2, no. 3 (March 1920): 47; or a photograph of "Hira Lal and Dr. Miller Baptizing Lepers at Mungeli, India," *World Call* 2, no. 10 (October 1920): 16.

[18]See, for example, photograph of "Mei Fan Swen," with promotion of related Sunday school material, *The Flag with Five Colors, World Call* 2, no. 3 (March 1920): 58; or of "A Sunday School Class in Damoh, India," *World Call* 2, no. 6 (June 1920): 26.

[19]See, for example, "Contrasting Heathenism and Christianity," *World Call* 2, no. 7 (July 1920): 40; or photograph captioned "A Hindu Idea of Religion" of a Hindu ascetic sitting on a bed of spikes, *World Call* 2, no. 3 (March 1920): 38.

[20]See, for example, "W. R. Warren, "Mission Fields from the Inside: Recipients of Christianity Tell Us About It," *World Call* 10, no. 1 (January 1928): 30.

[21]See the 1919 summary review of Disciples mission work in Tibet, Japan, India, the Philippines, the Congo, Mexico, Paraguay, and China in *World Call* 1, no. 10 (October 1919): 12–13 and 17–24.

[22]A phrase from the 1937 Oxford Conference, it was quoted by the editors of *World Call* in "Social Tasks for Churches," *World Call* 22, no. 1 (January 1940): 20.

[23]Stephen J. Corey, *Beyond Statistics: The Wider Range of World Missions* (St. Louis: Bethany Press, 1937), 13. Cited by the editors in *World Call* 19, no. 5 (May 1937): 11.

[24]See Stella Lewis Young, "Evangelizing Without Sermonizing," *World Call* 2, no. 8 (August 1920): 13.

[25] E. S. Muckley, "Should the Church Run Hospitals?" *World Call* 2, no. 7 (July 1920): 19.

[26]See DuBose, *Classics of Christian Missions,* 335.

[27]See "Association for the Promotion of Christian Unity," *World Call* 1, no. 6 (June 1919): 7.

[28]H. C. Armstrong, "Shall We Despair of Unity," *World Call* 2, no. 9 (September 1920): 31.

[29]As stated in the 1910 Edinburgh findings, "While the number of well-qualified foreign missionaries must be greatly increased in order to plant Christianity, to establish the native Church, to place at its disposal the acquired experience of the Christian Church, and to enlist and train effective leaders, nevertheless the great volume of work involved in making Christ known to the multitudinous inhabitants of the non-Christian world must be done by the sons and daughters of the soil." Quoted in DuBose, *Classics of Christian Missions,* 336.

[30]Charles T. Paul, "The New Home for the College of Missions: Hartford Seminary Foundation Opens Its Heart and Halls," *World Call* 10, no. 8 (August 1928): 25.

[31]DuBose reports that representatives from churches in Asia, Africa, and Latin America constituted only one-fourth of the total. See *Classics of Christian Missions,* 339.

[32]Stephen J. Corey, "Jerusalem 1928: Where Church History Was Made at the Enlarged Meeting of the International Missionary Council," *World Call* 10, no. 6 (June 1928): 33. Article also includes a photograph of the conference delegates.

[33]Ibid., 15.

[34]Wolfgang Günther and Guillermo Cook, "World Missionary Conferences," in *Dictionary of Mission: Theology, History, Perspectives,* ed. Karl Müller, et al. (Maryknoll: Orbis Books, 1997), 503.

[35]Bosch, *Transforming Mission,* 369. C. Howard Hopkins once referred to Mott as an "evangelical liberal" because, while emphasizing personal evangelism, he embraced the social gospel, which he often called the "whole gospel." See Hopkins, "John R. Mott (1865–1955): Architect of World Mission and Unity," in *Mission Legacies: Biographical Studies of Leaders of the Modern Missionary Movement,* ed. Gerald H. Anderson, et al. (Maryknoll: Orbis Books, 1996), 81.

[36]Günther and Cook, "World Missionary Conferences," 503.

[37]Stephen J. Corey, "Jerusalem 1928," 15.

[38]See William Richey Hogg, "Conferences, World Mission," in *Concise Dictionary of the Christian World Mission,* ed. Stephen Neill, et al. (Nashville: Abingdon Press, 1971), 136.

[39]"The Christian Message," chapter 13 in *The Jerusalem Meeting of the International Missionary Council, March 24–April 28,* vol. 1, *The Christian Life and Message in Relation to Non-Christian Systems of Thought and Life* (New York: International Missionary Council, 1928), 412. Quoted in DuBose, *Classics of Christian Missions,* 336.

[40]Corey, "Jerusalem 1928," 15. It is surely not insignificant that weaknesses (plural) are mentioned first and strength (singular) is listed second.

[41]Bosch, *Transforming Mission,* 369. See J. N. Farquhar, *The Crown of Hinduism* (London: Oxford University Press, 1913).

[42]A. W. Fortune, "Old Tasks in New Forms: Do Changing Conditions Require Changing Methods?" *World Call* 10, no. 3 (March 1928): 7–8.

[43]Ibid., 7.

[44]See Edwin Marx, "New Epoch in China Missions," *World Call* "China Supplement" (December 1932): 3.

⁴⁵Josephine M. Stearns, "Lure and Lessons of Foreign Travel: Upon the Completion of a Summer in Europe," *World Call* 10, no. 10 (October 1928): 25.

⁴⁶Ibid. Cf. E. Stanley Jones, *Christ at the Round Table* (New York: Abingdon Press, 1928), 11. Jones stated, "The deepest things of religion need sympathetic atmosphere. In an atmosphere of debate and controversy the deepest things, and hence the real things of religion, wither and die. In order to discover what is most delicate and fine in religion there must be an attitude of spiritual openness, of inward sensitiveness to the Divine, a willingness to be led by the beckoning spiritual facts…. Until a few years ago the usual attitude [of Christians] toward other faiths and cultures was criticism and lack of appreciation. Now the pendulum has swung back the other way to an attitude on the part of many of unqualified approval or to the attitude that all faiths are more or less the same. The time has come for an attitude between these extremes, namely, an attitude of appreciation with appraisal" (15, 17).

⁴⁷Stearns, "Lure and Lessons of Foreign Travel," 25.

⁴⁸Stephen J. Corey, "The Present-Day Summons to the World Mission of Christianity," *World Call* 14, no. 2 (February 1932): 32.

⁴⁹John R. Mott, *The Present-Day Summons to the World Mission of Christianity* (Nashville: Cokesbury Press, 1931), 197, 201.

⁵⁰See The Commission of Appraisal, William Ernest Hocking, Chair, eds., *Re-Thinking Missions: A Laymen's Inquiry After One Hundred Years* (New York: Harper & Brothers, 1932). Seven volumes of collected materials that informed the summary judgments in *Re-Thinking Missions* were published the following year.

⁵¹The seven denominations included the American Baptist, Congregational, Methodist Episcopal, Presbyterian (USA), Protestant Episcopal, Reformed Church in America, and United Presbyterian churches.

⁵²Here I will simply define theological pluralism as the view that the knowledge of the Divine, of the Absolute, is partial in all religions; that religious persons in all traditions may through dialogue with one another learn something new to all of them; and that there may well be more than one path to salvation–i.e., to right relations with God and neighbor.

⁵³The Commission of Appraisal, *Re-Thinking Missions,* 19.

⁵⁴Ibid., 44, 46–47. Emphasis mine.

⁵⁵Ibid., 28.

⁵⁶"Re-Thinking Mission," *World Call* 15, no. 1 (January 1933): 3.

⁵⁷Harold E. Fey, "Back of 'Re-Thinking Missions,'" *World Call* 16, no. 1 (January 1934): 41.

⁵⁸"Re-Thinking Missions," *World Call* 15, no. 1 (January 1933): 3.

⁵⁹Ibid.

⁶⁰Clarence H. Hamilton, "The Christian Mission and Other Faiths," *World Call* 15, no. 5 (May 1933): 19.

⁶¹Ibid.

⁶²Ibid.

⁶³Ibid., 20. First emphasis mine. Interested readers may find a striking account of a conversation on religious modernization and cross-cultural understanding between Hamilton and the renowned Chinese Buddhist master Taixu (T'ai Hsü) in Don A. Pittman, *Toward a Modern Chinese Buddhism: Taixu's Reforms* (Honolulu: University of Hawai'i Press, 2001), 115–17.

⁶⁴W. H. Lhamon, "Disciples and the Laymen's Report," *World Call* 15, no. 4 (April 1933): 19.

⁶⁵Joseph B. Hunter, "Evangelism at Home and Abroad," *World Call* 15, no. 3 (March 1933): 5.

⁶⁶Stephen J. Corey, "The Laymen's Foreign Missions Inquiry," *World Call* 15, no. 1 (January 1933): 7.

⁶⁷Robert Speer published his criticisms in a small book titled, *"Re-Thinking Missions" Examined: An Attempt at a Just Review of the Report of the Appraisal Commission of the Laymen's Foreign Mission Inquiry* (London: Fleming H. Revell Company, 1933).

[68]C. E. Lemmon, "A New Approach to Missions," *World Call* 16, no. 6 (June 1934): 5.

[69]M. Searle Bates, "The Laymen's Challenge: A Missionary View," *World Call* 15, no. 10 (October 1933): 12.

[70]Hendrik Kraemer, *The Christian Message in a Non-Christian World* (London: Edinburgh Publishing House, 1938).

[71]William Richey Hogg, "Conferences, World Missionary," in *Concise Dictionary of the Christian World Mission,* ed. Stephen Neill, et al. (Nashville: Abingdon Press, 1971), 136. Paul Knitter would classify Kraemer's theology of religions as a "partial replacement" model—i.e., a form of exclusivism slightly to the left of Barth. See Knitter, *Introducing Theologies of Religions,* chapter 2.

[72]"The Vision of God's Purpose," *World Call* 20, no. 7 (July 1938): 3.

[73]Robert E. Speer, "Approaching the Madras Conference," *World Call* 20, no. 7 (July 1938): 9.

[74]Neill, *A History of Christian Mission,* 456.

[75]Clarence H. Hamilton, "Living Trends in the World Christian Mission," *World Call* 21, no. 3 (March 1939): 6–7.

[76]"Then and Now," *World Call* 21, no. 1 (January 1939): 3.

[77]For example, regarding concerns about growing anti-Semitism, not only in Europe but in the United States, see Conrad Hoffmann Jr., "Anti-Semitism and America," *World Call* 22, no. 2 (February 1940): 13–14.

Chapter 6: It's about the Conversation

[1]David Tracy, *Plurality and Ambiguity* (San Francisco: Harper and Row, 1987), 27.

[2]Ibid., ix.

[3]William Adams Brown, *Imperialistic Religion and the Religion of Democracy* (New York: Charles Scribner's Sons, 1923), 134–35.

[4]Robert McAfee Brown, "Who Is This Jesus Christ Who Frees and Unites?" *The Ecumenical Review* 28 (January 1976): 11.

[5]Melanie A. May, "Response to Guenther Gassman," *Journal of Ecumenical Studies* 23 (Summer 1986): 376.

[6]Tracy, *Plurality and Ambiguity,* 18–20. In these "transcendental imperatives" for conversation, Tracy gives his own list and concludes with Bernard Lonergan's, which are the ones stated here.

[7]Paul S. Minear, *Images of the Church in the New Testament* (Philadelphia: Westminster Press, 1960).

[8]Alexander C. Zabriskie, *Bishop Brent* (Philadelphia: Westminster Press, 1948), 87, 158; Charles H. Brent, *The Inspiration of Responsibility* (Freeport, N.Y.: Books for Libraries Press, 1915), 24, 90–91; *Can the Churches Unite?* (New York: Century Company, 1927), vi.

[9]William Adams Brown, *The Church in America* (New York: Macmillan Company, 1922), 187.

[10]Samuel McCrea Cavert, "Christian Unity in America," in *The Church through Half a Century,* ed. Samuel McCrea Cavert and Henry Pitney Van Dusen (New York: Charles Scribner's Sons, 1936), 372–73; Cavert, "The Ecumenical Movement in Retrospect and Prospect," *The Ecumenical Review* 10 (April 1958): 318; William J. Schmidt, *Architect of Unity* (New York: Friendship Press, 1978), 114–16, 310.

[11]Henry P. Van Dusen, "The Ecumenical (World-Wide) Character of the Church Enables It and Its Members to Make a Unique Contribution Toward World Order," in *A Righteous Faith for a Just and Durable Peace,* ed. John Foster Dulles (New York: Federal Council of Churches in America, 1942), 21, 25; *World Christianity* (New York: Abingdon-Cokesbury Press, 1947), 232–34; "The Significance of Conciliar Ecumenicity," *The Ecumenical Review* 12 (April 1960): 314; *One Great Ground of Hope* (Philadelphia, Westminster Press, 1961), 61–62, 126–27.

[12]Robert McAfee Brown, "Whence and Whither?," in *The Challenge to Reunion*, ed. Robert McAfee Brown and David H. Scott (New York: McGraw-Hill Book Company, 1963), 17; *The Ecumenical Revolution* (Garden City, New York: Doubleday and Company, 1967), 137; "'Jesus Christ Frees and Unites'...and Divides," *The Ecumenical Review* 26 (July 1974): 430–38; "Who Is This Jesus Christ Who Frees and Unites?," 6–21. Also, in 1980 Brown stated this criterion for any future theology: "*It must be a theology that puts the welfare of children above the niceties of metaphysics.*" Brown, "Starting Over: New Beginning Points for Theology," *The Christian Century* 97 (May 14, 1980): 546. For a history of Brown's ecumenical thinking as expressed in print, see John T. Carmody, "The Development of Robert McAfee Brown's Ecumenical Thought," *Religion in Life* 43 (Autumn 1974): 283–93.

[13]Albert C. Outler, *The Christian Tradition and the Unity We Seek* (New York: Oxford University Press, 1957), 65–66, 81, 92, 96; id., *That the World May Believe* (New York: Joint Commission on Education and Cultivation, Board of Missions of the Methodist Church, 1966), 47, 53–54; "The Mingling of Ministries," *Mid-stream* 8 (Fall 1968): 106–18; "Ecumenism for Third Generation Ecumenists," *Mid-stream* 14 (October 1975): 531–33, 536–38; "A Memoir and a Prospectus–The Ecumenical Movement and the Cause of Christian Unity," *Mid-stream* 17 (January 1978): 13–23. For Outler's vision of Methodism as one of the orders, see Outler, "Do Methodists Have a Doctrine of the Church?," in *The Doctrine of the Church*, ed. Dow Kirkpatrick (New York: Abingdon Press, 1964), 12–28.

[14]Gerald F. Moede, "Members, Ministry, and Morphe," *Digest*, 14 (Princeton, N.J.: COCU, 1979): 209–27; "Preface" and "Eager to Maintain the Unity of the Spirit in the Bond of Peace," *Digest* 15 (1982): 42–50; "Response to Stuart G. Leyden," *Journal of Ecumenical Studies* 20 (Spring 1983): 282–83; "Striving Side by Side, With One Mind," *Circuit Rider* 13 (February 1989): 11–12; "Time to 'Own' COCU," *The Christian Century* 108 (January 16, 1991): 36–38. Paul Crow reported that Outler broached the subject of covenant unity in 1968. It fell on deaf ears then. But Moede reintroduced it in 1979 and 1980. See Paul A. Crow, "Covenanting as an Ecumenical Paradigm," *Mid-stream* 20 (April 1981): 131–32.

[15]Michael Kinnamon, "The Creative Edge," in *Unity in Each Place and in All Places: United Churches and the Christian World Communions*, ed. Michael Kinnamon (Geneva: World Council of Churches, 1983), 18; *Truth and Community* (Grand Rapids, Mich.: William B. Eerdmans; Geneva: WCC Publications, 1988).

[16]Frederick D. Jordan, "Address," *Digest* 8 (Princeton, N.J.: COCU, 1969): 148–53; John H. Satterwhite, "Church Union for Justice and Liberation," *Digest* 17 in *Mid-stream* 14 (April 1975): 251–53.

[17]Preston N. Williams, "An African-American Perspective on the Unity of the Church and the Renewal of Human Community," *Mid-stream* 28 (October 1989): 336–46.

[18]James H. Cone, *Speaking the Truth* (Grand Rapids, Mich.: William B. Eerdmans, 1986), 142–54.

[19]For a Roman Catholic African-American perspective, see Martin J. Carter, "An African-American Catholic Perspective on the Unity of the Church," *Mid-Stream* 28 (October 1989): 356–68.

[20]Gayraud Wilmore, "Race, Christian Unity, and the Unity of Humankind," in *Towards Visible Unity*, ed. Michael Kinnamon (Geneva: World Council of Churches, 1982), 146–52. The lamb-wolf image is drawn from William D. Watley, "Lambs and Wolves: A Vision of Hope," *Digest* 16 (1986): 45–47.

[21]Sallie McFague, *Metaphorical Theology* (Philadelphia: Fortress Press, 1982); *Models of God* (Philadelphia: Fortress Press, 1988), 3–40.

[22]Letty M. Russell, "Women in the WCC: Participation in a Symphony of Groaning," *Mid-stream* 14 (January 1975): 112; id., "Called to Account," *The Ecumenical Review* 30 (October 1978): 370; id., "Universality and Contextuality," *The Ecumenical Review* 31 (January 1979): 25; "Women and Unity: Problem or Possibility?," *Midstream* 21 (July 1982): 301–3.

[23]Melanie A. May, *Bonds of Unity* (Atlanta: Scholars Press, 1989), 5–6.

[24]For the role of Franklin Clark Fry in the World Council, see Dorris A. Flesner, *American Lutherans Help Shape World Council* (Dubuque, Iowa: Wm. C. Brown Company, 1981), 16, 85, 102–3, 114–17.

[25]Martin Marty asserts that the ecumenical movement exists for mission, but he believes confessional families have treasured qualities that deserve to survive in any future church ordering. For the links between unity and mission, see a series of articles by Martin E. Marty: "The Nature of the Mission We Seek," *The Christian Century* 77 (November 16, 1960): 1342–43; "Locating the Offense," *The Christian Century* 77 (November 30, 1960): 1404–5; "The Validity of Variety," *The Christian Century* 77 (December 14, 1960): 1464–65; "The Orders of Reunion," *The Christian Century* 77 (December 28, 1960): 1528–29; "Interim Ethics for Ecumenists," *The Christian Century* 78 (January 11, 1961): 44–46. For Marty's book-length argument, see *Church Unity and Church Mission* (Grand Rapids, Mich.: Wm. B. Eerdmans, 1964), 62, 110, 114. For more contemporary descriptions of church unity as a family of apostolic churches, see Marty's *Public Church* (New York: Crossroad, 1981), and "The Ecumenical Agenda: 2001," *Ecumenical Trends* 19 (October 1990): 132.

[26]For Lindbeck's discussion of the role of doctrine in religion see George Lindbeck, *The Nature of Doctrine* (Philadelphia: Westminster Press, 1984).

[27]See also William G. Rusch, *Ecumenism—A Movement Toward Church Unity* (Philadelphia: Fortress Press, 1985), 14, 119–21, for the concept of unity in reconciled diversity.

[28]The reference is to Charles Lamb's essay "A Dissertation on Roast Pig" as used by Rosabeth Moss Kanter, *The Change Masters* (New York: Touchstone Book, Simon and Schuster, 1984), 302.

[29]George Tavard objected to the "People of God" image, but because it smacked of "democratic permissiveness." See George H. Tavard, "Pluralism or Ecumenism," *One in Christ* 6, no. 2 (1970): 130–32.

[30]Avery Dulles, *A Church to Believe In* (New York: Crossroad, 1984), 1–15; id., *The Resilient Church* (Garden City, N.Y.: Doubleday and Company, 1977), 143.

[31]George H. Tavard, "The Recognition of Ministry: What Is the Priority?," *One in Christ* 23, nos. 1–2 (1987): 35.

[32]Avery Dulles, *The Catholicity of the Church* (Oxford: Clarendon Press, 1985), 79ff.

[33]This was John B. Sheerin's objection to the comparison in *Christian Reunion: The Ecumenical Movement and American Catholics* (New York: Hawthorn Books, 1966), 133.

[34]Alexander Schmemann, "Moment of Truth for Orthodoxy," in *Unity in Mid-Career*, ed. Keith R. Bridston and Walter D. Wagoner (New York: Macmillan Company, 1963), 48–55; John Meyendorff, *Orthodoxy and Catholicity* (New York: Sheed and Ward, 1966), 3–10, 19–20.

[35]This was Meyendorff's complaint in *Orthodoxy and Catholicity*, 47, 105, 115. See also John Meyendorff, *The Vision of Unity* (Crestwood, N.Y.: St. Vladimir's Seminary Press, 1987).

Chapter 7: Circling Back with Fresh Eyes

[1]A Tibetan title that can be translated, roughly, as "precious reincarnate Lama of Tarthang Monastery." It has been difficult to decide what name to use to refer to Tarthang Tulku Rinpoche. Strictly speaking Tarthang Tulku is a title and Rinpoche is an honorific. I have used Tarthang Tulku because his books have been published under this name.

[2]Tilden Edwards, *Living Simply Through the Day* (New York: Paulist Press, 1977), 23–24.

[3]Ibid., 32–33.

[4]From http://www.shalem.org/index.php/about-us/what-does-shalem-mean accessed March 25, 2009.

[5]Shalem Program Guide, Fall 1996, 2.

[6]Ibid., 5.

[7]Tilden Edwards, interview with the author at Shalem Institute for Spiritual Formation, Bethesda, Md. March 13, 1996.

[8]Tilden Edwards, interview with the author at Shalem Institute for Spiritual Formation, Bethesda, Md. March 15, 2001.

[9]Edwards, *Living Simply,* 24.

[10]Tilden Edwards, "Criss-crossing the Christian-Buddhist Bridge," in *Reflections of Mind,* ed. Tarthang Tulku (Berkeley: Dharma Press, 1975), 189.

[11]Gerald G. May, *Pilgrimage Home: The Conduct of Contemplative Practice in Groups* (New York: Paulist Press, 1979), 10.

[12]Connie Clark, ed., *Holy Meeting Ground: 20 Years of Shalem* (Washington, D.C.: Shalem Institute for Spiritual Formation, 1994), 13.

[13]May, *Pilgrimage,* v.

[14]Ibid., 182–83.

[15]Clark, *Meeting,* 17.

[16]Tarthang Tulku, *Kum Nye Relaxation: Parts 1 and 2* (Berkeley: Dharma Publishing, 1978).

[17]Edwards interview, 1996.

[18]Edwards, "Criss-crossing," 189.

[19]Gerald G. May, interview with the author at Shalem Institute for Spiritual Formation, Bethesda, Md. March 15, 2001.

[20]Ibid.

[21]Ibid.

[22]Ibid.

[23]Edwards interview, 2001.

[24]May interview, 2001.

[25]This emphasis in some Buddhist practices is seen clearly in Tarthang Tulku's *Time, Space, and Knowledge* series–books published by Dharma Press that link questions about the nature of reality with exploratory experiments–i.e., meditation practices. They are designed to offer experiential evidence that other ways of perceiving reality are possible.

[26]In my analysis of separation and connection I am drawing upon discussions in seminars led by Princeton Theological Seminary Christian education professors James Loder and Richard Osmer. These discussions, especially in Loder's seminars, were informed by the work of Michael Polanyi and the christological formula of the Council of Chalcedon.

[27]Edwards interview, 2001.

[28]Edwards interview, 1996.

[29]George E. Tinker, "Indian Culture and Interpreting the Christian Bible," claims American Indian cosmologies, unlike Euro-American cosmologies, tend to be more spatially than temporally oriented. See his *Spirit and Resistance: Political Theology and American Indian Liberation* (Minneapolis: Fortress Press, 2004), 88–99. Tinker argues that a narrow temporal orientation has flattened Euro American interpretations of the *basileia tou theou,* diminishing the *basileia*'s "right here and now" political relevance. As an example, on page 94 Tinker quotes former Phillips Theological Seminary professor M. Eugene Boring's argument for the "overwhelming temporal orientation" of the *basileia* sayings in Mark.

[30]Edwards interview, 1996.

[31]In *Restless Souls: The Making of American Spirituality* (San Francisco: HarperOne, 2006), Leigh Schmidt, a historian of American religions, gives convincing evidence that the leaders of several manifestations of "freestyle" spirituality in the United States did not divorce themselves completely from "traditional" religion.

[32]One point of contact that includes scholars grounded in the academy and those grounded in the monastery is the Society for Buddhist-Christian Studies. Its journal, *Buddhist-Christian Studies,* has published a wealth of articles on Buddhist and Christian approaches to conflict resolution.

[33]Tilden Edwards, "Spirituality in Ecumenical Perspective," in *Spirituality in Ecumenical Perspective*, ed. E. Glenn Hinson (Louisville: Westminster Press, 1993), 142.

[34]The initial research behind this paper was presented in 1996 to Robert Wuthnow's "Religion and Culture" seminar, which met as a weekly works-in-progress workshop of the Center for the Study of American Religion at Princeton University. His and the other participants' comments, esp. Marie Griffith's and Leigh Schmidt's, sharpened my focus quite helpfully. The paper itself was originally written for Princeton Theological Seminary's Spring 2001 doctoral seminar "Culture and *Oikoumene*" taught by Andrew Walls, whose work on Christian use of non-Christian religious practices is an ongoing inspiration. It was presented in March 2001 to Emory University's Graduate Conference "Religion, Identity, and Reconciliation." It was revised in light of the astute critiques of the participants, especially those of the primary speakers David Chidester and David Little and those of Laurie Patton, then chair of the Department of Religion.

Chapter 8: Labyrinth Walking as a Prelude to Spiritually Based Conversation

[1]Beatrice Bruteau, *Radical Optimism, Practical Spirituality in an Uncertain World* (Boulder, Colo.: Sentient Publications, 2004), 4.

[2]Hermann Kern, *Through the Labyrinth, Designs and Meanings over 5,000 Years,* (New York: Prestel Publishing, 2000), 23.

[3]Ibid.

[4]Ibid., 27.

[5]Ibid., 26–27.

[6]Ibid., 23

[7]Ibid.

[8]Ibid., 82–83, likely related to a sixth-century military exercise.

[9]Ibid., 306.

[10]Ibid., 106.

[11]Ibid., 153.

[12]Ibid., 306.

[13]Ibid., 23–31.

[14]Ibid., 305.

[15]Ibid., 306.

[16]Ibid., 30.

[17]Ibid.

[18]Ibid.

[19]Ibid.

[20]Ibid., 305.

[21]Cf: Genesis 2.

[22]Susan Rakczoy, "Developing Ecological Consciousness for a Planet in Peril," *Woodstock Report,* no. 87 (March 2007), http://woodstock.georgetown.edu/publications/reports/r-fea87e.htm accessed March 25, 2009.

[23]J. Philip Newell, *Christ of the Celts, the Healing of Creation* (San Francisco: Jossey Bass, 2008), vii.

[24]Ibid., x.

[25]Lauren Artress, "Foreword" in Jill Kimberly Hartwell Geoffrion, *Praying the Labyrinth: A Journal for Spiritual Exploration* (Cleveland: Pilgrim Press, 1999), viii.

[26]This evidence comes from the experience of people who have walked the labyrinth, but I could find no empirical evidence.

[27]J. Phillip Newell, "Love of Creation" (paper presented at McFarland United Methodist Church, Norman, Okla., June 28, 2008).

[28]Lauren Artress, *Walking a Sacred Path: Rediscovering the Labyrinth as a Spiritual Tool* (New York: Riverhead Books, 1995), 122.

[29]John O'Donohue, *Anam Cara: A Book of Celtic Wisdom* (New York: Harper Collins, 1997), 109–10.

[30]Bruteau, *Optimism,* 4.

[31]Ibid., 6.

[32]Ibid., 45–46.

[33]Roberta C. Bondi, *To Love as God Loves: Conversations with the Early Church* (Philadelphia: Fortress Press, 1987), 43, 54.

[34]Henri J. M. Nouwen, *Reaching Out: The Three Movements of the Spiritual Life* (Garden City, N.Y.: Doubleday & Company, 1975), 51.

Chapter 9: "Tell Me What You Want, What You Really, Really Want"

[1]Victoria C. Beckham, Melanie J. Brown, Emma L. Bunton, Melanie J. Chisholm, Geraldine E. Halliwell, Matthew P. Rowbottom, and Richard F. Stannard, "Wannabe," *Spice,* recorded by the Spice Girls (London: Virgin Records, 1996), title Code: 530427637, compact disc.

[2]John Koenig, *New Testament Hospitality: Partnership with Strangers as Promise and Mission* (Philadelphia: Fortress Press, 1985).

[3]Margaret Silf, *Inner Compass: An Invitation to Ignatian Spirituality* (Chicago: Loyola Press, 1999).

[4]Edward P. Hahnenberg, "Lay? Ministry? Christian Mission in a Pluralistic World" (plenary presentation, annual convention of the College Theology Society and the National Association of Baptist Professors of Religion, Salve Regina University, Newport, R.I., May 31, 2008) and Zeni Fox, "Snapshots of Laity in Mission: Consciousness of Responsibility for Ministry and Identity" (plenary presentation, annual convention of the College Theology Society and the National Association of Baptist Professors of Religion, Salve Regina University, Newport, R.I., May 31, 2008).

[5]Cynthia Bourgeault, *The Wisdom Jesus: Transforming Heart and Mind—a New Perspective on Christ and His Message* (Boston: Shambhala, 2008), 85–86.

[6]Priests for Equality, *The Inclusive New Testament* (Brentwood, Md.: Priests for Equality, 1996), 204.

[7]Paula M. Cooey, *Willing the Good: Jesus, Dissent, and Desire* (Minneapolis: Fortress Press, 2006).

[8]Jung Mo Sung, *Desire, Market and Religion: Reclaiming Liberation Theology,* ed. Marcella Althaus-Reid and Ivan Petrella (London: SCM Press, 2007).

[9]Ibid., 37.

[10]Carter Heyward, *Touching Our Strength: The Erotic as Power and the Love of God* (San Francisco: Harper and Row, 1989). Heyward attributes the church's predominately negative view of desire, as well as the religious conflation of desire with sexuality, to the church hierarchy's attempts to control certain forms of sexuality and to maintain certain forms of power.

[11]Don A. Pittman, Ruben L. F. Habito, and Terry C. Muck, eds., *Ministry and Theology in Global Perspective: Contemporary Challenges for the Church* (Grand Rapids, Mich.: William B. Eerdmans Publishing Co., 1996), 50.

[12]Daniel E. Tamburello, *Union with Christ: John Calvin and the Mysticism of St. Bernard,* Columbia Series in Reformed Theology (Louisville: Westminster John Knox Press, 1994).

[13]John B. Blevins, "Queer as This May Sound: Toward New Language and New Practices in Psychology, Theology, and Pastoral Care" (Th.D. diss., Emory University, 2005).

[14]Nancy J. Gorsuch, *Introducing Feminist Pastoral Care and Counseling: Introductions to Feminist Theology* (Cleveland: Pilgrim Press, 2001).

[15]Nathan Humphrey, "God equips the called," (2007), available at : http://episcopalchurch.org/34282_34032_ENG_HTM.htm?menu.=menu4542.

[16]The question to which they responded: "For you, what is the relationship between desire, your gifts for service, and your vocation in the world?" The timed response was intended to generate immediate and spontaneous thoughts, rather than edited and possibly self-censored reflections.

[17]Quotes in this section are from the respondents' questionnaires.

Chapter 10: Ties That Bind Too Tightly

[1]John Fawcett, lyricist, 1872, "Blest Be the Tie That Binds," *Chalice Hymnal* (St. Louis: Chalice Press, 1995), no. 433.

[2]Katherine Rhodes Henderson, *God's Troublemakers: How Women of Faith Are Changing the World* (New York: Continuum, 2006), 166.

[3]Susan Willhauck and Jacqulyn Thorpe, *The Web of Women's Leadership: Recasting Congregational Ministry* (Nashville: Abingdon Press, 2001), 48.

[4]Daniel Patte, *The Gospel According to Matthew: A Structural Commentary of Matthew's Gospel* (Valley Forge, Pa.: Trinity Press International, 1987), 154.

[5]M. Eugene Boring, "The Gospel of Matthew," in *The New Interpreter's Bible*, vol. 8 (Nashville: Abingdon Press, 1995), 100.

[6]Jerome H. Neyrey, *Honor and Shame in the Gospel of Matthew* (Louisville: Westminster John Knox Press, 1998), 21.

[7]Ibid., 53.

[8]Jesus' family's attempt to shame him is more clearly seen in the recounting of the episode in Mark. In the second gospel, his mother and brothers come because they thought he had "gone out of his mind" (Mk. 3:21). Matthew does not repeat the family opinion of Jesus, perhaps to mitigate the shame of the encounter.

[9]The phrase "kin-dom of God" as a paraphrase of "kingdom of God" was coined by Ada María Isasi-Díaz, "Solidarity: Love of Neighbors in the 1980s," in *Lift Every Voice: Constructing Christian Theologies from the Underside*, ed. Susan Brooks Thistlethwaite and Mary Potter Engel (San Francisco: Harper & Row, 1990), 31–48.

[10]Edwin H. Friedman, *Generation to Generation: Family Process in Church and Synagogue* (New York: Guilford Press, 1985), 229.

[11]For a good description of anxiety in an emotional system and its biological basis, see Peter L. Steinke, *How Your Church Family Works: Understanding Congregations as Emotional Systems* (Herndon, Va.: The Alban Institute, 1993), 13–25.

[12]Friedman, *Generation to Generation*, 27.

[13]Edwin H. Friedman, *A Failure of Nerve: Leadership in the Age of the Quick Fix*, ed. Edward W. Beal and Margaret M. Treadwell (Bethesda: The Edwin Friedman Estate/Trust, 1999), 236–37.

[14]Leroy T. Howe, "Self Differentiation in Christian Perspective," *Pastoral Psychology* 46, no. 5 (1995): 348.

[15]Ibid.

[16]Valerie Saiving, "The Human Situation: A Feminine View," in *Womanspirit Rising: A Feminist Reader in Religion*, ed. Carol P. Christ and Judith Plaskow (San Francisco: Harper and Row, 1979), 37.

[17]Ibid.

Chapter 11: Does Constructive Theology Matter?

[1]For an interesting and earlier take on viewing ministry in "political terms," see James Gustafson, "Political Images of the Ministry," in *The Church, The University, and Social Policy: The Danforth Study of Campus Ministries*, vol. 2: *Working and Technical Papers*, ed. Kenneth Underwood (Middletown, Conn.: Wesleyan University Press, 1969), 247–62.

[2]For the complete text of the speech, see http://www.cbsnews.com/stories/2008/03/18/politics/main3947908.shtml.

[3]From http://www.americanrhetoric.com/speeches/wjclinton1992dnc.htm.

⁴I am not trying to avoid the topic of God. After all, the phrase "under God" is significant for the different ways it has been interpreted in American political history. Moreover, in recent decades, it has become a virtual requirement for presidential candidates to affirm their belief in God–see footnote 5 below. Discussions of "civil religion" have also noted deference to God as a common theme in political life. See, for example, Robert Bellah, "Civil Religion in America," *Daedalus: Journal of the American Academy of Arts and Sciences* Winter (1967): 1–21, and Martin E. Marty, "Civil Religion: Two Kinds of Two Kinds," in his book *Religion and Republic: The American Circumstance* (Boston: Beacon Press, 1987), 77–94. Attend, in particular, to Marty's distinction between the "priestly" and "prophetic" modes of interpreting the phrase "under God." All that being said, while deference to God may function as a kind of rhetorical requirement in American political discourse, as frequently noted in speeches that invoke God's blessing on America, I have not found it to be one of the crucial topics/questions that political candidates need to address.

⁵A danger exists for both religion and politics in political appeals to religious themes and authority. While invoking America's religious faith has sometimes functioned to unify the nation, as in Lincoln's Second Inaugural or in Franklin Roosevelt's use of prayer in his speech following the bombing of Pearl Harbor, such appeals have also been used to arouse suspicions about the ultimate loyalty of religious minorities. Despite Article VI of the U. S. Constitution outlawing religious tests for political office, religious minorities–Catholics, Jews, Muslims, Mormons, and others–have been viewed skeptically by the public. In the election of 1800, for example, ministers supporting the Federalist candidate, John Adams, accused Jefferson of being an atheist. Christian faith was also used to help shape the single-issue politics of prohibition, especially in the 1890s, and in 1928, Republican candidate Hoover running against the Catholic Democratic candidate, Al Smith, played on anti-Catholic sentiments, especially in the South. Jack Kennedy had to face similar anti-Catholic voices in 1960, and argued in his now-famous address to the Houston Ministerial Association (http://www.npr.org/tempates/story/story.php?storyId=16920600)) that a candidate's private religious views should be separate from the public responsibilities of governance. Kennedy sought to display the attacks on his Catholicism as fundamentally un-American, invoking the American tradition of the separation of church and state. Since 1980, however, when Jerry Fallwell's Moral Majority helped return white evangelicals to political prominence, religion has functioned in a somewhat different way–namely, as a code of moral authenticity. Republican strategists, in particular, have used religiously related issues to create identity-tests for candidates. Candidates have been pressured not only to acknowledge their affiliation with a particular Christian denomination, such as the United Methodist Church, the United Church of Christ, the Roman Catholic Church, etc., but challenged to identify with the conservative tradition of that faith as a mark of authenticity. Is the candidate *really* a Christian or does he/she simply go through the motions of being one. For evangelical and Roman Catholic conservatives, for example, the litmus test of being a *real* Christian was often framed as opposition to abortion, or opposition to gay marriage. Using religious language to shape a public rhetoric of "traditional family values," Republican strategists used these religious tests to show that "liberals" were both "out of touch" with the core values of the American people and inauthentic in matters of religious faith. Liberals, they said, were "secular humanists," not to be trusted by true and faithful Christian Americans.

⁶While classic discussions of America's "civil religion," such as Robert Bellah's "Civil Religion" or Martin Marty's "Civil Religion: Two Kinds of Two Kinds," have tended to privilege presidential inaugural addresses, which emphasize the unity of American public life, convention addresses are equally revelatory, if not more so. Precisely insofar as they seek to inspire the party faithful and persuade those open to conversion, convention addresses illuminate the strategic divisions in our differing political theologies.

[7]The central task of political conventions could be described as the invention, or scripting, of political *heilesgeschichte*–the "myth" of the candidate–developed through Hollywood-directed biographies, nominating speeches, and keynote addresses, culminating in "the" speech by the candidate.

[8]Political challengers, regardless of party, always run, in theological terms, with a "theology of the cross" (i.e., one that identifies with people's suffering as "caused" by the party in office). Incumbents, however, tend to run with a "theology of glory" that urges voters to ignore the critics. Incumbents, again regardless of party, and due to the fact that they must defend their record of governance, tend to argue that "the country is on the right track; we have only to stay the course." See Clinton's 1996 convention address and Bush's 2004 address for evidence of that shift.

[9]For the full text of President Clinton's acceptance speech at the 1992 Democratic Convention see: From http://www.americanrhetoric.com/speeches/ wjclinton1992dnc.htm.

[10]The full text of George W. Bush's speech is at http://www.usatoday.com/news/ conv/118.htm.

[11]See Mark Lewis Taylor, *Religion, Politics, and the Christian Right: Post–9/11 Powers and American Empire* (Minneapolis: Augsburg Fortress, 2005), 62–70, where Taylor discusses "American greatness" as a central theme of neoconservative romanticism.

Chapter 12: Deep and New

[1]Mary Evelyn Tucker, *Worldly Wonder* (Chicago: Open Court, 2003), 149.
[2]Ibid., 3–4.
[3]Thomas Berry, *The Great Work* (New York: Bell Tower, 1999), 70–71.
[4]Intergovernmental Panel on Climate Change, http://www.ipcc.ch/about/ index.htm; and Al Gore, "Introduction," *An Inconvenient Truth* (Emmaus, Pa.: Rodale, 2006), 8; and David Hallman, "Climate Change: Ethics, Justice and Sustainable Community," in *Christianity and Ecology* (Cambridge: Harvard University Press, 2000), 453–57.
[5]Mary Evelyn Tucker and John Grim, "Series Foreword," *Christianity and Ecology* (Cambridge: Harvard University Press, 2000), xix–xx.
[6]Elizabeth Box Price, "Christian Nurture and the New Cosmology," *Religious Education* 103 (2008): 86–87.
[7]Tucker and Grim, *Christianity and Ecology,* xvi.
[8]Thomas Berry, *Dream of the Earth* (San Francisco: Sierra Club Books, 1988), 109–37.
[9]Tucker and Grim, *Christianity and Ecology.,* xvi.
[10]David G. Hallman, "The WC Climate Change Programme: History, Lessons and Challenges," available at World Council of Churches Web site, http://www.wcc-coe.org/wcc/what/jpc/pa-booklet-climate1.pdf.
[11]Tucker, *Worldly Wonder,* 38.
[12]Tucker and Grimm, *Christianity and Ecology,* xvi.
[13]Tucker, *Worldly Wonder,* 21.
[14]Paul Knitter, "Deep Ecumenicity Verses Incommensurability: Finding Common Ground on a Common Earth," in *Christianity and Ecology* (Cambridge: Harvard University Press, 2000), 365.
[15]Ibid., 377.
[16]Ibid., 368–69.
[17]Ibid., 370.
[18]Ibid., 372. See a similar view from the perspective of process theology by Jay McDaniel, "Ecotheology and World Religions," *Ecospirit,* ed. Laurel Kearns and Catherine Keller (New York: Fordham University Press, 2007), 38–39, 41.
[19]Bill McKibben, foreword to *The Greening of Faith: God, the Environment, and the Good Life,* ed. John E. Carroll, Paul Brocelman, and Mary Westfall (Hanover, N.H.:

University Press of New England, 1997), 38; as quoted by Paul Knitter in "Deep Ecumenism Versus Incommensurability," *Christianity and Ecology,* ed. Dieter Hessel and Rosemary Radford Ruether (Cambridge: Harvard University Press, 2000), 377.

[20]Knitter, "Deep Ecumenism," 378.

[21]Tucker, *Worldly Wonder,* 4.

[22]Ibid., 7.

[23]Ibid., 8, 9.

[24]Matthew Fox, *One River Many Wells: Wisdom Springing from World Faiths* (New York: Jeremy P. Tarcher/Penguin, 2000), 2.

[25]Ibid., 7.

[26]Tucker, *Worldly Wonder,* 55.

[27]Brian Swimme and Thomas Berry, *The Universe Story* (San Francisco: Harper, 1992).

[28]Tucker, *Worldly Wonder,* 86.

[29]Price, "Christian Nurture," 92.

[30]Ibid., 92–99.

[31]A Course Programs Award from the Center for Theology and the Natural Sciences, Berkeley, California, was received by Elizabeth Box Price, Ed.D. for her course "Christian Nurture and the New Cosmology." Dr. Price also received several grants from the Association of Theological Schools and from the Templeton Foundation to support her course research and to explore natural science and ecological education for clergy and persons of faith. She has studied in residence at the Earth Literacy Program of Genesis Farm, Blairstown, New Jersey, and in residence at the Whidbey Institute, Whidbey Island, Washington.

[32]See Margaret J. Wheatley, *Leadership and the New Science: Discovering Order in a Chaotic World* (San Francisco: Berrett-Koehler Publishers, 1999). Wheatley demonstrated implications of the new science for the field of organizational theory and action moving from Newtonian ways to principles of organization that include what is presently known about how the universe organizes. Education has a similar task.

[33]For an example see Norman C. Habel, *Seven Songs of Creation* (Cleveland: The Pilgrim Press, 2004). Also see interpretation of scripture from the perspective of Earth through the Earth Bible Project, such as Norman C. Habel, ed., *Readings from the Perspective of Earth* (Sheffield, England: Sheffield Academic Press, 2000).

[34]Sallie McFague, *Super, Natural Christians: How We Should Love Nature* (Minneapolis: Augsburg Press, 1997), 26–34.

[35]See Howard Gardner, *Frames of Mind* (New York: Basic Books, 1983).

[36]See Riane Eisler, *Tomorrow's Children* (Boulder, Colo.: Westview Press, 2000).

[37]Ibid., 14.

[38]Ibid., 16.

[39]Brian Swimme, *Hidden Heart of the Cosmos* (Maryknoll, N.Y.: Orbis Books, 1996), 24.

[40]Price, "Christian Nurture," 100.